BTEC
Level 2

707

edexcel
advancing learning, changing lives

ART AND DESIGN | LEVEL 2

BTEC First

Tamar MacLellan | Alan Steven Parsons | Jan Wise

Published by Pearson Education Limited, a company incorporated in England and Wales, having its registered office at Edinburgh Gate, Harlow, Essex, CM20 2JE. Registered company number: 872828

www.pearsonschoolsandfecolleges.co.uk

Edexcel is a registered trademark of Edexcel Limited

Text © Pearson Education Limited 2010

First published 2010

13 12 11 10
10 9 8 7 6 5 4 3 2 1

British Library Cataloguing in Publication Data
A catalogue record for this book is available from the British Library
.
ISBN 978 1 846 90612 1

Edited by Davina Thackara and Janine de Smet
Designed and typeset by Brian Melville
Original illustrations © Pearson Education Limited 2010
Illustrated by John Hallett, Alex Green and Brian Melville
Cover design by Pearson Education Limited
Picture research by ZooID and Pearson Education Limited
Cover photo/illustration © Superstock/moodboard
Back cover photos © Photos.com; Clark Wiseman/Pearson Education Ltd; attem/Shutterstock;
Clark Wiseman/Pearson Education Ltd.
Printed in the UK by Scotprint

Websites and Hotlinks

There are links to relevant websites in this book. In order to ensure that the links are up to date, that the links work, and that the sites are not inadvertently linked to sites that could be considered offensive, we have made the links available on the Pearson website at www.pearsonschoolsandfecolleges.co.uk/hotlinks. When you access the site, search for either the express code 6121V, title BTEC Level 2 First Art and Design Student Book or ISBN 9781846906121.

Disclaimer

This material has been published on behalf of Edexcel and offers high-quality support for the delivery of Edexcel qualifications.

This does not mean that the material is essential to achieve any Edexcel qualification, nor does it mean that it is the only suitable material available to support any Edexcel qualification. Edexcel material will not be used verbatim in setting any Edexcel examination or assessment. Any resource lists produced by Edexcel shall include this and other appropriate resources.

Copies of official specifications for all Edexcel qualifications may be found on the Edexcel website: www.edexcel.com

Contents

About your **BTEC Level 2 First Art and Design course** vii

Section 1: Knowledge

Unit	Credit value	Title	Author	Page
1	10	Contextual references in art and design	Jan Wise	1
2	5	2D visual communication	Tamar MacLellan	25
3	5	3D visual communication	Alan Steven Parsons	49
4	10	Using ideas to explore, develop and produce art and design	Jan Wise	69
5	5	Building an art and design portfolio	Alan Parsons	87

Section 2: Skills

Unit	Credit value	Title	Author	Page
S1	–	Planning skills	Jan Wise	103
S2	–	Preparing and making skills	Tamar MacLellan	119
S3	–	Evaluating skills	Alan Steven Parsons	135

Section 3: The Works

Unit	Credit value	Title	Author	Page
6	5	Working in the art and design industry	Tamar MacLellan	151
7	10	Working with graphic design briefs	Alan Steven Parsons	157
8	10	Working with photography briefs	Tamar MacLellan	165
9	10	Working with fashion design briefs	Jan Wise	171
10	10	Working with textiles briefs	Jan Wise	177
11	10	Working with 3D design briefs	Alan Steven Parsons	183
12	10	Working with interactive media briefs	Alan Steven Parsons	191
13	10	Working with visual arts briefs	Tamar MacLellan	199
14	10	Working with 3D design crafts briefs	Alan Steven Parsons	207
15	10	Working with digital art and design briefs	Alan Steven Parsons	215
16	10	Working with accessory briefs	Jan Wise	223
17	10	Working with moving image briefs	Alan Steven Parsons	231
18	10	Working with site-specific briefs	Jan Wise	239

Glossary   245

Index   249

Credits

We would like to thank Bedford and Oxford and Cherwell Valley Colleges for their invaluable help in the development and trialling of this course.

The authors and publisher would like to thank the following individuals and organisations for permission to reproduce photographs:

Shelagh rmstrong/iStockphoto p. **1**; Clark Wiseman/Pearson Education p. **3**; 2009 Banco de México Diego Rivera Frida Kahlo Museums Trust, Mexico, D.F./DACS/Christie's Images/Superstock Ltd. p. **3**; Vivienne Westwood Ltd p. **4**; Wallace Collection, London/Bridgeman Art Library p. **4**; ADAGP, Paris and DACS, London 2009/Musee National d'Art Moderne/Lauros/Giraudon/Bridgeman Art Library p. **6**; Succession Marcel Duchamp/ADAGP, Paris and DACS, London 2009/Bridgeman Art Library p. **7**; Salvador Dali, Gala-Salvador Dali Foundation, DACS, London 2009./Salvador Dali Museum, St. Petersburg, Florida/Bridgeman Art Library p. **8**; The Willem de Kooning Foundation, New York/ ARS, NY and DACS, London 2009/Thyssen-Bornemisza Collection, Madrid, Spain/Bridgeman Art Library p. **8**; L & M Services B.V p **10**; Mark Glean p. **10**; Alia Thomas p. **11**; Michael Ochs Archives/Getty Images p. **12**; The Print Collector/Alamy p. **13**; Historical Picture Archive/Corbis UK Ltd. p. **13**; Tracey Emin. All rights reserved, DACS 2009./Press Association Images p. **14**; Michael Boys/CORBIS p. **16**; Justin Kase Zonez/Alamy p. **17**; Zooid Pictures p. **17**; John Glover/Alamy p. **17**; ADAGP, Paris and DACS, London 2009/Giraudon/Bridgeman Art Library p. **19**; Jan Wise p. **19**; Jan Wise p. **19**; Absodels/Getty Images p. **21**; Ruth Facey p. **23**; Private Collection/Bridgeman Art Library p. **23**; Tamar MacLellan p. **25**; Pearson Education Ltd/Studio 8/Clark Wiseman p. **27**; Tamar MacLellan p. **27**; JinYoung Lee/iStockphoto p. **28**; The Art Archive / Usher Art Gallery Lincoln / Eileen Tweedy p. **29**; Tamar MacLellan p. **31**; Tamar MacLellan p. **31**; Philip Gatward/Dorling Kindersley p. **32**; Darko Novakovic/Shutterstock p. **32**; Joe_Potato/iStockphoto p. **32**; Stephen Whitehorn/Dorling Kindersley p. **33**; Diane Labombarbe/iStockphoto p. **33**; Neil Lang/Shutterstock p. **35**; Maxim Petrichuk/Shutterstock p. **36**; DREAMWORKS/AARDMAN ANIMATIONS / THE KOBAL COLLECTION p. **37**; Ирина Татарникова/iStockphoto p. **38**; Image Source Pink/Alamy p. **40**; Image Source/Corbis p. **40**; Tamar MacLellan p. **41**; Tamar MacLellan p. **42**; Tamar MacLellan p. **42**; Tamar MacLellan p. **42**; Dave Robinson/Key Publishing p. **47**; Hemis/Alamy p. **49**; Felix Mizioznikov/Shutterstock p. **51**; Shutterstock p. **51**; murat $en/iStockphoto p. **53**; Third Angle p. **53**; yuyangc/Shutterstock p. **53**; Karen Gentry/Shutterstock p. **53**; Jane Brennecker/iStockphoto p. **55**; Solodovnikova Elena/Shutterstock p. **55**; From the University of Derby, Year One Student Work web page. Reproduced by permission of The University of Derby. p. **55**; DOUG RAPHAEL/Shutterstock p. **55**; Terry Walsh/Shutterstock p. **57**; Getty Images p. **59**; Sony UK Limited p. **59**; Anglepoise Ltd. p. **59**; Photos.com p. **60**; Pearson Education/Studio 8/Clark Wiseman p. **61**; Pearson Education/Studio 8/Clark Wiseman p. **61**; Pearson Education/Studio 8/Clark Wiseman p. **61**; Pearson Education/Studio 8/Clark Wiseman p. **61**; Pearson Education/Studio 8/Clark Wiseman p. **61**; Anthony d'Offay, London/Anthony d'Offay Ltd p. **62**; Pearson Education/Studio 8/Clark Wiseman p. **63**; Pearson Education/Studio 8/Clark Wiseman p. **63**; Pearson Education/Studio 8/Clark Wiseman p. **63**; Pearson Education/Studio 8/Clark Wiseman p. **63**; Pearson Education/Studio 8/Clark Wiseman p. **63**; Aaron Hayhurst p. **64**; Pearson Education/Studio 8/Clark Wiseman p. **66**; Pearson Education/Studio 8/Clark Wiseman p. **66**; Pearson Education/Studio 8/Clark Wiseman p. **66**; Marc Friend p. **67**; balaikin/Shutterstock p. **69**; Jan Wise p. **71**; Jan Wise p. **71**; Jan Wise p. **71**; Jan Wise p. **71**; Jan Wise p. **71**; Corbis p. **72**; Randy Faris/Corbis p. **73**; Private Collection/Christie's Images/Bridgeman Art Library p. **74**; Paul Reynolds/Nicki Williams p. **76**; Jan Wise p. **77**; Jan Wise p. **77**; Jan Wise p. **77**; Jan Wise p. **77**; Jan Wise p. **79**; Jan Wise p. **79**; Succession Picasso/DACS 2009/Bridgeman Art Library p. **80**; Paul Reynolds/Nicki Williams p. **81**; Jan Wise p. **85**; Elpiniki/iStockphoto p. **87**; Pearson Education Ltd/Jules Selmes p. **89**; Alan Parsons p. **89**; Alan Parsons p. **95**; Alan Parsons p. **95**; Alan Parsons p. **95**; Alan Parsons p. **96**; Alan Parsons p. **96**; Alan Parsons p. **96**; Pearson Education/Studio 8/Clark Wiseman p. **96**; Alan Parsons p. **98**; Alan Parsons p. **98**; Ben Copperwheat p. **101**; Jeremy Hoare p. **103**; Gareth Boden/Pearson Education p. **104**; Pearson Education/Studio 8/Clark Wiseman p. **104**; Pearson Education/Studio 8/Clark Wiseman, Tacu Alexei/Shutterstock, Epic Stock/Shutterstock p. **106**; Alia Thomas, Baloncici/Shutterstock, Colour/Shutterstock p. **106**; Alia Thomas, juliengrondin/Shutterstock, Megan Gayle/Shutterstock p. **107**; Martin Valigursky/Shutterstock, Andrey Armyagov/Shutterstock, helissente/Shutterstock, Francesco Carta fotografo/Shutterstock, crystalfoto/Shutterstock, Dimitri/Shutterstock, Buturlimov Paul/Shutterstock, dendong/Shutterstock, Konrad Bak/Shutterstock, Kadroff/Shutterstock, boumen&japet/Shutterstock, Kadroff/Shutterstock, lev radin/Shutterstock p. **107**; Logo reproduced by kind permission of Next Plc. p. **109**; Logo reproduced by kind permission of New Look .p. **109**; Alia Thomas p. **111**; Jan Wise, saranvaid/Shutterstock p. **112**; Paul Reynolds/Nicki Williams p. **113**; Paul Reynolds/Nicki Williams p. **113**; Courtesy of Millais Gallery, Southampton Solent University p. **114**; Jan Wise p. **117**; Gratien JONXIS/Shutterstock p. **119**; Photos.com p. **120**; Tamar MacLellan p. **120**; Tamar MacLellan p. **120**; Tamar MacLellan p. **120**; Tamar MacLellan p. **121**; Tamar MacLellan p. **122**; Tamar MacLellan p. **124**;

Tamar MacLellan p. **125**; Tamar MacLellan p. **126**; Tamar MacLellan p. **127**; Tamar MacLellan p. **128**; Tamar MacLellan p. **128**; Tamar MacLellan p. **129**; Sally Moret p. **133**; Vlade Shestakov /Shutterstock p. **135**; Pearson Education/Jules Selmes p. **136**; Mouse in the House/Alamy p. **136**; Achim Prill/iStockphoto p. **137**; R. MACKAY PHOTOGRAPHY/Shutterstock p. **137**; Milos Luzanin/Shutterstock p. **137**; Alan Parsons pp. **139**, **142**; Alan Parsons pp. **139**, **140**, **142**; Alan Parsons pp. **139**, **140**, **142**; jallfree/iStockphoto p. **140**; jallfree/iStockphoto p. **141**; jallfree/iStockphoto p. **141**; jallfree/iStockphoto p. **141**; Alan Parsons p. **144**; Alan Parsons p. **144**; Alan Parsons p. **144**; Alan Parsons p. **146**; Alan Parsons p. **146**; Alan Parsons p. **146**; Marc Friend p. **149**; Plush Studios/Getty Images p. **151**; TommL/iStockphoto p. **153**; Pearson Education Ltd/Jules Selmes p. **153**; Uygar Ozel/iStockphoto p. **154**; Sergey Chirkov/Shutterstock p. **154**; Ashley Cooper/Alamy p. **157**; From Neville Brody and Research Studios © - some rights reserved pp. **159–160**; Logo reproduced with kind permission of Reebok. p. **161**; Logo reproduced by kind permission of New Look p. **161**; Logo reproduced by kind permission of Next Plc. p. **161**; Logo reproduced by kind permission of Hyundai p. **162**; From images taken from World Football Yearbook 2002-3. Reproduced by permission of Dorling Kindersley Books. p. **162**; Orange Advertisement reproduced with kind permission of Orange. p. **163**; Front Page from The Times. Reproduced by kind permission of The Times and NI Syndication and Image from World Trade Towers used in the Times Newspaper © Spencer Platt. Used by permission of Getty Images. p. **164**; Front Page from The Sun. Reproduced by kind permission of The Sun and NI Syndication and Image of Neill Kinnock used in the Sun newspaper © Stewart Kendall. Used by kind permission of Sportsphoto Agency p. **164**; Magazine Cover from Elle Magazine UK. Reproduced by permission of Elle Magazine UK/Paris p. **164**; Cover of 'PC Gamer' used by permission of Future Publishing Ltd. p. **164**; Photos.com p. **165**; Article titled "Credo / Jenny Pitman" by Adam Jacques. Reproduced by permission of Independent Newspapers and Donald MacLellan p. **168**; Donald MacLellan p. **169**; Gina Smith/Shutterstock p. **171**; Clare Allington p. **173**; Clare Allington p. **173**; Radius Images/Corbis p. **174**; Tom Klima/Shutterstock p. **177**; Jules Selmes/Pearson Education Ltd p. **179**; Jan Wise p. **179**; Jan Wise p. **180**; Paul Reynolds/Nicki Williams p. **182**; Elizabeth Whiting & Associates/Alamy p. **183**; webking/iStockphoto p. **185**; Pearson Education Ltd/Gareth Boden p. **187**; annastock/Shutterstock p. **187**; Studio 37/Shutterstock p. **187**; John Hurst/Shutterstock p. **187**; Tatiana Popova/Shutterstock p. **189**; Justin Paget/Shutterstock p. **189**; magicoven/Shutterstock p. **189**; Ronen/Shutterstock p. **189**; COLUMBIA / THE KOBAL COLLECTION p. **189**; Ferran Traite Soler/iStockphoto p. **189**; lavitrei/Shutterstock p. **189**; Agb/Shutterstock p. **189**; ArcadeImages/Alamy p. **191**; Jay Crihfield/Shutterstock p. **196**; Nikita Rogul/Shutterstock p. **196**; Milkos/Shutterstock p. **196**; Konstantin Yolshin/Shutterstock p. **196**; Monkey Business Images/Shutterstock p. **197**; Chris Schmidt/iStockphoto p. **197**; ozkan/Shutterstock p. **199**; Mark Glean p. **201**; Mark Glean p. **201**; Mark Glean p. **201**; Mark Glean p. **201**; Mark Glean p. **202**; Mark Glean p. **203**; Mark Glean p. **203**; Daniela Andreea Spyropoulos/iStockphoto p. **207**; Matthew Ward/Dorling Kindersley p. **209**; RexRover/Shutterstock p. **211**; Suzanne Long/Alamy p. **213**; Steve McBeath/iStockphoto p. **213**; Natalie Adamov/Shutterstock p. **213**; attem/Shutterstock p. **213**; artida/Shutterstock p. **215**; Alan Parsons p. **217**; APaterson/Shutterstock p. **220**; scoutingstock/Shutterstock p. **220**; Amy Nichole Harris/Shutterstock p. **220**; siloto/Shutterstock p. **220**; michaeljung/Shutterstock p. **220**; Theodore Scott/Shutterstock p. **220**; Juanmonino/iStockphoto p. **220**; Nathan Holland/Shutterstock p. **220**; Dean Mitchell/Shutterstock p. **221**; Planner/Shutterstock p. **221**; Supertrooper/Shutterstock p. **221**; luchschen/Shutterstock p. **221**; Umbar Shakir/iStockphoto p. **223**; Sarah Cant p. **225**; Sarah Cant p. **226**; Sarah Cant p. **226**; Yann Layma/Stone/Getty Images p. **228**; Time & Life Pictures/Getty Images p. **229**; LOU OATES/iStockphoto p. **231**; Dragan Trifunovic/iStockphoto p. **233**; Nathan Jones/iStockphoto p. **234**; claudia veja/Shutterstock p. **234**; Tiplyashin Anatoly/Shutterstock p. **234**; Alan Parsons p. **235**; Alan Parsons p. **235**; July Flower/Shutterstock p. **239**; Tim Green/The Green Album p. **241**; Tim Green/The Green Album p. **242**.

The authors and publisher would like to thank the following individuals and organisations for permission to reproduce their materials:

Case Studies (Professionals)

Joe Lam and Suite101.com p. **37**; The Graphics Design Team, Marketing Department, Southampton Solent University p. **74**; Nicki Williams p. **76**; Jason Noble (quote only) p. **93**; Mark Gaynor p. **114**; Danny Stijelja pp. **159-160**; Donald MacLellan pp. **167-169**; Clare Allington pp. **173-174**; Alison Willoughby p. **180**; Joshua Ashmore pp. **185-186**; Adam Oliver pp. **193-194**; Mark Glean pp. **201-203**; Ruth Parsfield pp. **209-211**; Deanne Cheuk pp. **217-218**; Sarah Cant pp. **225-226**; Gennie Altas pp. **233-235**; Jon Buck pp. **241-242**.

WorkSpace case studies

Ruth Facey p. **23**; Dave Robinson and Key Publishing p. **47**; Marc Friend p. **67**; Ann Wise p. **85**; Ben Copperwheat p. **101**; Tim Williams p. **117**; Sally Moret p. **133**; Marc Friend p. **149**.

Every effort has been made to contact copyright holders of material reproduced in this book. Any omissions will be rectified in subsequent printings if notice is given to the publishers.

About your BTEC Level 2 First Art and Design course

Choosing to study for a BTEC Level 2 First Art and Design qualification is a great decision to make for lots of reasons. Art and Design can lead into you into a whole range of professions and sectors and allows you to explore your creativity in many different ways.

Your BTEC Level 2 First in Art and Design is a **vocational** or **work-related** qualification. This doesn't mean that it will give you all the skills you need to do a job, but it does mean that you'll have the opportunity to gain specific knowledge, understanding and skills that are relevant to your chosen subject or area of work.

What will you be doing?

The qualification is structured into **mandatory units** (ones that you must do) and **optional units** (ones that you can choose to do). How many units you do and which ones you cover depend on the type of qualification you are working towards.

- BTEC Level 2 First **Certificate** in Art and Design: 1 mandatory and 1 optional unit that provide for a combined total of 15 credits

- BTEC Level 2 First **Extended Certificate** in Art and Design: 3 mandatory units and optional units that provide for a combined total of 30 credits

- BTEC Level 2 First **Diploma** in Art and Design: 6 mandatory units and 9 optional units that provide for a combined total of 60 credits

Unit Number	Credit value	Unit Name	Cert	Ext Cert	Diploma
1	10	Contextual references in art and design	M	M	M
2	5	2D visual communication	O	M	M
3	5	3D visual communication	O	M	M
4	10	Using ideas to explore, develop and produce art and design	N/A	O	M
5	5	Building an art and design portfolio	N/A	O	M
6	5	Working in the art and design industry	N/A	O	M
7	10	Working with graphic design briefs	N/A	O	O
8	10	Working with photography briefs	N/A	O	O
9	10	Working with fashion design briefs	N/A	O	O
10	10	Working with textiles briefs	N/A	O	O
11	10	Working with 3D design briefs	N/A	O	O
12	10	Working with interactive media briefs	N/A	O	O
13	10	Working with visual arts briefs	N/A	O	O
14	10	Working with 3D design crafts briefs	N/A	O	O
15	10	Working with digital art and design briefs	N/A	O	O
16	10	Working with accessory briefs	N/A	O	O
17	10	Working with moving image briefs	N/A	O	O
18	10	Working with site-specific briefs	N/A	O	O

How to use this book

This book is designed to help you through your BTEC Level 2 First Art and Design course. It has three sections:

- **Knowledge:** the chapters cover Units 1 – 5 (mandatory), giving detailed information about each of the learning outcomes

- **Skills:** this section takes you through the process of 'plan, prepare and make, evaluate and reflect', helping you to develop these skills in relation to your chosen specialism

- **The Works** showcases a range of artists and industry professionals, giving first hand experience of working to briefs across different sectors including fashion and textiles, lens-based media, graphic design and visual arts. These map to Units 7 – 18 and provide links to Unit 6 Working in the art and design industry.

This book contains many features that will help you use your skills and knowledge in work-related situations and assist you in getting the most from your course.

Introduction

These introductions give you a snapshot of what to expect from each unit – and what you should be aiming for by the time you finish it!

Assessment and grading criteria

This table explains what you must do to achieve each of the assessment criteria for each of the mandatory and optional units. For each assessment criterion, shown by the grade button **P1**, there is an assessment activity.

Assessment

Your tutor will set **assignments** throughout your course for you to complete. These may take the form of projects where you research, plan, prepare, make and evaluate a piece of work, sketchbooks, case studies and presentations. The important thing is that you evidence your skills and knowledge to date.

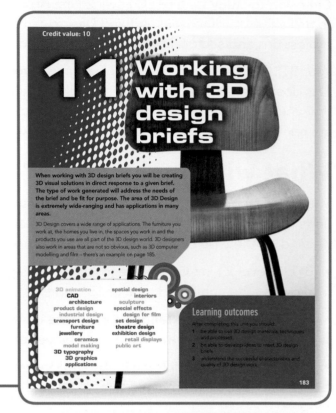

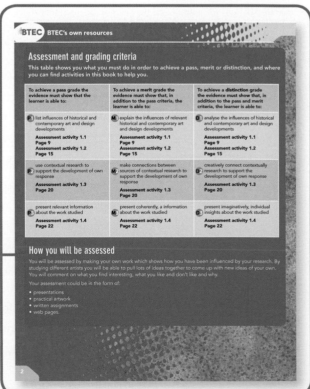

Learner experience

Stuck for ideas? Daunted by your first assignment? These learners have all been through it before…

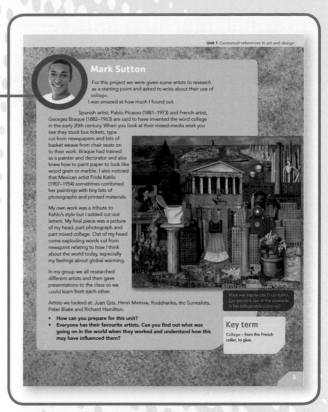

Mark Sutton

For this project we were given some artists to research as a starting point and asked to write about their use of collage.
I was amazed at how much I found out.

Spanish artist, Pablo Picasso (1881–1973) and French artist, Georges Braque (1882–1963) are said to have invented the word collage in the early 20th century. When you look at their mixed-media work you see they stuck bus tickets, type cut from newspapers and bits of basket weave from chair seats on to their work. Braque had trained as a painter and decorator and also knew how to paint paper to look like wood grain or marble. I also noticed that Mexican artist Frida Kahlo (1907–1954) sometimes combined her paintings with tiny bits of photographs and printed materials.

My own work was a tribute to Kahlo's style but I added cut-out letters. My final piece was a picture of my head, part photograph and part mixed collage. Out of my head come exploding words cut from newsprint relating to how I think about the world today, especially my feelings about global warming.

In my group we all researched different artists and then gave presentations to the class so we could learn from each other.

Artists we looked at: Juan Gris, Henri Matisse, Rodchenko, the Surrealists, Peter Blake and Richard Hamilton.

- How can you prepare for this unit?
- Everyone has their favourite artists. Can you find out what was going on in the world when they worked and understand how this may have influenced them?

Mark was inspired by Frida Kahlo. Can you pick out the elements in her collage-style painting?

Key term

Collage – from the French coller, to glue.

Activities

There are different types of activities for you to do: **Assessment activities** are suggestions for tasks that you might do as part of your assignment and will help you develop your knowledge, skills and understanding. **Grading tips** clearly explain what you need to do in order to achieve a pass, merit or distinction grade.

BTEC **Assessment activity 5.5: Presenting 3D work**

Get your 3D work together. Arrange the two lights as in the diagram shown on page 97. They should be at 45 degrees to the work, and the camera should be on a tripod, facing the work square. Put one of the lights slightly nearer the work – this will act as the key light. The second light will add detail to the shadows. If you only have one light, you can still reflect light into the shadows by putting a reflective surface at an angle and out of shot. This will reflect some of the light back into the shadows. If you don't have a pull-down backdrop, bend a sheet of clean white paper and arrange it behind the work, so that it forms a curved surface.

Take photographs of your work and experiment with close-ups of the surfaces.

Grading tips

When you are working through this kind of activity you need to balance two things: working safely to a high technical standard and working creatively. Make sure you know how the camera and lights operate to get technically sound pictures – this will meet **P2**. To reach **M2**, you need to show that you can manage the technical process and get strong shots consistently. This will make for an effective set of photographs. To reach **D2** you can also explore creative approaches, such as camera angles, using just one light for some of the shots, details and so on, as well as making sure you have a consistent and effective set of photographs.

There are also suggestions for activities that will give you a broader grasp of the industry, stretch your imagination and develop your skills.

 Activity 2: Keep a visual diary

Buy a small pocket sketchbook. Collect bits and pieces that represent or remind you of things you do during the week and glue them in. Keep a tiny packet of crayons with the sketchbook and make sketches of what you see or do. Write a few words to record your thoughts, feelings and ideas.

Use your visual diary as a starting point for an assignment.

What sort of bits and pieces?

Keep and use: sugar packets, bus and train tickets, tickets to gigs and shows, photos, postcards of places you've visited. The term for bits and pieces like this is 'ephemera'. A fashion student might collect labels from garments.

Personal, learning and thinking skills

Throughout your BTEC Level 2 First Art and Design course, there are lots of opportunities to develop your personal, learning and thinking skills. Look out for these as you progress.

PLTS

Independent enquirers

Gathering research about art and design organisations will evidence your independent enquiry skills.

Functional skills

It's important that you have good English, maths and ICT skills – you never know when you'll need them, and employers will be looking for evidence that you've got them too.

Functional skills

ICT and English

Using the Internet to undertake research and presenting your findings will evidence your ICT skills.

Key terms

Technical words and phrases are easy to spot. The terms and definitions are also in the glossary at the back of the book.

Key term

Contemporary – usually means 'of now' but often means trendy/cutting edge.

WorkSpace

Workspace provides snapshots of real workplace issues, and show how the skills and knowledge you develop during your course can help you in your career.

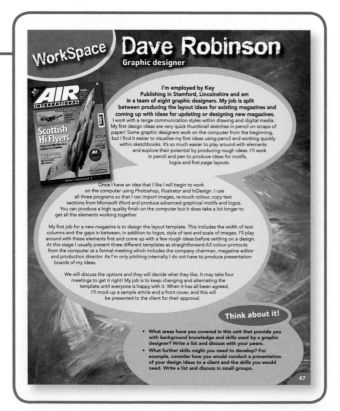

WorkSpace **Dave Robinson**
Graphic designer

I'm employed by Key Publishing in Stamford, Lincolnshire and am in a team of eight graphic designers. My job is split between producing the layout ideas for existing magazines and coming up with ideas for updating or designing new magazines. I work with a range communication styles within drawing and digital media. My first design ideas are very quick thumbnail sketches in pencil on scraps of paper! Some graphic designers work on the computer from the beginning, but I find it easier to visualise my first ideas using pencil and working quickly within sketchbooks. It's so much easier to play around with elements and explore their potential by producing rough ideas. I'll work in pencil and pen to produce ideas for motifs, logos and first page layouts.

Once I have an idea that I like I will begin to work on the computer using Photoshop, Illustrator and InDesign. I use all three programs so that I can import images, re-touch colour, copy text sections from Microsoft Word and produce advanced graphical motifs and logos. You can produce a high quality finish on the computer but it does take a lot longer to get all the elements working together.

My first job for a new magazine is to design the layout template. This includes the width of text columns and the gaps in between, in addition to logos, style of text and scale of images. I'll play around with these elements first and come up with a few rough ideas before settling on a design. At this stage I usually present three different templates as straightforward A3 colour printouts from the computer at a formal meeting which includes the company chairman, magazine editor and production director. As I'm only pitching internally I do not have to produce presentation boards of my ideas.

We will discuss the options and they will decide what they like. It may take four meetings to get it right! My job is to keep changing and alternating the template until everyone is happy with it. When it has all been agreed, I'll mock up a sample article and a front cover, and this will be presented to the client for their approval.

Think about it!

- What areas have you covered in this unit that provide you with background knowledge and skills used by a graphic designer? Write a list and discuss with your peers.
- What further skills might you need to develop? For example, consider how you would conduct a presentation of your design ideas to a client and the skills you would need. Write a list and discuss in small groups.

47

Just checking

When you see this sort of activity, take stock! These quick activities and questions are there to check your knowledge. You can use them to see how much progress you've made, or as a revision tool.

Edexcel's assignment tips

At the end of each chapter, you'll find hints and tips to help you get the best mark you can, such as the best websites to go to, checklists to help you remember processes, and really useful facts and figures.

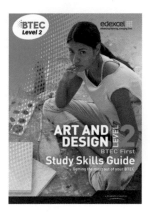

Have you read your **BTEC Level 2 First Study Skills Guide**? It's full of advice on study skills, putting your assignments together and making the most of being a BTEC Art and Design student.

work Ask your tutor about extra materials to help you through your course. You'll find interesting videos, activities, presentations and information about the Art and Design sector.

Your book is just part of the exciting resources from Edexcel to help you succeed in your BTEC course. For more detais visit:

- www.edexcel.com/BTEC
- www.pearsonfe.co.uk/BTEC

Websites and Hotlinks

There are links to relevant websites in this book. In order to ensure that the links are up to date, that the links work, and that the sites are not inadvertently linked to sites that could be considered offensive, we have made the links available on the Pearson website at www.pearsonschoolsandfecolleges.co.uk/hotlinks. When you access the site, search for either the express code 6121V, title BTEC Level 2 First Art and Design Student Book or ISBN 9781846906121.

1 Contextual references in art and design

150 years ago art and design students, in order to learn, had to copy exactly the work of famous artists. From this way of working, they learned how to draw, paint and sculpt as well as to make jewellery, furniture and buildings. You don't have to do that anymore but you are expected to find out about the work of other artists from the past and the present. You'll find out how materials have been used, and how artists have used information from the world around them for inspiration.

This unit will introduce you to key movements in art and design and how artists responded to what was going on in their time. Finding the answers to how society changed because of new ideas in science and manufacturing and how life changed because of world wars can all be discovered by studying art and design.

If you look at how artists worked at the start of the last century you'll find out that they were influenced by the technology that was being invented then. For example, paintings and sculptures reflected the discovery of speed through the invention of cars and planes. Fast forward to artists of the last 40 years and you can discover how Pop, Rock and Punk music changed fashion and graphic design forever. By knowing about contextual references in art and design you will find out how the past links with the work of artists today.

movement
abstract art
realism
historical art

Learning outcomes

After completing this unit you should:

1   know the influences of historical and contemporary art and design developments

2   be able to use historical and contemporary references to support research and development of own response

3   be able to present information about the work studied in an appropriate format.

Assessment and grading criteria

This table shows you what you must do in order to achieve a pass, merit or distinction, and where you can find activities in this book to help you.

To achieve a **pass** grade the evidence must show that the learner is able to:	To achieve a **merit** grade the evidence must show that, in addition to the pass criteria, the learner is able to:	To achieve a **distinction** grade the evidence must show that, in addition to the pass and merit criteria, the learner is able to:
P1 list influences of historical and contemporary art and design developments **Assessment activity 1.1 Page 9** **Assessment activity 1.2 Page 15**	**M1** explain the influences of relevant historical and contemporary art and design developments **Assessment activity 1.1 Page 9** **Assessment activity 1.2 Page 15**	**D1** analyse the influences of historical and contemporary art and design developments **Assessment activity 1.1 Page 9** **Assessment activity 1.2 Page 15**
P2 use contextual research to support the development of own response **Assessment activity 1.3 Page 20**	**M2** make connections between sources of contextual research to support the development of own response **Assessment activity 1.3 Page 20**	**D2** creatively connect contextual research to support the development of own response **Assessment activity 1.3 Page 20**
P3 present relevant information about the work studied **Assessment activity 1.4 Page 22**	**M3** present coherently, information about the work studied **Assessment activity 1.4 Page 22**	**D3** present imaginatively, individual insights about the work studied **Assessment activity 1.4 Page 22**

How you will be assessed

You will be assessed by making your own work which shows how you have been influenced by your research. By studying different artists you will be able to pull lots of ideas together to come up with new ideas of your own. You will comment on what you find interesting, what you like and don't like and why.

Your assessment could be in the form of:

- presentations
- practical artwork
- written assignments
- web pages.

Mark Sutton

For this project we were given some artists to research as a starting point and asked to write about their use of **collage**.
I was amazed at how much I found out.

Spanish artist, Pablo Picasso (1881–1973) and French artist, Georges Braque (1882–1963) are said to have invented the word collage in the early 20th century. When you look at their mixed-media work you see they stuck bus tickets, type cut from newspapers and bits of basket weave from chair seats on to their work. Braque had trained as a painter and decorator and also knew how to paint paper to look like wood grain or marble. I also noticed that Mexican artist Frida Kahlo (1907–1954) sometimes combined her paintings with tiny bits of photographs and printed materials.

My own work was a tribute to Kahlo's style but I added cut-out letters. My final piece was a picture of my head, part photograph and part mixed collage. Out of my head come exploding words cut from newsprint relating to how I think about the world today, especially my feelings about global warming.

In my group we all researched different artists and then gave presentations to the class so we could learn from each other.

Artists we looked at: Juan Gris, Henri Matisse, Rodchenko, the Surrealists, Peter Blake and Richard Hamilton.

- **How can you prepare for this unit?**
- **Everyone has their favourite artists. Can you find out what was going on in the world when they worked and understand how this may have influenced them?**

Mark was inspired by Frida Kahlo. Can you pick out all the elements in her collage-style painting?

1. Know the influences of historical and contemporary art and design developments

Can you connect Punk Rock with Marie Antoinette?

Dame Vivienne Westwood is a fashion designer who invented Punk Rock fashions in the 1970s. Clothes were often offensive printed slogans on torn fabrics which were pinned together again with safety pins. Twenty years later, Westwood started to look at paintings of wealthy people such as Marie Antoinette (1755–1793) to inspire her work.

Look at portraits of wealthy women from 1600 to 1850 and at Westwood's work from the late 1980s onwards. Compare this example of a Westwood top with the painting that inspired it. Discuss the common points.

Discuss the points that are common to the paintings and Westwood's fashions. See the Wallace Collection on Hotlinks.

This Westwood article of clothing has been photographically printed with a detail from François Boucher's *Daphnis and Chloë* (1743–5) in the Wallace Collection, London

Boucher's *Daphnis and Chloë* (1743–5) in the Wallace Collection, London

1.1 Influences

Artists and designers have always been inspired by what has happened in the world around them and have shown this in their work. Sometimes artists work on their own and their ideas seem to sit in isolation, but usually they can be grouped into movements. Key movements in art and design provide a timeline from which you can see how artists relate to each other.

The timeline below names some key movements and gives you an idea about some of the events and inventions that affected the way artists and designers have worked.

Figure 1.1: Key art movements and events from 1850 to the present day

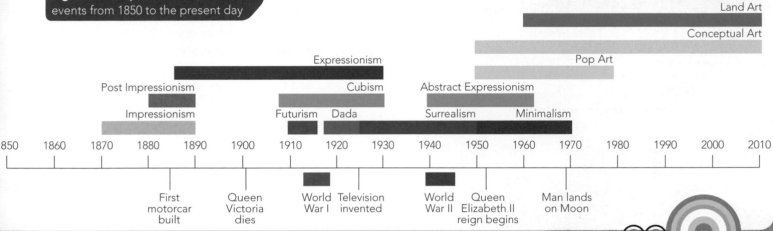

Land Art
Conceptual Art
Pop Art
Expressionism
Abstract Expressionism
Post Impressionism
Cubism
Impressionism
Futurism   Dada
Surrealism   Minimalism

850 1860 1870 1880 1890 1900 1910 1920 1930 1940 1950 1960 1970 1980 1990 2000 2010

First motorcar built
Queen Victoria dies
World War I
Television invented
World War II
Queen Elizabeth II reign begins
Man lands on Moon

Impressionism and Post Impressionism

Impressionism came about because someone found out how to put oil paint in tubes! Before the 1840s, artists ground up paint in their studios using pigment and oil. This was a messy business and it was difficult to take paints outside to work. Artists would sit outside and sketch and then go back into their studios to make paintings. They would often incorporate drawings they had made from copying the old masters.

When oil paint in tubes was invented, artists began to move outside with their easels and canvases, capturing the effects of the sun, wind and rain. The most famous of these artists were known as the Impressionists because they painted an impression of what they saw. The group painted quickly outdoors and had a loose painting style. Among them were:

- Edouard Manet (1832–1883)
- Claude Monet (1840–1926)
- Pierre Auguste Renoir (1841–1919)
- Alfred Sisley (1839–1899)
- Camille Pissarro (1830–1903)
- Berthe Morisot (1841–1895).

If you look closely at their work you can sometimes see tiny flies and bits of sand stuck in the dried paint.

Impressionism
Cubism
Futurism
Dadaism
Surrealism
Abstract
Expressionism

Look at the style of brushstrokes used by the Impressionists

Get out some books from your library on the Impressionist painters. Compare the different ways that they apply paint and think about their use of colour

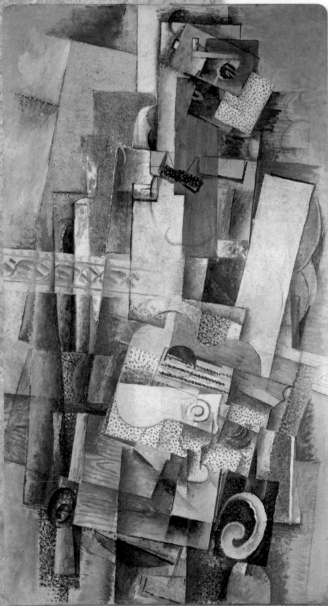

Notice how Georges Braque has flattened perspective in this Cubist work

Post Impressionism came later and included artists such as Georges Seurat (1859–1891) who looked at colour in a more scientific way, Paul Cézanne (1839–1906) who explored pictorial structure and Paul Gauguin (1848–1903) and Vincent van Gogh (1853–1890) who considered the symbolic use of line and colour.

Cubism

In the early 20th century Picasso and Braque began to work in a style that became known as Cubism, which revolutionised European painting and sculpture. In Cubist works objects are depicted from different angles, which are shown in one picture. The surface of a painting can look random, but the artist is showing you the object from different viewpoints to give you more information about it.

Many artists adopted Cubist ideas and you can trace Cubist influences throughout the 20th century in painting and sculpture.

What invention may have given Picasso and Braque the idea to change the way we look at art?

Futurism

The Futurists were an Italian group led by Filippo Marinetti (1876–1944) who were enthralled by the invention of the motor car and the speed they could suddenly travel. Technology took a while to be embraced by Italy, which was a very poor country in the early 20th century, so artists hadn't experienced steam trains and fast travel like their contemporaries in some other European countries.

'We declare that the splendour of the world has been enriched by a new beauty: the beauty of speed' – Marinetti from the Futurist Manifesto, 1909.

The Futurists analysed speed and depicted movement in their paintings. They were also influenced by early film and began to look at everything on a frame-by-frame basis. Very famous paintings of this time include work by Giacomo Balla (1871–1958) – see for example *Dynamism of Dog on a Leash* (1912) and a 1913 sculpture *Unique Forms of Continuity in Space* by Umberto Boccioni (1882–1916).

Marcel Duchamp (1887–1968), an artist who tended to have a go at many different styles, made a famous Futurist painting in 1912 called *Nude Descending a Staircase*, in which he analysed and painted every step of a model going down a staircase on to one canvas.

Dadaism

The Dada movement developed as a result of the turmoil that came out of the First World War (1914–1918). Many painters, actors and writers moved to Switzerland in 1916 and played around with art that had no meaning. They made art from found objects and incorporated 'chance' into their work. Duchamp was a member of this anarchic movement, and one thing he did was to attach an obscene caption to a postcard of Leonardo's *Mona Lisa*. Duchamp had started experimenting with found objects in 1913 and his 'ready-mades', which were everyday items such as a snow shovel, were displayed unaltered in a gallery. Duchamp claimed that any object is art as long as the artist defines it as such.

Can you see how Duchamp depicts movement in his painting?

Key term

Surreal – sur-real means unreal, something which is bizarre or relates to surrealism.

Surrealism

Surrealism grew out of Dadaism as artists began to react to the political and philosophical thoughts of the time. Surrealist artists made 'automatic' drawings and tried to illustrate what was happening in their unconscious minds. During the early 1920s scientific theories about how the mind worked were beginning to develop. Practitioners such as Sigmund Freud invented psychoanalysis and artists were keen to reflect these theories in their work. From the 1920s the Surrealist movement spread around the globe, affecting painting, photography, drawing, sculpture, film, poetry, writing and music.

Artists to look at include Man Ray (1890–1976), Meret Oppenheim (1913–1985), Leonora Carrington (1917–), Roland Penrose (1900–1984), Lee Miller (1907–1977) and Salvador Dali (1904–1989). Dali turned himself into a self-publicist and appeared on television and directed films. In 1973 Dali met the rock star Alice Cooper and produced a three-dimensional hologram of him.

In what ways was Dali's preoccupation with the unconscious mind reflected in this painting?

Abstract Expressionism

Jackson Pollock (1912–1956) painted drip paintings between 1947 and 1956, which are concerned with rhythm and harmony. Pollock flicked and dripped paint on to large boards and canvases as they lay on the floor. His abstract work was part of Abstract Expressionism which emerged in America after the end of the Second World War in 1945. Artists were responding to the horrors of war as well as to the emerging Cold War and mass consumerism. Look at the work of Harold Rosenberg (1906–1978) and Willem de Kooning (1904–1997) to find out more and then link these to the work of Andy Warhol (1928–1987).

What is being expressed in this painting by Willem de Kooning?

Minimalism

This was an offshoot of modern art that appeared in New York in the 1950s in the shape of sculptures and paintings. Carl Andre (1935–), Donald Judd (1928–1994) and Tony Smith (1912–1980) are among the best-known Minimalist artists. Canvases were large and, to many people, looked blank – just filled with one or two colours. This art was extremely unpopular with the public because it looked like nothing.

Unexpectedly in the 1980s, Minimalism seemed to be adopted by ordinary people. Interiors became Minimalist as contents of rooms were either thrown away or hidden behind floor-to-ceiling cupboards that often were concealed. Many magazines featured the Minimalist interiors of architects and designers, which then influenced and inspired other designers. Furniture also became less fussy. Designers began to adopt industrial materials to make furniture, and floors were covered with rubber tiles or tamped-down concrete, as you might find in factories. Of course not everyone went Minimalist, but this example shows how ideas circulate among artists and designers.

 Assessment activity 1.1: Key movements  **P1 M1 D1**

List the key movements you are familiar with. Can you put any important events against these movements?

If you are interested in a specialist pathway, can you answer any of the following about the key movements you have listed?

- What were the dates of the movement?
- What fashions did women wear?
- What sort of transport was used?
- What materials were used to make furniture?
- How did people communicate?
- What did houses built at the time look like?
- What sort of music did people listen to? **P1**

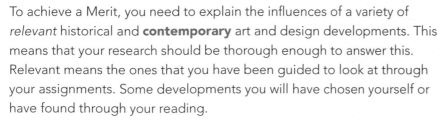

Grading tip **M1**

To achieve a Merit, you need to explain the influences of a variety of *relevant* historical and **contemporary** art and design developments. This means that your research should be thorough enough to answer this. Relevant means the ones that you have been guided to look at through your assignments. Some developments you will have chosen yourself or have found through your reading.

Grading tip **D1**

To achieve a Distinction, you need to show that you can analyse. This means that you should read or listen to enough information to show that you understand how one thing influences another.

 PLTS

Creative thinkers and self–managers

Personal learning and thinking skills are practised when you use your own initiative to explore historical and contemporary references.

Note on a mind map or spider diagram how artists are linked.

Use the information to give yourself new directions to explore.

Key term

Contemporary – usually means 'of now' but often means trendy/cutting edge.

1.2 The wider context

Here are some examples of how art and design has been influenced by developments in construction, technology and travel.

> **height and speed**   radio waves   **polymer technology**
> **trading**   **photography**   **travel**

Can you see how height and speed are depicted in this painting by Robert Delaunay?

How did going up in the world affect artists?

The Eiffel Tower was built from 1887 to 1889, and gave Parisians the opportunity to look at their great city from above. Until then height was only really experienced from the top of seven-storey apartment blocks or from the steps of Sacré Cœur, which is a church on a hill in Montmartre, the highest point in Paris.

In 1903 the Wright Brothers invented the first flying machine and suddenly height and speed merged.

Robert Delaunay (1885–1941) is an artist who embraced the principles of Cubism yet took inspiration from his fascination with height and speed. His paintings include the Eiffel Tower and bi-planes. Early broadcasting transmitters were attached to the Eiffel Tower and Delaunay used the idea of radio waves to segment his paintings. Delaunay was also influenced by early abstract artists such as Franz Marc and Wassily Kandinsky from 'The Blue Rider' group.

Polymer technology

Acrylic paint came about because of the technology involved in polymers. It became available commercially in the 1950s. Acrylic paint dries very quickly, and artists soon discovered that they could paint straight lines that had crisp edges as the colours didn't bleed. Look at the early Op Art work of Bridget Riley. The technology changed the way she painted, but she looked at the illusion of movement and the interaction of colour relationships for her inspiration.

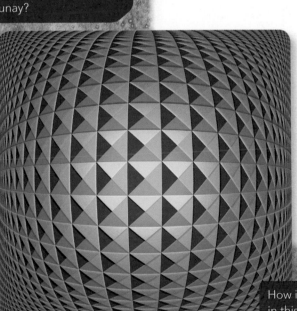

How is the illusion of movement created in this optical print by Mark Glean?

Trading

Imports of china tableware such as plates and bowls started to come from Japan in the 19th century when trading restrictions between Japan and the West were lifted. The china was often wrapped up in Japanese woodcut prints which did not use perspective and tended to have cropped views. European artists who saw these images started to look at their own world differently. Vincent van Gogh is an example.

Can you find any other artists who were influenced by Japanese woodcuts?

The introduction of photography

When photography was invented in the mid-19th century, artists gradually began to lose interest in painting 'reality' and to paint more personal subjects. Many artists had previously made their living by painting rich people and their possessions, and would often make their customers look more beautiful and younger than they really were. When photography came along, more people could afford photographs and so didn't buy portraits of themselves. Artists therefore began to paint other things. They made paintings of subjects they wanted to paint and then sold them rather than working to commission. As artists had more control over what they painted, they began to be more experimental and so 'modern art' started to happen.

Travel

Travel is also a big influence on the way artists have worked. Look especially at the work of Paul Gauguin, who travelled to the South Seas and painted exotic women and landscapes.

These sketchbook pages are the work of BTEC Level 2 First learner Alia Thomas. They are based on the work of Henry Rousseau. How might you respond to influences from cultures and countries other than your own?

Did you know?

Henri Rousseau
also painted faraway jungles but only ever visited his local botanical gardens!

Case study: Jamie Reid and the Sex Pistols

Jamie Reid (1947–) broke new design ground with a record cover for the Sex Pistols in 1977. The record was called 'God Save the Queen'. Why was the cover of the record (below) seen as shocking?

How were the letters made and how would you describe the style? Reid's work defined the image of Punk Rock, especially in the UK. Reid did this because, apart from pre-cut letters called transfer letters (one of the brand names was Letraset), stencil shapes and ready-made type, most typography was hand crafted and took skill and time to produce. At the start of the 20th century artists had experimented with collage, and Reid's record cover echoed their subversive methods.

In the 21st century computer-generated type makes large numbers of fonts available to designers, although new fonts still evolve. Today's graphic designers use computer applications to generate ideas, relating images with typefaces to communicate in exciting ways.

1 Look up the word 'subversion' in a dictionary or online. Can you explain why this word is used to describe the record cover?

2 Can you identify fonts that relate to periods in art history?

3 Can you find artwork that relates the image to the style of the font?

The cover of the Sex Pistols album *God Save the Queen* by Jamie Reid was seen as shocking when it was released in 1977

1.3 Historical art and design developments

Exhibitions have played a prominent role in showcasing the developments in art and design starting with the Great Exhibition in 1851.

Exhibitions

The Great Exhibition, London 1851

'The Great Exhibition of Works of Industry of All Nations' brought exhibits of art, design, technology and industry under the same roof for the first time, and included work from around the world. Visitors saw some of the latest ideas in furniture, iron work, china and gold and silverware design, from countries such as India, Australia, North America and Europe. This insight into design helped artists and designers breathe new ideas into their work.

Among the fine art and applied art exhibits were:

- Hiram Powers' *The Greek Slave*
- a group of Indian art objects
- sculpture displays in front of the Indian Pavilion
- Stained Glass Gallery
- The Medieval Court
- Pugin's Gothic-style stove
- a heating stove in the form of a suit of armour.

More images of the Crystal Palace and exhibits at the Great Exhibition can be found on Hotlinks.

Over 6 million visitors came to see displays from over 17,000 exhibitors, and the profits from the exhibition enabled the building of other museums in London, most notably the Victoria and Albert Museum.

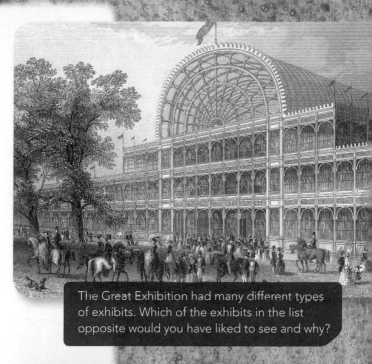

The Great Exhibition had many different types of exhibits. Which of the exhibits in the list opposite would you have liked to see and why?

Exposition Internationale des Arts Décoratifs et Industriels Modernes Paris, 1925

This exhibition gave the name 'Art Deco' to the geometric style of design and interior decoration that was popular in the 1920s and 1930s in Europe and America. It also displayed the latest technology, such as tubular steel furniture, as well as ivory, jade and objects made from lacquer.

The Festival of Britain, London, 1951

This exhibition was designed to boost morale after the devastation of the Second World War. The exhibition displayed good quality public design, interiors, fabrics, furniture and everyday items, including the latest designs from Scandinavia. Some of the exhibition was in the Royal Festival Hall, Southbank in London, which still exists today.

Stained Glass Gallery, Great Exhibition, 1851

- **Can you find out which artists and designers worked at the Festival of Britain?**
- **Can you discover which designer made stacking chairs which are similar to those sold today?**

This is Tomorrow, 1956

In 1956 Richard Hamilton made a collage called *Just what is it that makes today's homes so perfect, so appealing?* for this exhibition held at the Whitechapel Gallery in London. Hamilton used photographs of all the things around him that were changing his world, which included bird's-eye views of people lying on beaches and grainy pictures of lunar surfaces.

1.4 Contemporary art and design developments

The Internet and the speed at which we communicate have changed the way that artists see the world and respond to it. You can draw inspiration and ideas from artists' online blogs and RSS feeds.

The Creative Opera Design blog is an example of an online blog where designers can find advice and discuss their work and developments in their sector. Artsmonitor is an example of a RSS feed which provides news, articles and bookmarks to those in the art and design sector. To view the Creative Opera design blog go to Hotlinks.

Banksy

Look at the spray-can work of Banksy as an example of an artist who has succeeded in getting what was seen as vandalism accepted as art.

Banksy is an anonymous graffiti artist who has become famous for combining graffiti art with stencilling techniques in street art. He has never been seen making this guerrilla art in the public places that he works and his true identity has never been confirmed. His work comments on political, social and cultural affairs.

In the summer of 2009 Banksy took over Bristol City Museum with a free exhibition of his work as a thank you to the city that inspired him with its underground scene of artists and musicians.

Tracey Emin

Tracey Emin, a contemporary **conceptual** artist, proclaimed her unmade bed and all its surrounding rubbish a work of art in 1999. Emin's influences were her unhappy adolescence and the way she felt about herself. However, the public wasn't as shocked by it as visitors were by Duchamp's ready-made works 85 years earlier.

Key terms

Conceptual Art – a term used in the 1960s to describe art where the idea behind the work is more important than the end result.

Tracey Emin's bed wasn't shocking to the public. Can you think of any reasons why 'anything goes' now as art and design?

1.5 Interactive museums and galleries

WebExhibits is an American website which includes 'exhibits' on individual artists such as Andy Warhol, historical paintings and artefacts such as Bellini's *Feast of the Gods*, as well as art and design topics and themes, such as the use of colour. To view the exhibits on WebExhibits go to Hotlinks.

This is also an online design gallery which showcases work by designers at UCreative. It contains images of work created by current and ex-students, and is searchable by discipline (3D Design, Digital Design, Sculpture) and exhibition. To view the design work on UCreative go to Hotlinks.

BTEC Assessment activity 1.2: The influence of technology

Examples of how technology influenced artists can be brought up to the present day as you explore how contemporary artists and designers use digital art, sound and fibre technologies in their work. First though, explore the Bauhaus which was a German art school from 1919 to 1933.

Work in small groups and answer the following:

1. Which new technologies did Bauhaus art students explore?

2. Which of these technologies are still used today?

3. Identify contemporary digital artists – where can their work be seen?

4. What is the link between sound technology and art?

5. How is fibre technology used apart from in fashion design?

Grading tips

- Explain the importance of the Bauhaus technologies. Show that you understand how they influenced ideas about design.
- Record the designers' names and give examples of their work. Find out if any of their work has become a 'design classic' and explain why, nearly 90 years later, people still want to have it.
- When you look for digital artists, do research artists who have achieved recognition, but don't overlook up-and-coming artists.

museums and
galleries
artists' houses
open studios
public art

Key terms

Contextual – the context in which something was made. For example, Picasso painted *Guernica* in 1937 as his response to a town being bombed in the Spanish Civil War.

Primary sources – are those that you experience for yourself first-hand.

Secondary sources – are those that another person has reviewed or experienced for you to refer to.

Who lived at Charleston Farmhouse? What art movement were they linked to? Write 100–150 words about them

2. Be able to use historical and contemporary references to support research and development of own response

The golden rule for this learning outcome is 'research, record, respond'. Have a go at researching an area that you are interested in but are unfamiliar with – this will expand your **contextual** understanding. Brainstorm your ideas with others and really think about what is achievable in the time you have. You might find a mind-mapping software tool useful or construct your spider map in your sketchbook or work journal. Then focus on your research – what do you need to find out in order to develop your artwork?

2.1 Using primary and secondary references

Make sure that your research contains both **primary** and **secondary sources**.

Primary sources

Primary research enables you to make your own mind up about the artist from your first-hand experience. Researching primary sources is essential, so go to galleries, museums and exhibitions whenever you can, and if possible try to make sure your response to an assignment is based around a local resource. Collect leaflets and postcards and record any interviews you have with artists.

Visiting museums and galleries

One example of primary research is when you see the original artist or designer's work, such as a painting, hanging on a wall for yourself. If you're lucky, you can get close enough to see all the detail and can experience the colours and textures. The benefit of seeing something for yourself is also to appreciate the size of the work. A good art book will give you the dimensions of an artwork, but it's always best to see the real thing. Exhibitions will often gather together important works of art belonging to private collectors that are never seen in books. Although rich collectors such as royalty and large companies still collect paintings, so do pop stars and footballers.

Part of the fun of an exhibition is to see who has lent their collection. The curator will have hung each piece so that it has some relation to the work next to it. You should read the text next to each piece and any synopsis about the exhibition for information about the work displayed.

Visiting artists' houses

A really exciting form of primary research is to visit an artist's house. Artists who have died sometimes have their homes preserved by independent trusts. Tour guides will tell you how the artists lived, and you can see how rooms are decorated and the art and decorative objects that filled their home.

Open Studio events and local art weeks

Artists group together in country areas, cities and towns and sometimes open their studios to display their work for sale. Studios tend to be open from a week up to a month, with opening times and details published in catalogues and through websites: type 'artists' studios open events + UK' into a search engine and you will find a list of events near you.

Here are some questions you could ask an artist and about his or her work:

- What is your background? (name, nationality, date of birth)
- What was your education?
- What was your early work like?
- Are you part of a movement?
- Who are your contemporaries? (other artists working at the same time)
- Have you been influenced by any significant events? Why do you work in the way you do?
- What has contributed to your success?

You can adapt this format to a movement or use the same questions to investigate a particular decade of art and design.

Public art

Public art is usually large, found out of doors and very accessible to see. Most towns and cities sponsor artists to make major sculptures and much of this art will be listed on council websites. Once you've seen the real thing and made up your mind about it, you can then research details about the artist to support your findings.

On this page are three examples of public art in different settings.

Secondary sources

Secondary sources includes a variety of things, so look at art books, CD-ROMs, DVDs, magazines and journals, as well as reading about artists on the Internet.

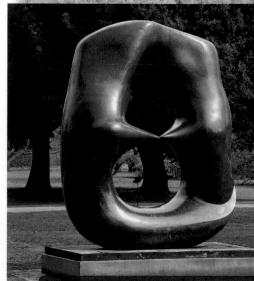

What reasons can you think of why Henry Moore intended his sculptures to be sited in landscape?

art books
CD-ROMs
DVDs
magazines and journals
Internet

In what ways do you think Barbara Hepworth's sculpture 'works' in relation to the building and its setting?

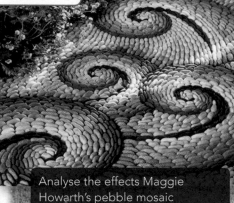

Analyse the effects Maggie Howarth's pebble mosaic pavement is creating

2.2 Recording your sources

Record your findings – Make your own notes as you find information from looking, reading and listening. If you print out notes from the Internet, highlight the parts you have read to show that you have read the information. No one gets extra marks for using up trees and then presenting piles of unread printouts as part of the assignment. Be smart and take detailed notes which show that you have engaged with the subject you are researching.

Record your sources – You may want to look at your sources again for further information. Note down accurately where you obtained the information from so that you can find it again. See below for details on how to do this. You should also evidence your sources throughout your work or at the end of an assignment, as this is professional practice as well as being a Pass criteria requirement.

Why bother to record this kind of detail?

Working in a professional way is a smart way of working. It looks good and shows that you've taken a mature approach to your studies. Plus, if anyone reading your work is interested they can look it up too. If you look at the criteria for **M3** you will see that it requires you to present a variety of information about the work studied. By recording your sources you show that you have used a variety of information and not only that it was from different places and media.

If you've looked at a website and taken down your own notes make sure that the URL information is recorded before you change sites – don't waste time searching again for information you've already used and finished with.

For a web page such as Wikipedia – record it like this:

Guggenheim Museum Bilbao: http://en.wikipedia.org/wiki/Guggenheim_Museum_Bilbao (accessed 11 May 2009)

For a DVD:

presenter, title, production company and the year it was made in the same format as for a book. Use the same idea for a television programme, but give information about the channel and the date you watched the programme. Make a note of all the books, magazines, newspapers, journals, websites, DVDs, television programmes that you have used to obtain information from. Use this format:

For books: author, *title in italics*, (publisher and year of publication, in brackets), as in

Beaney J. & Littlejohn J., *A Sketch in Time* (Double Trouble Enterprises, 2003)

For magazines, newspapers and journals: author, article, magazine/journal, date and page, as in

Caro A. 'The Sculptural Architecture of Mughal India' (*The World of Interiors,* April 2002, p. 198)

For a journal article from a website: author, article, web journal, web address plus the date accessed as in

Soll A. (2009), 'Pollock in Vogue: American Fashion and Avant-garde Art in Cecil Beaton's 1951 Photographs', *Fashion Theory*, Vol. 13, Issue 1, http://docserver.ingentaconnect.com (accessed 29 April 2009)

2.3 Developing your own response

You've brainstormed the assignment and researched historical and contemporary art and artists to help you develop your response. Next, analyse how this research has helped your ideas. Here is a list of things that may have influenced you – can you add some more?

subject matter
form
colours
techniques

Case study: Jessica Ryles

Part 1: Secondary source research

For a project on our senses, I followed up my primary research (which involved responding to music by painting shapes and colours) with research using secondary sources on Wassily Kandinsky. I used a range of Internet sites as well as art books. I discovered that Kandinsky had a condition called synaesthesia, where you see music in colours and shapes.

On the Internet, I was able to see how Kandinsky used this condition to his advantage: he used colour and different shapes in a way that you wouldn't normally think of doing and that's why his work is so good.

Part 2: Developing your own response

After I finished my research, I started to develop my own work for the project (on our senses). I was

inspired by the way Kandinsky worked when he saw music in colours.

Here are some examples of the paintings I created in response to music.

Wassily Kandinsky's painting emphasises how he could see colours when listening to music

19

Make a spider diagram of ideas so you can think through responding with your own artwork.

Grading tips

To achieve **M2** you need to show you have made connections between your research and your response. To show that you have made connections your research needs to be linked to your outcome and you need to be able to explain this. Make sure that you are able to mention a selection of artists and be able to describe their work and how they connect. The paragraph about Minimalism shows very clearly how to make connections, so if your outcome was a Minimalist piece then you would develop this idea further.

To achieve **D2** you need to work independently and show that you have been insightful. This means that you have read as much as you can about a topic and have drawn your own conclusions. You've thought about the issues and also shown that you have your own opinions. If you find that hard to do, try asking an adult (not the tutor) to talk to you and ask questions. This will make you think about the work you've researched and help give shape to your ideas and thoughts.

3. Be able to present information about the work studied in an appropriate format

3.1 Presenting information

You need to present your work in an appropriate format. This could be:

- a case study presented as a written essay
- an oral presentation using visual images presented on display boards or as a PowerPoint
- annotated images in a file or sketchbook
- web pages
- pages for the course VLE
- a poster presentation made using an IT package
- supported by an oral presentation.

3.2 Making judgements and commenting on your work

However you present your information you need to give an indication of your research and explain how it has influenced your work.

There are different ways that you can do this. Here are some examples:

- **Annotating your sketchbook**
  Annotating images in a sketchbook is not necessarily the easy option. Think of it a bit like an essay that you have cut up and pasted around your work, in a sequence that is easy to follow and makes reference to the pictures. When you work in a sketchbook you have the choice of handwriting or pasting text in. Clear, well-formed handwriting always looks good in sketchbooks, but you will need to work out exactly what to write before you do so. Make sure that your words are legible and spelling, grammar and punctuation are correct.

- **Oral presentation** – If you opt for an oral presentation – which you can support with a poster, a PowerPoint presentation or A1 illustrated display boards – you still need to hand in the text of what you intend to say as evidence. Unless you present a recording of your presentation, then you have to evidence your work with written words.

- **Written presentation** – Use the structure to help shape your writing. Decide (if you haven't been given a word count) how much to write to complement your choice of presentation:

Being able to present your research well is an important skill in art and design – make the most of the tips provided here

  1 Introduction – why you researched what you did
  2 Findings/results/discussion – reflections about artists, relevant details about art movements
  3 Conclusion – what you think about what you found out and how it influenced the art you made

Illustrate your findings. This can be with postcards, pictures from magazines, gallery leaflets or discarded books, the Internet or your own samples of small sections of another artists' work where you have tried to copy the way they worked. Sounds familiar – that's where we started!

Assessment activity 1.4: Illustrated presentation

What areas have you covered in this unit? Give a 5-minute illustrated presentation to your peers and conclude your talk by giving out a one-page handout on your findings. Use bullet points to make your findings clear, and give everyone the chance to ask you questions. By listening to your group and collecting their handouts, you will find out much more about historical and contemporary influences in art and design than on your own.

Grading tips

Make sure you:

- recommend books and websites
- talk about a favourite gallery or museum
- are enthusiastic about your topic.

To achieve **M3** you have to present coherently a variety of information about the work studied. This means that your work needs to be clear and well presented. The reasons that you did your research need to be explained.

D3 requires you to present imaginatively. This means that you have ideas, can make connections and have opinions. However, you can also be imaginative in the presentation of your work, by designing original covers or unusual presentation boards, or by packaging your work in a memorable way.

 ## Case study: Jessica Ryles, 'What is Art?'

Part 3: Writing an essay

I organised my essay into three parts:

- introduction
- discussion points, supported by findings from my research
- conclusion.

I also included a bibliography of the websites I visited and the books that I read. As part of my essay, I handed in illustrated research notes about all the artists I explored in my 'Senses' project.

Conclusions:

Some people think art needs to be shocking and unusual to really be noticed and appreciated, and to be honest it works; sometimes shocking and unusual can definitely not be ignored.

But just because shocking art may seem like it steals the limelight doesn't mean that less shocking art is less interesting. Just because today's crowd is more used to shocking scenes, it doesn't mean that nothing can be shocking any more!

There is always something new and OLD out there that STILL and WILL have the power to shock!

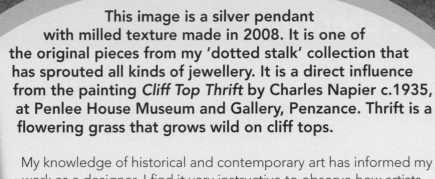

This image is a silver pendant with milled texture made in 2008. It is one of the original pieces from my 'dotted stalk' collection that has sprouted all kinds of jewellery. It is a direct influence from the painting *Cliff Top Thrift* by Charles Napier c.1935, at Penlee House Museum and Gallery, Penzance. Thrift is a flowering grass that grows wild on cliff tops.

My knowledge of historical and contemporary art has informed my work as a designer. I find it very instructive to observe how artists have approached their view of subjects and how designers have responded to demands of functionality and decoration when making objects.

It is important to observe how the great periods of art and design have remained as inspirations to subsequent generations. Creative practitioners must filter the knowledge of historical and contemporary art to understand its original context and its current relevance – if any. I use this as a springboard for an individual response, and to deliver a fresh and original piece of work. In this way my work acknowledges the examples of others but remains true to the personal style that develops. Therefore an artist should maintain an interest in the output of other artists, not just from one's own discipline but from wider sources. This revitalises ones own perception and understanding of creative energy and helps to balance these within one's working life.

Think about it!

- Have you ever produced a piece of work influenced by someone else's art?
- What inspires your work?

Just checking

1 What does 'contextual' mean?

2 Why is technology important to art and design? Can you list how ideas and inventions have made a difference to the way artists have looked at things?

3 List four different ways of presenting your work.

4 What is the best way to show that you have read information found on the Internet?

edexcel

Assignment tips

Experiencing artists' work

You can really appreciate the size, texture, detail and colours of paintings, textiles, fashions, graphics, furniture, products, jewellery, glass and ceramics if you can experience them first-hand. Always take the opportunity to look at artists' sketchbooks and worksheets that might be on display, as these can inform you about how ideas have been developed.

Websites

The galleries and museums listed below represent just a few of the great places to visit. They all have websites and most have virtual galleries full of art and design work:

- Tate: Tate Modern, Tate Britain, Tate Liverpool and Tate St Ives

- Fashion Museum, Bath

- Design Museum, London

- Victoria and Albert Museum, London

- Warner Textile Archive, Braintree

- Geffrye Museum, London (furniture and interiors)

- National Trust (buildings and interiors)

- English Heritage (buildings and interiors)

To visit the websites go to Hotlinks.

2 2D visual communication

Being able to get your ideas across is a core skill in the art and design industry and there are techniques and skills in 2D visual communication that are used across drawing, painting, digital work, photography and printmaking which will help you do this.

Think about designs, products or brand names, for example, that really stand out – the artists, designers and craftspeople behind them have all experimented with different ways of communicating, often 'breaking the rules' to come up with innovative and memorable designs.

This unit introduces you to using skills that will help you to best record and communicate your ideas visually. You will explore, experiment with and apply mark-making skills with a range of art and design materials and investigate all stages of the design process: from gathering research and starting points within your sketchbooks, producing initial thumbnail, compositional and layout sketches through to design development.

communicating ideas
hand-drawn ideas
concept boards
computer-generated visuals
storyboards
visuals
design roughs
presentation boards
thumbnail sketches
final illustrations
diagrams
layouts

Learning outcomes

After completing this unit you should:

1 be able to use 2D mark-making techniques

2 be able to communicate design ideas using 2D visual communication techniques

3 be able to use formal elements in 2D visual communication.

Assessment and grading criteria

This table shows you what you must do in order to achieve a pass, merit or distinction grade, and where you can find activities in this book to help you.

To achieve a **pass** grade the evidence must show that the learner is able to:	To achieve a **merit** grade the evidence must show that, in addition to the pass criteria, the learner is able to:	To achieve a **distinction** grade the evidence must show that, in addition to the pass and merit criteria, the learner is able to:
P1 demonstrate use of 2D mark-making techniques safely when working from primary and secondary sources **Assessment activity 2.1 page 34** **Assessment activity 2.2 page 35** **Assessment activity 2.3 page 38**	**M1** demonstrate consistent and effective use of 2D mark-making techniques when working from primary and secondary sources **Assessment activity 2.1 Page 34** **Assessment activity 2.2 Page 35** **Assessment activity 2.4 Page 39**	**D1** demonstrate imaginative and independent use of 2D mark-making techniques when working from primary and secondary sources **Assessment activity 2.1 Page 34** **Assessment activity 2.2 Page 35** **Assessment activity 2.4 Page 39**
P2 communicate design ideas using 2D visual communication techniques **Assessment activity 2.3 Page 38**	**M2** communicate ideas effectively and consistently using 2D mark-making techniques **Assessment activity 2.4 Page 39**	**D2** communicate ideas imaginatively and independently using 2D mark-making techniques **Assessment activity 2.4 Page 39**
P3 use formal elements in 2D visual communication **Assessment activity 2.5 Page 43**	**M3** explain the use of formal elements in 2D visual communication **Assessment activity 2.5 Page 43**	**D3** evaluate the use of formal elements in 2D visual communication **Assessment activity 2.5 Page 43**

How you will be assessed

You need to provide evidence that shows your skill in using your chosen art and design techniques and that you can work safely in producing your work. You also need to demonstrate that you worked from both primary and secondary sources and that you understand and can use art and design language and terms appropriately.

Your assessment could be in the form of:

- a one-to-one or group recorded oral or visual presentation
- a display or exhibition of your work
- a sketchbook review
- a portfolio presentation of your work with a recorded or written review.

Bonny Cannon

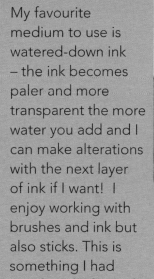

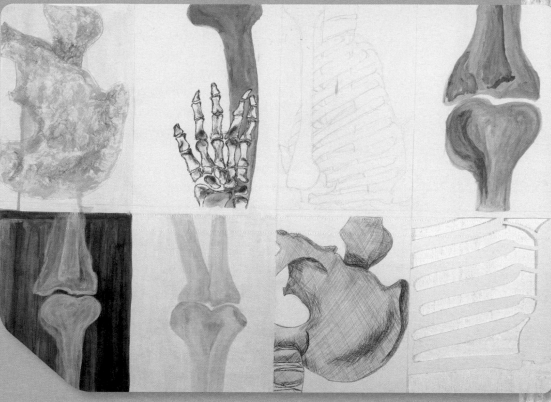

My favourite medium to use is watered-down ink – the ink becomes paler and more transparent the more water you add and I can make alterations with the next layer of ink if I want! I enjoy working with brushes and ink but also sticks. This is something I had not done before. I find thin wooden skewers really good to use. They have a point at one end and you can make lots of different types of marks with them. Biros can also be really good to draw with. You can make very light lines and dark lines which can be very effective when drawing. I have learned about cross hatching which is using lines to describe the form of an object or how light and dark something is. Using lines like this can really help to make objects look three dimensional. This worked very well when we drew the skeleton. We had to choose different sections and make use of a range of media and these techniques really helped me.

At the beginning of my course, I struggled with painting as I had not done very much before. I found it very hard to mix colours and get the shades right. But the tutors helped and showed me how to do this with paint and a range of other media too – they often suggest new ideas you haven't thought of and help you develop an individual style.

I have definitely learned a new skill and now feel confident about painting in light and dark areas.

- **Think about the mark-making techniques and media you have used. What has worked well for you?**
- **How confident do you feel about experimenting?**

Experiment with tone

Select any pencil and get started experimenting with **tone**. Draw a rectangle and divide it into six sections. Fill in each section so that it is a different shade of grey to produce your own **tonal range**. Aim for the first section to be as dark as possible and get steadily lighter so that the last one is as light as possible. Remember to note down which grade of pencil you used and try other grades to see how they differ.

Key terms

Tone – the variation of light and dark areas which can be used to describe 3D forms in 2D.

Tonal range – the different shades of grey between solid black and absolute white.

All artists and designers use 2D visual communication exploring a range of materials and techniques to best express their ideas and show other people their designs. For example:

- animators often start by using pencils, pens and paper to produce initial linear visuals of ideas for scenes and they may then develop these using storyboarding software to add emotion and further detail with layers of colours and textural effects

- textile designers select groups of colours to combine within their work and may explore scale, complexity and different pattern repeats within their seasonal collections

- product designers record dimensions, construction details and 3D form accurately in order to construct prototypes and final pieces

- photographers may explore composition and placement and direction of light both when setting up a shot and within the post-production stage when images can be changed using different qualities of paper and printing techniques

- graphic designers will produce initial page layouts considering the style of text, colour range and white space left within their work to ensure readability, consistency and the effectiveness of their designs.

1. Be able to use 2D mark-making techniques

1.1 2D mark-making

Effective and imaginative 2D mark-making can be produced using any medium or material capable of making a mark on a surface. Materials can be used separately or combined to add further texture and depth to a piece of work. The mark-making you choose to use will be dependent on the end purpose of your work and may be incredibly economical or minimal such as Henri Matisse's refined single line drawings in which he explored pattern and form within still life or traditional Japanese drawings produced with a fluid brush line and ink.

Try using fluid brush lines and ink to create a Japanese-style brush drawing

More complicated, layered mark-making can be produced using different combinations of media. Contemporary illustrator Lauren Child uses a combination of collage, Photoshop and coloured pencils, while the architectural paintings of John Piper use a combination of wax resist with ink, paint, charcoal and graphite.

Materials

A great way to get started developing mark-making skills is to explore drawing materials first. These are readily available and the range of effects, styles and skills learned here can be made use of within design assignments and then translated into a wider range of materials. Experiment with how you hold each material, the scale you work at and how you apply them. For example, ink could be applied with a stick, drawing pen, brush or sponge to make different types of marks.

Ink and mixed-media image by John Piper. Think about using ink, charcoal and collage in your illustrations

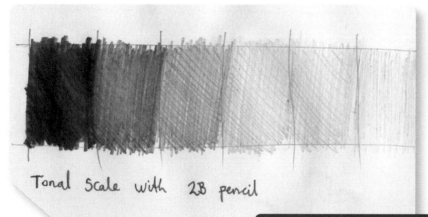

Figure 2.1: Tonal scale with 2B pencil

Pencils

Pencils are divided into 'B' and 'H' grades. The higher the 'B' grade the softer the pencil. This results in a wider tonal range – from black to very pale grey – and more texture. The 'B' refers to 'black' as 'B' grade pencils will produce deeper black tones. You will also find that this pencil goes blunt quickly and you have to sharpen it a lot. The higher the 'H' grade the harder the pencil will be, resulting in paler tones and more accurate, sharper marks.

pencils – graphite, charcoal, coloured
inks – drawing, fabric dyes, food colouring
paints – watercolour, gouache, acrylic
pastels – chalk, oil, wax

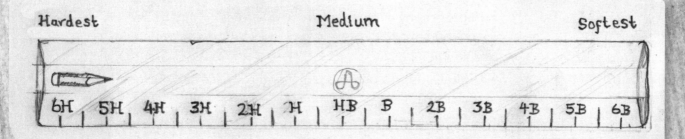

Figure 2.2: The HB pencil scale

Paper

The surface you choose to work on will affect the range of marks you make.

Paper type	Description	Application
cartridge paper	white or cream, different weights and textures available	good for drawing, painting and printing onto
newsprint	cream, smooth	good for mono-prints can be used for quick initial pencil studies
sugar paper	rough, textured, different colours available	good for charcoal and pastel drawings can be used with paint but tends to absorb the colour
wallpaper lining	cream, smooth, different weights and lengths available	good for large scale working
photographic paper	matt, pearl, gloss, different weights available	good for colour work and printing final designs
layout paper	smooth, white, semi-see through	used for developing and refining design ideas
tissue paper	thin, see through, lots of colours available	used in collage work and can be good to layer using PVA glue mixed with water can be drawn onto although it can rip easily – this quality can be exploited
graph paper	grid paper, different styles available	used to develop accurate ideas
sand paper	rough, textured	can be used in collage or painted over and drawn onto good for large scale work but difficult for detailed studies
watercolour paper	different weights and textures available	used with soft drawing materials, watercolour and ink washes and paint

Table 2.1: Which of these paper types might you use in your work?

Did you know?

You can create different marks by changing the way you hold a pencil, pen or paint brush. If you hold the tool at the very end it will produce very light and loose flowing lines, while rolling it and drawing with the edge will produce a textural softer mark.

The mark-making that you produce can be developed using materials found within printmaking, photography and digital media, such as:

- **Printing** – carving or drawing marks into lino, card, polystyrene, wood blocks, and cutting or painting stencils for screen printing
- **Photography** – using sepia toning, increasing and decreasing the contrast, printing onto matt, pearl or gloss paper, dodging or burning the image when printing
- **Digital** – using a pen and tablet or the mouse and exploring drawing and painting tools such as the brush, eraser, pen, blur and burn within Photoshop.

1.2 Techniques

Specialist materials and each process area can be used in different ways to produce a range of techniques.

- Different drawing techniques such as stipple, smudge, cross hatch, single and multiple-line can be used to create different mark-making styles.
- In printmaking the techniques of silkscreen printing, mono-printing, lino cuts and wood blocks will all produce different styles of work.

The two photographs below show how learners have taken a primary source object and explored how they can draw it to best represent its shape, form and pattern in order to produce their own interpretation of the object. They have experimented with techniques such as line, smudge, blending and wash and tried each material several times before moving on to the next.

Use your sketchbook to develop your mark-making skills and techniques and record your progress (see Figure 2.3). Be imaginative: experiment with different ways of using materials and techniques to develop your own style.

Experimenting with techniques and materials is a great way to test their physical properties as well as your imagination

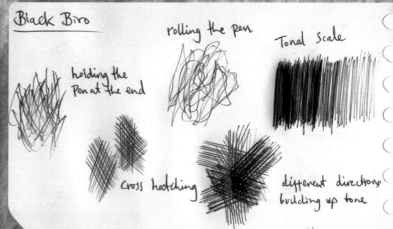

Figure 2.3: 2D mark-making techniques

Experimenting with techniques

Some techniques are often linked to specific media but it can be interesting to explore using different techniques in one piece of work so that you create imaginative and original drawings, visuals and design work. Here are some examples of 2D visual communication techniques which are often linked to specific media:

Sgraffito drawing and painting technique

Digital art

digital blending, digital painting, cloning

Printmaking

mono-print, collagraph, block printing, etch, silkscreen

Drawing

stipple, smudge, sgraffito

Cloning digital art technique

Silkscreen printmaking technique

Painting

blend, wash, scumble, sgraffito

Photography

dodge, focus

The diagram below identifies different types of media with suggested techniques for you to try out for yourself.

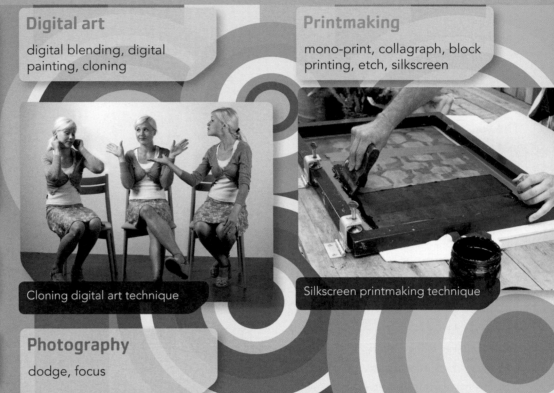

Ink
- Apply with a thin stick or skewer for scratchy mark-making.
- Apply with a round tipped brush for thin and thick fluid lines.
- Water down and apply as a thin layer.
- Apply over resist materials to create a different effect e.g. wax, masking fluid.

Printing
- Cut into a rubber, polystyrene block or lino to form a block and print with using an ink pad.
- Cut away sections in a piece of paper or acetate and stencil through colour – produce different textures by using a toothbrush, sponge, rage, spray paint, screen print.

Materials and techniques

Acrylic paint
- Add lots of water to make into a thin and pale wash – apply this to a background area with a large DIY brush or sponge.
- Mix sand or sawdust into your paint to make it more textural and apply onto the paper with a palette knife.
- Use masking fluid or masking tape to cover sections of your work then paint over.
- Mix into a smooth consistency and apply with a dip pen or stick to change the range of mark-making.
- Mix into a thick consistency and apply to the edge of a piece of card and print with it.
- Mix into a thin consistency with lots of water when you start a painting so that these first marks are very pale and can be easily corrected.
- Mix PVA glue into your paint so that it dries with a shine.

Figure 2.4: How many of these materials and techniques have you used? Try experimenting with new combinations.

1.3 Recording

Artists and designers often draw, paint, photograph and record primary sources as starting points for their work. By looking at real objects, places and forms artists can:

- select what to record and what to leave out
- select sections they are interested in to observe and develop into designs
- choose the angle from which to draw in order to observe particular colours, shapes or forms
- decide on how the object is positioned and composed on the page.

They may also work from a range of secondary source materials which could be imagery found within books, magazines or on the Internet. Working with secondary sources means that artists can focus on:

- sourcing a specific object or theme for their work
- creating an original image by combining and or making collages of text and images
- using cameras, photocopiers and software packages to work on scale, placement and composition.

No matter what your assignment or brief, you are likely to use both primary and secondary sources to record ideas. You may experiment with creating a range of compositions using primary sources, recording first in a realistic and accurate way before moving on to drawing styles suitable for specific areas of art and design such as abstracting and repeating patterns or surface pattern design, for example.

- Architect, designer and watercolourist Charles Rennie Mackintosh worked initially in watercolour producing paintings from the primary source of real flowers. The shapes within the petals from a rose were transformed into his stylised rose design which he applied to fabric, furniture and glass windows.
- Contemporary designer Claire Coles draws inspiration from historical floral images on wallpapers (secondary source materials), ceramics and jewellery combining sections of old wallpapers and 'drawing' onto them with stitching to produce accessories, illustrations and ceramics.

1.4 Health and Safety

In the studio or workshop, it is important that you follow safe systems of working to ensure your own safety and that of others. Your tutor will introduce media, techniques and processes with explanations and practical demonstrations so that you understand how to use them safely. It is important that you take notes and apply the same safety procedures when working on your own. Further information about how to use media and equipment safely can be found on instruction sheets when you buy media and on a range of health and safety websites.

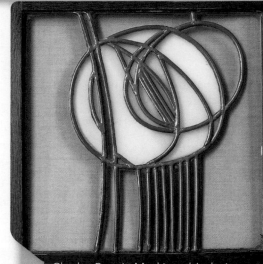

Charles Rennie Mackintosh's design simplifies the structure of a rose

This stitch design uses found materials to create something new, in the style of work by Claire Coles

The following websites provide practical advice on working safely:

- NSEAD (The National Society for Education in Art and Design) Health & Safety Guide
- Visual Arts Career Guide
- Health & Safety in the Arts: Painting & Drawing Techniques
- Drawing & Sketching Techniques
- Art Safety Training Guide.

Go to Hotlinks to view them.

1.5 Developing your observation and recording skills

A 2D designer, such as a photographer, graphic designer, animator or illustrator, will search out interesting shapes, patterns, colour palettes and compositions to use as inspiration and reference for future work. A 3D designer such as a fashion or furniture designer will record form and structure to use as the silhouette and shape. Whichever direction you choose and whatever media you work in, you will need to practise your observation and recording skills as often as you can.

BTEC Assessment activity 2.1: Primary sources

Natural forms contain a great selection of shapes, textures, colours and forms which can be recorded as a starting point for a range of different design outcomes. The 3D forms can be used for sculptures, fashion designs or packaging designs and the 2D shapes and colours can be used for illustrations, textiles or print. Try developing your drawings into ideas for print.

Select a form which contains colours, textures, shapes and a structure that you are interested in. Turn it around until you find the viewpoint and angle you want to record, then sit it on a white piece of paper in front of you. This will help to show off the colours and shapes clearly.

Use drawing materials and a digital camera to record different viewpoints so that you can produce a logical sequence of studies which record the front, back, top, underneath and sides of your natural form. Experiment with linear drawing media (e.g. pencils, fine liners, paintbrushes) to produce directional mark-making to describe the surface of your chosen form. Colour it to record texture and tonal qualities and use your digital camera to zoom in and select detailed sections of pattern.

Consider the composition of your drawings and experiment with a range of different picture plane formats including: a square, a portrait or landscape rectangle, and an elongated rectangle. Think about varying the complexity of your work so that some images are very detailed and some are very refined. Think about varying the scale at which you work so that some designs are huge and some are tiny.

Grading tips

Be imaginative and make use of a wide range of 2D mark-making techniques within your studies, for example:

- single line and multiple lines – clone, rotate, cut, rip
- tone – cross hatch, stipple, smudge, blend, wash
- texture – dodge, focus, scumble, layer media, use glue/sand/collage
- form – perspective, silhouette
- colour – collage, paint, pastels
- scale. **P1**

Talk through your work with your tutor or peers, recording the media used and explain the type of the marks you can make. **M1**

Review and select your most successful studies to use for print. Discuss your reasons for choosing them and which techniques, materials and mark-making styles you have used. What else could you use to develop your drawings and produce a final study? **D1**

BTEC Assessment activity 2.2: Secondary sources   P1 M1 D1

Building upon Assessment activity 2.1, now switch to using secondary source materials as a starting point. Collect a range of images of natural forms.

Review what you have collected and group images into a collage. Use a viewfinder to select different shapes and compositions. You could cut, rip, enlarge or reduce images, photograph or manipulate them using a photocopier or software package such as Photoshop or Illustrator. **P1**

Grading tip M1 D1

You need to show that you can work independently and use mark-making skills which are effective and imaginative in order to meet the merit and distinction criteria. Think about how you can change the scale of your work or the composition within your drawings. Take risks with this and produce studies which are very different from each other. Try combining techniques such as paint on top of computer-generated imagery or machine stitched lines on top of ink washes. Select your mark-making carefully so that the media and styles you choose convey natural form in an imaginative way.

Take time to review your work regularly and think about what is successful and what can be improved. Act on these decisions so that you further develop your own original style of working.

Remember

Keep a scrapbook of work by practising artists and designers that you like in order to develop your understanding of historical and contemporary art, craft and design practices. These are great for reference and to make use of if you become stuck in an assignment. File them in different sections depending on the media and their speciality.

Patterns and structures from natural forms find their way into product design, architecture and design

Functional skills

ICT and English

Making use of the Internet to research both secondary source imagery and techniques used by practising artists and designers will evidence ICT skills. Analysing the information you collect and adding notes about the media and techniques you have used next to your drawings will evidence English skills.

Activity

Combining media and materials

Be imaginative and inventive with how you use materials and try combining and layering them within your work. Try some of these ideas:

- Alter oil pastels by blending with white spirit using a brush or rag. This will 'melt' the waxy surface and create a watercolour paint-like quality. Try working back over it with coloured pencils for extra detail.
- Experiment with layering a range of black and white media on one drawing using the linear qualities of pencil, the tonal qualities of charcoal and the boldness of paint or ink to develop a greater range of tonal marks.
- Use inks as pale washes or strong colour sections painted on top of graphic pencils.
- Add machine or handstitched lines for further texture and variety of mark-making.
- Print out photographs or digital images and work back into them with paint, pastels and ink.

2. Be able to communicate design ideas using 2D visual communication techniques

2.1 Communicating

How you communicate and the 2D visual communication techniques you use are often related to what you are recording and why. Here are some examples.

Interior designers

Interior designers will produce mood boards containing swatches of paint, fabrics and wallpaper supported by sketches of the finished room to fit with their client's requirements in addition to accurate computer-generated 3D visuals produced to scale. From the outset, they will need to consider time-frames and budgets in order to manage and fulfil their client's expectations.

Photographers

Photographers will often produce very quick pencil or pen compositional sketches or test shots of an intended photograph to show a client or a picture editor. These are used to make sure that the final photograph will fit with the page layout of the website, magazine or newspaper.

Jewellery designers

Jewellery designers will visualise their initial ideas on paper and make use of their 3D modelling software packages to render their designs in order to show a client the overall style of the finished piece. They need to consider raw materials, processes, techniques and complexity in light of available budgets and whether their pieces are hand-crafted or intended for mass production.

User-interface software designers

Software designers who create user interfaces will use a range of storyboarding and 'mocking up' techniques to test out their potential products with real people. These may include simple records of user needs and actions; possible screen layouts; navigational routes; screen, button, icon design.

Processes
- Are the processes in a step-by-step, linear order?
- What machinery or equipment do I need?

Timescale
- How much time for planning?
- How much time for production?
- Do I need a prototype?
- When's the deadline? Is it negotiable?

Audience
- Customer profile (What are they like? What do they do?)
- Age range?
- Gender?
- How do they expect me to communicate with them?

Competition
- Who are my competitors?
- How much do their products cost?
- What is unique and innovative about my work? Where does it fit in the market?

Factors affecting design outcomes

Budget
- What's the budget – is it fixed?
- Do I know how much each process costs me?
- What is the cost of materials?
- Where can I make savings?
- Does the budget match the desired end-product? How can I get them to match?

Figure 2.5: Think about your next 'assignment' – use these questions to draw up a detailed plan for your work

Creating prototypes is essential in this field – before costs are incurred in developing assets and in the technical build. As you begin to answer these questions and determine the end purpose of your work, have a look at the work of artists and designers who are producing work for your target market. What techniques are they using? What materials? This is a great way of extending your ideas and seeing the possibilities of materials and techniques. It is also a great way of looking for a gap in the market, and by understanding what has already been produced you can search out a new and innovative design idea.

Research the work of Nick Park at Aardman Animations to find out how animators record their design ideas

2.2 Design ideas

The style, techniques and presentation of your design ideas will depend on the final purpose and audience for your work. Here are some examples of how different people use visual communication techniques.

Animators

During the planning and ideas stage of producing a film an animator uses 2D visual communication techniques and may also use 3D techniques later on. The animator will:

- develop the storyline and produce an initial pen and paper storyboard illustrating each frame of the film as a quick linear study
- illustrate the characters either by hand using marker pens or using illustration software and also begin to design the sets, props, surfaces and colour range to be used
- sculpt models of the characters either by hand and then scan the 3-dimensional forms into the computer or model them directly on the computer using 3D software.

Case study: Llyn Hunter, storyboard artist

Llyn Hunter, a storyboard artist for major TV and Film animated cartoons, describes the process of storyboarding for online magazine Suite101.

For TV, you have to turn things around pretty fast. Most television is 22 minutes because of the commercials. A writer will have to come up with a script, which is then given to the storyboard artist. We work on an 8 ½ x 14in legal size sheet of paper and it'll have three or four panels across the top. In the middle you'll have sections for action, dialogue, and slugging, which is how they time out things for the animation.

Usually two people work on the storyboards, each doing 600 drawings, 1200 drawings total for the 22 minutes. So it looks like a giant comic book and serves as a blueprint for the cartoon. It will be used

by the Director, Timing Director, and Animators. And everyone refers back to the storyboards to make sure everything is working together.

Suite101: What tools do you use?

Hunter: A pencil, pencil sharpener, sheet of paper and an eraser. As time goes on, we are starting to work on the computer, but these tools are still the most widely used.

Suite101: What advice can you give new storyboard artists entering the industry?

Hunter: My biggest advice is to first learn the computer because everybody is switching to it. So learn to draw with a Waycon Tablet, Photoshop, or Maya. If you know a background to them it will help you out.

What fabrics are going to be used to make these garments?

Fashion designers

Fashion designers also work with a range of techniques throughout the process of researching, designing and constructing a fashion collection.

They may produce inspiration or mood boards at the beginning of the process containing collaged imagery, colours and samples of fabrics to communicate the theme of the collection. These are then developed into first ideas and designs as line drawings with the designers working on a thin paper called layout paper. Using layout paper means that a template of a figure can be seen through it and the design idea for a garment can be drawn on top.

The next step is to work up technical drawings, either by hand or on the computer. Each seam, fastening and detail is drawn accurately so that patterns can be made for the garment. The design is then illustrated to convey the type of fabric used and to give an impression of someone wearing it. These drawings are often stylised and developed using image manipulation software packages (such as Photoshop) or programs specifically developed for garment and textile design (such as Colour Matters) so that materials can be scanned in and manipulated to convey movement, surface texture and decoration.

BTEC Assessment activity 2.3: Collecting design ideas

You can get ideas from anywhere! It can help to look at what other artists and designers produce to see how your own work fits in and to extend your own knowledge of media, techniques and processes. A great way to do this is to visit a museum or gallery and have a look at the work being displayed.

In order to get the most out of your visit you need to get prepared before you go. Take a digital camera with you and think about the size of the sketchbook you will be able to use and if you need to prepare the pages before you go by changing the colours or sizes of pages to suit what you are going to be recording. Check which media you will be allowed to work with in the gallery. Many places will only allow you to photograph work without using the flash and only work in 'dry' media (pencils, pencil crayons, biros, felt tip pens, and fine liner ink pens).

When you are there have a quick look around and then select one piece of work to study. Note down as much information as possible by collecting relevant postcards, exhibition leaflets, photographing, drawing what you can see and making notes. Use your camera to record how the object is displayed and zoom in on interesting sections to record more detail. As you gather information start with the facts:

- Who produced the work?
- What is the subject matter?
- Where was it produced?
- When was it made?
- How was it produced?

Assessment activity 2.4: Recording design ideas

Following on from Assessment activity 2.3, as you observe an object of study in a museum or gallery think about why you like it and how you could use it in your design work. To help you get started work through the following list of suggestions:

- **Fashion or interior textile design** – Record the colour palette, either by photographing, making written notes or shading small swatches of coloured media. Note down the proportions of each colour used so you can reflect this in your own work. Record any pattern elements in the piece and the range of mark-making that has been used.

- **Portrait or landscape photography** – Draw the whole piece, roughly noting down the main shapes and composition in line. Divide your drawing into a 3 x 3 grid and note the key elements in each third. Think what your eye is drawn to first and how you look across the image. Record the key angles which are used and the overall balance of the work.

- **Technical or book illustration** – Choose your favourite section and make several studies so that you build up your knowledge of the piece and draw accurately making use of guide lines and construction lines adding as much detail as possible. Note the range of media, the mark-making and surface texture so that you can make use of this.

- **Ceramics or mixed media sculpture** – Select a 3D piece of work, photograph and draw it from all sides to build up a complete picture of the whole object. Use contour lines when you draw so that you begin to describe the surface and form.

- **Graphic design or advertising** – Select a piece of work containing text and record this. Note the colours used by photographing, making written notes or drawing colour swatches. Produce a compositional study in line only noting the centre lines and the key structure to the piece.

Discuss the work that you have chosen, make written and visual notes recording which elements you will use in your own design work – is it the colour palette? the structure? the composition? the media used?

Grading tip **D2**

You will need to be able to work independently in the gallery to select your piece of work and communicate your ideas imaginatively to meet the distinction criteria. Try to produce as many varied ideas as possible. Take time to prepare the pages of your sketchbook before the visit with different types of papers and coloured backgrounds and also organise your camera and drawing materials you will need before a trip. Then make the most of the time you have in the gallery to produce a wide range of studies. These should include both written and colour notes in addition to ideas about how you could use them in your later design work. The more you think about the end result and evidence it, the better!

2.3 Presenting final ideas

It is important that you allow lots of time to produce the final piece. You will need to make use of everything you have learned when producing rough ideas, samples and mock-ups to ensure that you demonstrate your skills and ability to their full.

Functional skills

English

Producing drawn and written notes in your sketchbook to develop your design ideas will evidence your English skills.

Presentation can help or hinder your final piece. Take some time to research how practising artists and designers present their work to clients. Take a look at art and design books and magazines, and look at examples in galleries. For example, fashion designers and graphic designers will often produce presentation boards where their final designs are displayed on foam board with word-processed type explaining their final ideas. Textile designers present their designs on white paper so that the colours in their patterns are shown off against the clean white paper.

It is important that you allow plenty of time to produce the final piece as presentation can help or hinder the success of the outcome. You will need to make use of everything you have learned about materials, mark-making and techniques required when producing rough ideas, samples and mock-ups to ensure that you demonstrate your skills and ability to their full.

Ensure you have sourced all the materials you will need and that you have enough space to make the finished piece. Take photographs of your final piece as it develops so that you can record all stages. These will document the range of mark-making, techniques and processes that you have used.

Many designers work in a sketchbook adding supporting 'colour notes' in words alongside quite sketchy first observations. Often, they will use photographs and images from books, galleries or websites to develop their ideas back in their studio. Designers then translate their ideas into a range of samples to evaluate and work up further, before constructing final prototypes at the actual scale. Last of all they produce their final piece.

Here are some ways of presenting your work:

What methods will you use to present your final ideas?

- Hang fabrics using see through fishing line from hooks in strips of wood or pinned into boards.

- If you have made wearable pieces (fashion, costume, accessories, jewellery) you may want to take photographs of people wearing these and print these out to be displayed alongside your work. Keep the background simple in these photographs – perhaps photograph against a brick wall or a white sheet so that your design stands out and remember to check that your model is not wearing clothes or jewellery which may conflict with your designs.

- Use double-sided sticky fixer tape or hook and loop tape to display your work for a wall presentation. Avoid attaching your work with a staple gun or drawing pins as these will be seen. Use a tape measure, ruler and spirit level to ensure your work is displayed straight.

- If a group of you are displaying your work together decide on a top height and stick to this same level for all your work so that your exhibition flows. Take some time to consider where each of your works is shown so that you complement each other's work with colour, image, scale and type of work.

3. Be able to use formal elements in 2D visual communication

Having experimented with a range of mark-making techniques and explored different styles of drawing for design to suit your purpose, you also need to develop formal elements so that you can best make use of the qualities of each material. Developing your skills is an ongoing process!

Case study: Jonah Wimbush

I produced this charcoal drawing in the first week of my course.

I taped the branch on to the wall in front of me so that I could easily see the positive and negative shapes and then produced a page of line drawings in my sketchbook to experiment with composition. Then we drew the main lines of the branch on our page and used charcoal to work into the shadows by blending out to produce shapes of the leaves.

I found the charcoal very difficult to work with to start with but it is worth persevering. It was hard to get all the different shapes of light and dark and is a lot softer than pencils. At the beginning I found it a bit hit and miss but I got better and am now a lot more confident about re-working

areas and developing them by going over them again with a rubber to erase the tone or by adding more tone.

Can you see the use of formal elements in Jonah's charcoal drawing?

3.1 Formal elements

Formal elements include:

- proportion – the relationship and size of one shape next to another
- composition – the arrangement of shapes with a picture plane: this could be symmetrical, asymmetrical, balanced, unbalanced, sections, the whole object
- line studies – an idea or observation shown in a drawn line without the use of shading: this could be an outline describing the shape, a contour line describing the form or directional lines describing the structure and texture
- tonal work – with charcoal, light and dark shades of grey
- texture – the surface quality, i.e. rough, smooth, wet, shiny.

More formal painting elements can be seen in the example below. A range of media has been used in the painting to represent the form, shape and texture in the best way. The artist started with a rough, pale outline using coloured pencils to show the general shape and to ensure that the composition was strong. At this stage the artist observed both the object and the negative shapes around it to ensure that the proportion was correct. Then thin washes of paint were applied to 'map in' the solid mass.

Corrections were made to the original drawing so that these thin washes were in a different place to the original outline where necessary.

Gradually the paint was thickened and the tonal values of the colours corrected to represent each section and to convey the 3D form and structure.

The striking background was added as a contrast and to add impact to the painting.

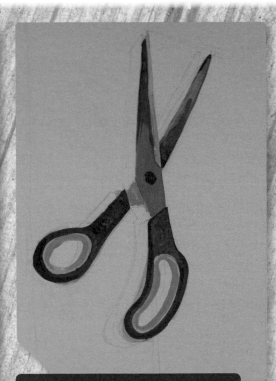

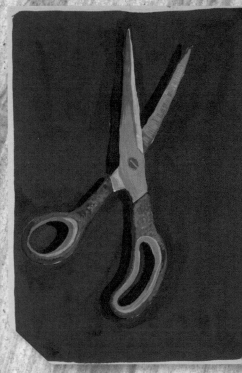

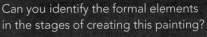
Can you identify the formal elements in the stages of creating this painting?

PLTS

Creative thinkers and reflective learners

Developing, reviewing and refining skills with 2D techniques and processes will evidence your ability to make use of creative thinking and reflective learning skills.

The higher the level of skill you can develop with each media the better your final outcomes will be. Keep looking and don't be afraid to correct and alter your painting at all stages of your work to ensure accuracy within your final piece. Developing, improving and refining skills is incredibly important if you want to stand out and progress within the world of art and design, and the best way to do this is to practice!

Assessment activity 2.5: Developing your skills

Artists and designers develop their own individual styles of working. Many choose to work with one specific subject matter for many years or only work in one material, fully exploiting its characteristics and developing original and innovative techniques and processes.

This activity gives you the chance to take one object and one style of working and explore its potential, while developing your skills in using formal elements.

Choose a starting point and a focus for your work – this could be anything from landscapes to people, manmade objects or natural forms, domestic or industrial buildings or furniture for example. Gather together a selection of images or objects to work from, and then in the studio, create a range of studies using your selected formal element.

Explore a range of media, expanding and refining your work to exploit the qualities of the formal element you selected. For example, if you selected 'line' you could produce a variety of lines by:

- drawing with coloured wire, thick or thin fuse wire and creating 2D or 3D drawings
- stitching by hand or with a sewing machine with thread, yarn, string or rope
- attaching a stick of charcoal or pastel to the end of a cane and drawing with this
- covering your paper with glue and using thread or string to draw with to produce a continuous line drawing
- using the edge of a short or long piece of card, or a ruler dipped in black, white or coloured paint and printing with it
- printing with a screen, sponge, or spray paint through a cut or ripped stencil
- mono-printing lines by drawing on the back of paper pressing lightly onto ink or by drawing into the ink itself and pressing the paper down on this
- drawing with strips of masking, gum, brown or coloured tapes. Try ripping it or cutting it to different thicknesses
- using ink with sticks, skewers, ends of paint brushes, DIY brushes, sponges
- using contour lines in pencil or pen to describe the surface and form of the object
- using drawing and painting tools within Photoshop to create 2D and 3D lines
- using a camera to record lines
- scoring into or creasing a negative when printing to create lines
- masking out sections of the photographic paper to create lines.

Grading tip

In order to achieve the merit and distinction criteria you need to be able to explain and evaluate the use of formal elements within 2D visual communication. You can do this by reviewing your work as it develops and noting the formal elements used. Discuss your work with your tutor and peer group. Consider what is the most successful and think of ways to extend what you have produced – perhaps by combining techniques or by being more ambitious with the scale, the composition selected or the colour palette. Evidence your ideas by producing further studies which make use of your observations and demonstrate how you have evaluated your work and used this to extend your visual communication skills.

3.2 Materials

There is a range of generic and specialist materials that you can use within drawing, painting, printmaking, photography and digital media. It is good to build up your own collection of general materials which you can use within assignments.

It is not important to have top brand names or expensive equipment but it is a good idea to have a good range of equipment and materials, and also replace materials when they run out. For example, household emulsion paint works very well and food colouring can be used as a cheaper alternative to drawing ink.

Some assignments may require more specialist equipment such as different types of photographic paper to print upon or different types of fine liner or marker pens. There are lots of art shops and online art suppliers where you can buy these. You may also find that some materials can be bought from book shops, DIY stores, home stores or garden centres at a cheaper price.

3.3 Disciplines

2D visual communication covers the disciplines of drawing, painting, printmaking, photography and digital media. Although some skills, techniques and formal elements are usually associated with one of the disciplines, you can produce inventive and original work if you layer and transfer from one discipline to another. The following table gives you some suggestions of the range of activities within each discipline.

Drawing	Using dry media: pencils, crayons, charcoal, stitch etc. Observational studies Mark-making techniques	Thumbnail sketches Design development Layouts and technical diagrams Compositional drawings
Painting	Using wet media: gouache, acrylic, watercolour, oil etc. Colour notes	Observational studies Illustrations Final pieces
Printmaking	Screen printing Transfer printing Block printing	Lino printing Mono-printing Collagraph printing
Photography	Black and white, colour, sepia Traditional	Digital Pin-hole camera
Digital media	Photoshop Illustrator	InDesign Microsoft Word

Table 2.2: 2D visual communication disciplines

3.4 2D visual communication

The range of media, mark-making and formal elements you use will be dependent on what stage you are at within the design development cycle and also the purpose of your final outcome. The examples below describe how formal elements are used within areas of art and design.

Composition

Photographer

A photographer may use a 3 x 3 grid to help frame images. In shots of landscapes, for example, the sky could be one third and the landscape two thirds of the photograph.

In post production stages, shots can be cropped or have Photoshop filters added to lighten or darken sections. This emphasises different areas and strengthens the composition so that the viewer is drawn to a focus area within the photograph.

Designer for print

A designer working in the print industry constructs templates and specimen page layouts, making decisions about the placement and flow of text and images to create a memorable design that is clear and has consistency of design.

Colour palettes are selected to best convey the message of the product being advertised and choice of typeface and white space left to emphasis important sections.

Textile designer

A textile designer may arrange shapes in a range of repeating patterns such as: block repeat, brick repeat, half-drop and multi-directional. These need to be at the correct scale to fit a garment for fashion fabrics or the width of interior fabrics.

A collection of coordinating fabrics are often produced using the same shapes at different scales and placed in different repeating patterns so that they can be used together.

Storyboard artist

A storyboard artist may develop a series of specific storyboards to communicate different sections of a film to show action sequences and to develop character profiles. The composition within each frame of the storyboard is explored thoroughly before a final decision is made on the camera angle to be used.

These would be produced quickly as thumbnail sketches using line and tone and then further developed and refined using colour.

Colour

Interior designer

An interior designer may put together a palette of paint colours and flooring and fabric surface textures to be used in a room and present these on a mood board to a client.

The colours selected would be dependent on the end use of the room and the mood required by the client, for example, tranquil, bold, modern.

A main colour would be selected and then supporting tones of this colour would be added with contrasting colours as small accents. A tranquil and relaxing colour scheme many include a neutral beige plus shades of blues and greens.

Activity

Experiment with composition

Make a rectangular viewfinder and use it to look at architecture. Select a composition to draw. Try working with your viewfinder in a 'portrait' and 'landscape' format and note the differences.

Activity

Experiment with colour

Scan a portrait photograph into the computer and produce different colour versions of the same image. You could look at the pop art prints by Andy Warhol to give you some ideas of the variety of colour combinations and the range possible.

Animator

An animator would use pencils or black pens to create linear first ideas. Tone would be added to create contrast and strong light and shade to convey emotion. Finally a range of colours would be added to the final pieces to create the particular mood and emotion required within their work, for example, comedy, horror, romance, thriller, science fiction.

Animators may use: marker pens, watercolour paint, inks, and Photoshop to add colour to their work.

Ceramicist

A ceramicist would begin by producing a linear drawing of the ceramic form and then develop this into a 3D model on the computer. Different colours and textures would be explored and the final finish selected.

An example of this style of working can be seen in the work of Michael Rice – please go to Hotlinks to view this.

Printmaker

A printmaker can produce multiple colour prints. One technique used is called the reductionist technique. This involves the printmaker starting with a lino or wooden block and cutting away the first section of the image. This is inked and printed and then the second section is cut away on the same block. The process continues until all colours have been printed.

Alternatively, the printmaker can produce one plate for each colour to be printed. The main or 'key' block containing the structure and main descriptive elements of the image would be printed first and the subsequent blocks registered to this.

Each colour will interact with the colours already printed which may result in the colour changing or 'overlaps' being created.

Line

Fashion designer

A fashion designer would use pencil lines drawn onto layout paper to develop their first design ideas.

These linear studies would be refined and redrawn by tracing through onto the next sheet of layout paper until a clear accurate design is produced. The final design would be translated into a working drawing which is a flat diagram showing all seams, detailing and fastenings with measurements so that the garment pattern pieces can be made. Finally, an illustration would be produced using colour and textural mark-making to represent clearly the range of different fabrics used.

Graphic designer

A graphic designer may use lines to visualise first ideas as thumbnail sketches or 'scamps'. These ideas would be realised using Photoshop, Illustrator or Word.

Sculptor

A sculptor may visualise their first ideas using contour lines to describe the 3D surface of their form. This style of visualising can be seen in the drawings produced by Henry Moore – please go to Hotlinks to view work by Henry Moore.

Activity

Experiment with line in wire

Using wire, draw a self portrait. You could choose to work from a photograph or work from a mirror.

Activity

Experiment with line in stitch

Using stitch, draw a self portrait. You could use hand or machine stitching and may want to collage together different types of fabrics and surfaces. You could look at the work of Claire Coles to give you some ideas. Stitch over a photograph and then use the reverse side of the paper.

WorkSpace Dave Robinson

Graphic designer

I'm employed by Key Publishing in Stamford, Lincolnshire and am in a team of eight graphic designers. My job is split between producing the layout ideas for existing magazines and coming up with ideas for updating or designing new magazines.

I work with a range communication styles within drawing and digital media. My first design ideas are very quick thumbnail sketches in pencil on scraps of paper! Some graphic designers work on the computer from the beginning, but I find it easier to visualise my first ideas using pencil and working quickly within sketchbooks. It's so much easier to play around with elements and explore their potential by producing rough ideas. I'll work in pencil and pen to produce ideas for motifs, logos and first page layouts.

Once I have an idea that I like I will begin to work on the computer using Photoshop, Illustrator and InDesign. I use all three programs so that I can import images, re-touch colour, copy text sections from Microsoft Word and produce advanced graphical motifs and logos. You can produce a high-quality finish on the computer but it does take a lot longer to get all the elements working together.

My first job for a new magazine is to design the layout template. This includes the width of text columns and the gaps in between, in addition to logos, style of text and scale of images. I'll play around with these elements first and come up with a few rough ideas before settling on a design. At this stage I usually present three different templates as straightforward A3 colour printouts from the computer at a formal meeting which includes the company chairman, magazine editor and production director. As I'm only pitching internally I do not have to produce presentation boards of my ideas.

We will discuss the options and they will decide what they like. It may take four meetings to get it right! My job is to keep changing and alternating the template until everyone is happy with it. When it has all been agreed, I'll mock up a sample article and a front cover, and this will be presented to the client for their approval.

Think about it!

- What areas have you covered in this unit that provide you with background knowledge and skills used by a graphic designer? Write a list and discuss with your peers.
- What further skills might you need to develop? For example, consider how you would conduct a presentation of your design ideas to a client and the skills you would need. Write a list and discuss in small groups.

Just checking

1 What is a primary source?

2 What is a secondary source?

3 What media could you use to produce linear mark-making?

4 What can you add to paint to change its appearance (to make it shiny or textured for example)?

5 List at least three different types of paint and describe how you could use them.

6 Can you identify formal elements in the work of a designer of your choice?

Assignment tips

Keep a sketchbook

It is a great idea to make use of a sketchbook and carry it around with you. It is an excellent place to start assignments and record first research, initial drawings and trials with materials and mark-making, in addition to practising favourite techniques and developing individual ideas independently.

Keep a research file

Collect information about artists and designers and keep a file of images and styles of work. These are great to refer to and will be vital in developing your understanding of different techniques and processes.

Practise your techniques and develop your own style

Spend time exploring techniques and refining your style. You might find you are particularly interested in figure drawing or developing characters or tonal work and could choose to keep working on these themes to further develop skills and the range of mark-making styles you can create.

Log your work for your final assessment

Document your work, describing processes and using technical terms that will help you work towards the merit and distinction criteria. This doesn't always need to be in written form – you can record using video or audio. You could include details such as:

- **primary** sources or **secondary** sources

- the range of **media** you have used and **mark-making styles**

- the **formal elements** you have used such as line, tone, texture, colour

- explain **why** you selected particular media, mark-making and formal elements

- review **what** has been the most successful and **why**

- explain what you could do to **extend** your work.

3 3D visual communication

3D visual communication is widely used in the art and design industry. It has applications in areas as diverse as:

- packaging
- 3D graphics
- furniture design
- product design
- transport design
- interiors

- ceramics
- jewellery
- body adornment
- sculpture
- public art

There are many different materials, processes and techniques available to the artist, craftsperson or designer when working in 3D. This unit looks at some of the ways you can use these in your work.

formal elements
technical information
materials
techniques
processes
health and safety
design ideas
design development

Learning outcomes

After studying the unit you should:

be able to use 3D making techniques

be able to communicate design ideas using 3D visual communication techniques

be able to use formal elements in 3D visual communication.

Assessment and grading criteria

This table shows you what you must do in order to achieve a pass, merit or distinction, and where you can find activities in this book to help you.

To achieve a **pass** grade the evidence must show that the learner is able to:	To achieve a **merit** grade the evidence must show that, in addition to the pass criteria, the learner is able to:	To achieve a **distinction** grade the evidence must show that, in addition to the pass and merit criteria, the learner is able to:
P1 demonstrate use of 3D making techniques safely when working from primary and secondary sources **Assessment activity 3.1** **Page 54** **Assessment activity 3.2** **Page 56** **Assessment activity 3.7** **Task 2, Task 3, Task 4** **Page 65**	**M1** demonstrate consistent and effective use of 3D making techniques when working from primary and secondary sources **Assessment Activity 3.1** **Page 54** **Assessment activity 3.7** **Task 2, Task 3, Task 4** **Page 65**	**D1** demonstrate imaginative and independent use of 3D making techniques, when working from primary and secondary sources **Assessment activity 3.1** **Page 54** **Assessment activity 3.7** **Task 2, Task 4** **Page 65**
P2 communicate design ideas using 3D visual communication techniques **Assessment activity 3.3** **Page 59** **Assessment activity 3.4** **Page 60** **Assessment activity 3.5** **Page 61** **Assessment activity 3.7** **Task 1, Task 3, Task 4** **Page 65**	**M2** communicate ideas effectively and consistently, using 3D making skills **Assessment activity 3.3** **Page 59** **Assessment activity 3.4** **Page 60** **Assessment activity 3.5** **Page 61** **Assessment activity 3.7 Task 1,** **Task 3, Task 4** **Page 65**	**D2** communicate ideas imaginatively and independently using 3D making techniques **Assessment activity 3.3** **Page 59** **Assessment activity 3.4** **Page 60** **Assessment activity 3.5** **Page 61** **Assessment activity 3.7 Task 1,** **Task 3, Task 4** **Page 65**
P3 use formal elements in 3D visual communication **Assessment activity 3.6** **Page 62** **Assessment activity 3.7** **Task 4** **Page 65**	**M3** explain the use of formal elements in 3D visual communication **Assessment activity 3.6** **Page 62** **Assessment activity 3.7** **Task 4** **Page 65**	**D3** evaluate the use of formal elements in 3D visual communication **Assessment activity 3.6** **Page 62** **Assessment activity 3.7** **Task 3, Task 4** **Page 65**

How you will be assessed

You will be given 3D assignment/s by your tutor. You will be assessed through your performance in:

- developing design ideas to 3D design brief/s
- your understanding of 3D materials
- your use of making techniques
- your use of formal elements
- how you observe health and safety legislation and guidelines
- your practical work.

Loretta Hamzat

I have really enjoyed exploring 3D materials. We got the chance to work with clay, which I hadn't done before. It was an eye-opener to see the different construction techniques available. We watched a video on a Nigerian potter called Ladi Kwali who fired the pots in a bonfire. We are going to use a process called Raku firing. I'm really looking forward to it.

There's a lot of health and safety stuff to look at. I thought this would be boring until I saw the fact sheets on what happens if you don't follow the guidelines – it's really important to work safely. There is a lot of noting down of technical information, which I got more used to as I worked on the unit. I've got my own 'dictionary of terms' now, which I can refer back to when I need to.

I was amazed at how designers use formal elements – we had learned about them before, but when I considered how they were used by others it really helped me understand them. I also looked at the design process, and learned how to make test pieces and **maquettes** to help see the designs in progress. I can now understand how designers use things like shape to **communicate ideas**. I described the different shapes used in cars to my mum when we were in a traffic jam recently, and how the different designs were matched to people's aspirations. She was really impressed.

- Why is it important to follow health and safety guidelines in the workshop?
- Next time you go shopping see if you can identify how product designers have used shape to communicate ideas.

An example of a raku-fired pot. In which country did Raku ceramics develop?

Design in the home

Take your sketchbook or journal, and go into each room in your home. In the first room, list the items you can recognise that have been designed using 3D visual communication. If you know the different construction or manufacture processes used to make them, list these as well. Go into the second room, and so on until you have worked through all the rooms.

Looking at the results, are you surprised at how many you recorded?

1. Be able to use 3D making techniques

In this learning outcome you will be introduced to different materials, techniques and processes used in 3D. Examples of 3D making techniques include: cutting, joining, shaping, carving, weaving, 3D digital techniques, sanding, fusing, casting, slotting, piercing and stitching. 3D making techniques are used when you make models, carry out experiments and create finished pieces. 3D visual communication is the communication of volume, spatial size and shape, tactile qualities, weight, ergonomics, softness, structure and so on.

Here are some of the other terms you are likely to encounter when working with 3D visual communication.

Key terms

Aesthetics – how something looks and feels. The aesthetics of a piece involves aspects such as beauty, balance and use of materials. If something is clumsily made, or difficult to use, or looks awkward, it might be described as having poor aesthetics.

Communicate ideas – by responding to themes, identifying the constraints of a design brief, investigating materials, techniques and processes, presenting ideas (such as through maquettes), creating working models through sketchbooks/work journals and by completing a finished piece.

COSHH – stands for Control of Substances Hazardous to Health. COSHH relates to hazards that have to be controlled by safety measures and equipment.

Maquette – a model or rough version of a sculpture or 3D form or product.

PPE – stands for Personal Protective Equipment. PPE includes respirators, safety goggles, gloves, gauntlets and so on.

Recording from primary sources – using any combination of drawing, lens-based and written techniques to record directly from sources first-hand.

Recording from secondary sources – using images and examples from postcards, magazines, video, film, printed materials and so on, as starting points for a design.

1.1 3D making techniques

Let's look at some materials and what you could use them for in this unit.

Material	Applications
Clay	pottery; modelling; sculpture; tiles; casting process
Wood	furniture; sculpture; storage systems; interior design; joining; framing; supporting; finishing
Metal	jewellery; sculpture; fabrication; body adornment; patinas;
Plastics	models; sculpture; jewellery; body adornment; accessories; vacuum forming
Plaster	sculpture; mould-making; casting; making sprigs
Card	model-making; maquettes; forming shades in lighting
Paper	maquettes; sculpture
Wire	sculpture; jewellery; mixed media work
Resin	sculpture; jewellery; mixed media work

clay
wood
plastics
metal
plaster
resin
cardboard

Table 3.1: Materials and their potential uses

You may use other materials, or combine these in different ways. The possibilities are endless. Here are some examples of how different artists and designers have used different techniques in a range of pieces.

Collage of images showing work with card, clay and glass

BTEC **Assessment activity 3.1: Making a 3D Form based on a hand** P1 M1 D1

Make some quick studies of your hand. Take some photographs as well. Use these as a starting point for a 3D form based on your hand. You will need your tutor's/technician's permission to work on this activity.

In your 3D workshop, there will probably be 'scraps bins'. These are where off-cuts of materials are put – it's better than just throwing them away, as they can be used for tests or the kind of activity here. You might have separate bins – such as a wood scraps bin, a plastics scrap bin and so on.

Take a selection of scraps in different materials and combine them to construct an abstract 3D version of your hand. Don't worry too much about whether it looks exactly like it. The aim is to get used to exploring materials while working from primary and secondary sources. Work to the following guidelines:

- You must combine at least three different types of materials.
- You can't use glue or nails/screws, so you will have to work out how to join them.
- If you are able to, try using materials to articulate some of the joints.
- Use hand tools only.
- Observe all health and safety guidelines and legislation.

Take photographs of the finished form. Make more than one if you have time, and make notes in your sketchbook or work journal. We'll go on to how to create a technical log next.

Grading tips

When you are exploring materials and making techniques, try to be aware of their inherent qualities. This term means the nature of the materials – the 'hardness' of wood, the 'thinness' and 'bendiness' of wire. To achieve a merit grade **M1** you will need to understand these qualities and combine them sympathetically, or with awareness. To be working at distinction level **D1** you will need to be imaginative with the materials and making techniques that you use, and show that you can manage the making processes independently.

1.2 Recording

Primary sources are those that you can record from directly, such as an object or environment; **secondary sources** are those that are reproduced or already made. Artists, designers and makers use primary and secondary sources as starting points for their work. The range of potential sources is very wide, and practitioners often build up a personal visual library of images that they have drawn, photographed and recorded, which they then use to help produce artefacts.

Rob Forbes leads the design company Design Within Reach, making 'simple designs that are available to all'. He uses photography to record aspects of design in contemporary life that influence his thinking and ideas.

To view a video of Rob Forbes on ways of seeing go to Hotlinks.

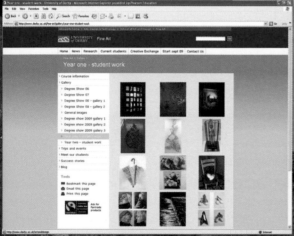

What are the differences between these primary and secondary sources?

Activity: Primary and secondary sources

Take the list of sources shown below, and organise them according to whether they are primary or secondary sources:

- natural environments
- plants
- humans
- animals
- insects
- shells
- landscapes
- made environments
- architecture
- artefacts
- street furniture.

- galleries
- exhibitions
- museums
- magazines
- journals
- video
- film
- Internet
- printed material
- CD-ROM

Check with your tutor. How many did you get right?

Functional skills

ICT

Searching for examples of primary and secondary sources using the Internet and online publications, as well as selecting and using information and evaluating its fitness for purpose, will evidence your ICT skills.

1.3 Creating a technical log

Get a separate sketchbook or ring binder. Use it to store all your notes about technical information and handouts your tutor or technician gives you. Once you get going on the design work you can refer back to it. You can also use it to keep fact sheets about materials.

1.4 Health and Safety

Induction

Before you use any 3D materials, you need to have an induction into using them properly. There is legislation on using equipment, materials and processes provided by the manufacturers, organisations and the Health and Safety Executive (HSE). These are all designed to protect you and others sharing the studio or workshop from harm. Sometimes it's tempting to ignore them and just get the job done, especially if you're in a hurry. DON'T – it only takes a second for something that seems straightforward to become dangerous, especially if you get casual because you have done it before.

BTEC Assessment activity 3.2: Health and safety

Look at the legislation and guidance terms below. With the permission of your tutor, go around the 3D workshops and studios and make a note of all the machines that have signs, guidance notes and warnings. Note down which machines require you to follow specific legislation and guidance. Some of them might require you to observe more than one health and safety rule:

- no loose clothing
- long hair tied back
- **PPE** – goggles
- PPE – aprons
- PPE – ear defenders
- danger – heat
- no unauthorised use
- no student use.

There may be other signs – include these as well.

Keep this information in your work journal. You can use it for assessment.

COSHH

COSHH stands for Control of Substances that are Hazardous to Health. It is a system for telling users about the chemical characteristics of the raw materials they are using. It also informs users of hazards associated with the cutting, shaping, mixing, applying and so on of the specified materials. They are provided by the manufacturers, and can be obtained from websites or sent with materials when ordered. You can keep copies of COSHH sheets in your technical log.

2. Be able to communicate design ideas using 3D making techniques

In this outcome you are working with 3D making techniques to communicate a message or intention. You'll also get the chance to demonstrate more evidence towards using 3D making techniques.

2.1 Communicating ideas

Designers use 3D to communicate ideas about brands or products – sometimes this includes both the packaging and the product. When this is related to the products function, it has a harmony or simply just feels 'right'. Sometimes this is through the shapes used, or the materials, colours, textures and so on, or combinations of these formal elements.

Artists also communicate ideas through 3D making techniques. The artist Antony Gormley created the iconic public art piece *The Angel of the North*.

Activity

What kinds of hazards do COSHH sheets show?

Make a list of the materials you can use, and get some examples of COSHH sheets to go with them. Ask your tutor about materials that are no longer used in centres because of concerns about health and safety – there is a well-known example from recent years. How many materials did you find? Why are they no longer used?

PLTS

Independent enquirer
This activity will help you to become more confident about raising questions and will help you to analyse information effectively, illustrating your independent enquiry skills.

Use the Internet to find out what Anthony Gormley has famously said about the meaning of this piece of public art

2.2 Responding to briefs

When you are communicating your design ideas you need to:

- establish the purpose of the brief
- come up with initial ideas on how to meet the brief
- identify and work from appropriate primary and secondary sources
- get interim feedback from clients
- select materials and processes that best fit the idea, design and brief
- organise the making of all models, maquettes and prototypes.

Case study: Andrew Ellis, 3D designer

Andrew is a designer who has experience in the field of 3D design. He has produced designs for high street names, specialising in product design and branding.

'It's vital to understand the purpose of the brief. If you don't know what clients are looking for, how can you deliver what they want? So I spend a lot of time asking questions to establish clearly what's needed. I also research existing examples of this and similar products. The design process begins with my looking at possible primary and secondary sources to help meet the brief. I will do a lot of drawings and marker pen work, and present these to the client to get feedback. I'll also explain what materials I plan to use. I then experiment with different models, maquettes and prototypes until I get the right result. Sometimes the ideas change due to projected manufacturing costs, or the arrival on the market of a similar product that I didn't know about. I have a small workshop, but once my design has been approved it goes to production workshops and fabrication.'

Functional skills

Note on a mind map or spider diagram how artists are linked.

Use the information to give yourself new directions to explore.

Activity: The craft market

You are a recent graduate who wants to develop the commercial side of your 3D craftwork. You are planning to submit work to important craft fairs. You understand that vital industry contacts can be made at these events. They are also a really good opportunity to sell work. To make the event a success you have identified that you need to:

- have an overall production budget
- get quality marketing/publicity materials together, such as postcards of your work for sale on the day, cards and catalogues
- arrange a photographic shoot of your work
- organise display equipment – cases, plinths and so on
- plan a practical activity to undertake on the day.

What would you leave out?

It's a significant amount of effort and work. To make it a success, you want your work to stand out from the crowd. What devices, ideas or methods could you use to achieve this?

To do this you may need to research examples of craft fairs – look at the established ones, such as Origin and Art in Clay.

Assessment activity 3.3: Identifying the characteristics in iconic designs

To help you work to 3D Design briefs you need to develop an understanding of what makes effective and exciting design. To do this you can look at examples of iconic design, and evaluate the ways they are designed and produced.

Look at the following design icons.

Apple iMac, 1996 – Apple Design Team and Jonathon Ive

Sony Walkman, 1979 – Sony Design Centre

Anglepoise lamp, 1932 – George Carwardine

Grading tips

Make notes about their use of:

- sources or starting points
- materials
- shape/form
- 3D visual communication – what did the designers set out to say?
- target audience
- what makes them stand out from other designs?

Some of the ideas you find out will be quite interesting – for instance, have you found out what the Anglepoise lamp was inspired by?

This activity is designed to help you introduce aspects of strong design into your own work, by recognising what practitioners have done. From the examples you have chosen, think about what makes them effective and try to use this in your own work. If you do this, you will be meeting the merit criteria **M2**. Develop the task to identify which ones were imaginative in meeting the design ideas – thinking and working in this way will help you reach distinction level **D2**.

2.3 Communicating and design briefs

Let's see how 3D visual communication is applied to design briefs. A designer needs to identify the target group for their brief. This enables them to produce designs that are in keeping with the requirements and tastes of the target group. You can see examples of this in any high street or major retailer. Think about the types of materials, colours and fabrics that are used in 'contemporary' styled furniture and then contrast these with the materials and colours used in 'traditional' styled furniture. We'll use lighting as an example.

PLTS

Independent enquirers and creative thinkers

Researching examples of lighting, analysing information and generating ideas to meet the brief will evidence your independent enquiry and creative thinking skills.

Functional skills

English

Communicating information, ideas and opinions effectively and persuasively, and writing up your conclusions will evidence your English skills.

 BTEC **Assessment activity 3.4:** Communicating design ideas

You are a designer commissioned to submit designs for a full range of contemporary standing, table and ceiling lighting. The client is a well-known retailer in the home furnishings sector. The target group is defined as couples between 20 to 30 years of age with above average income. You are working towards presenting your initial design ideas in drawing form.

Produce a series of design ideas for the range of lighting. Use drawing and model-making/construction.

To do this you will need to:
- research existing examples of contemporary lighting design
- select primary and secondary source material
- use drawings to show initial ideas and developments
- propose materials and finishes
- make a model of one of the designs.

Evaluate your final designs and model; use feedback from your peers and tutor to help you do this.

Grading tips

As long as you are meeting the brief and the design functions you can work towards the merit and distinction grades by being consistent, imaginative and independent. Presentations are a good way of showing your design work and explaining the design process, and can help you reach higher grades. Whatever method of showing your work you choose, make sure that you explain how your designs are consistent and effective **M2** and, if possible, how you have been imaginative in effectively generating the ideas and meeting the brief **D2**.

BTEC

Assessment activity 3.5: Public art

P2 M2 D2

A development in your town includes a major supermarket site, new leisure area and communal gardens. These are replacing the site of some local factories, which were the mainstay of the town's economy in the past, but have fallen into disrepair. The committee of local council officers and representatives from organisations involved have to include a piece of public art as part of the development as one of the conditions of planning permission. You are a local artist and are going to submit for the commission for the public artwork, which is on the theme of 'past industrial heritage'.

Submission for a public art commission

Consider your local town or city. Find out if it had an industrial heritage that has now vanished or been replaced. Use this subject as the theme for your submission for a piece of public art. You will need to:

- research examples of public art
- select primary and secondary source material
- develop ideas in drawing formats
- identify materials for production
- make a model of the sculpture
- evaluate your final drawings and model.

Grading tips

You might be able to find examples of public art in your area, and possibly meet the artist if he or she is local, to discuss how the brief was met. Again, you will be working at merit level **M2** if you can identify how you have been consistent in meeting the brief. You can show this in your notes, design ideas and final pieces. If your ideas are imaginative and your solutions to the brief are exciting and original, you will be working at distinction level **D2**.

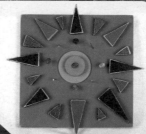

In these examples the learners have used different formal elements to create effects – what do you think they are trying to communicate?

PLTS

Team workers and self–managers

Collaborating with peers will evidence your teamwork skills. Working towards goals and organising your time and resources will evidence your self-managing skills.

What is it about this Mueck sculpture makes the women seem real?

3. Be able to use formal elements in 3D communication

3.1 Formal elements

Artists, craftspeople and designers use different combinations of formal elements. Formal elements include:

- line
- tone
- colour
- form
- shape.

- texture
- proportion
- scale
- volume

Artists and designers also use formal elements for 3D visual communication. Here are just a couple of examples to get you thinking about how you could use formal elements in your own work.

Scale

Ron Mueck is an Australian sculptor (1958–). His work, *Two Women* (2005, mixed media, 85.1 x 47.9 x 38.1 cm), shown on the left, features two aged women at a much smaller scale than they would normally be, and uses production techniques and making processes that mark the work as Hyperrealist. This is artwork that is so realistic in surface detail, colour and shape that it challenges the viewer to believe that it is real – it's quite a shock seeing his work. These two figures are smaller than the metre rule you have in your design studios.

 BTEC **Assessment activity 3.6: Communicating design ideas**    P3 M3 D3

In groups of four, think of artists who you know work in 3D. Make a list of their names on a sheet of A1 paper. Spend some time in your group discussing each artist, and researching visual examples of their work. Next to their names you are going to write up the formal elements they use, how they use them and to what effect.

Write up your responses. Translate the conclusions to your sketchbook or work journal.

Take 30 minutes to write up a summary of what you have learned so far on formal elements. List the different ones you have researched or experimented with, and think about how you used them. Keep your explanations simple.

What did you learn from using formal elements in 3D visual communication?

Grading tips

Look at the differences in the wording of the grading criteria for P3, M3 and D3, shown in the grid on page 50. Aim to *explain* the elements and how they meet the brief. *Evaluate* if they were successful in communicating the intention – look at their use in more depth.

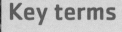

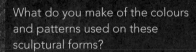

What do you make of the colours and patterns used on these sculptural forms?

Key terms

Raku – Raku ceramics are of Japanese origin and were associated with the Tea Ceremony. Work is rapidly fired in kilns where it can be extracted quickly and placed red-hot in a reduction chamber, where the oxygen is burnt away and then quenched. Alternatively it can be left to cool gradually. This produces the range of crackle glazes and metallic or iridescent effects associated with this way of firing ceramics.

3.2 Ceramic sculptural forms

The artworks above show ceramic forms, and close-ups of the surfaces. In these examples the artist has used a combination of formal elements to create ceramic pieces that work on different levels – as shapes, and then closer up as detailed surface planes. All of these pieces have been **Raku** fired.

3.3 3D digital techniques

It is also possible to work in 3D using computer software, again using formal elements. This image shows screenshots from animations, where the texture, colour and scale have been used to convey objects and scenes. Although using a different set of 'making' techniques, the designers still have to understand how the shapes and colours work – in this case to re-create a suburban garden from the point of view of an ant.

Did you know?

Ceramicists will often spend a long time developing glazes and techniques, and making sure they can recreate the effects – if it doesn't work, they can only sell them as 'seconds', and so can't charge high prices.

shapes
colours
textures
materials
overall concept

It's time to bring the different aspects of the unit together. Let's recap: the designer will work to a brief, and this will involve being able to communicate design ideas. He or she will need to use 3D making techniques when working on models, maquettes or interpreting drawings (if working as part of a team this may involve working from other people's 2D and 3D drawings). It is also important to be able to understand how the elements (see left) relate to the purpose of the brief and that the client's needs have been met.

Artists working on public art-related schemes also have to use 3D making techniques to produce scale models and visualise their ideas. They need to use formal elements to communicate the feel or message of the piece, especially when it has to relate to a local theme.

Aaron Hayhurst – animations screenshot. In this shot the learner has worked on a computer-based animation platform, called Cinema 4D, which allows you to create characters and environments in 3D. To do this you need to understand formal elements like perspective and scale and use drawing and evaluation skills

BTEC Assessment activity 3.7: Recycled bag design

For this brief, you are asked to design and make a bag that uses recycled materials. This could be fabric based, or use alternative approaches. You should research available materials/ techniques suitable for constructing your bag and record them within your sketchbook. From this research you should develop a range of possible ideas that will lead you to designing and making your final idea. You will also need to choose a theme and target audience. Your bag designs should focus more on the aesthetic appeal than on the function of the object, but in some areas there will be a crossover of both craft and function. It is important that you refer to formal elements and visual communication in the construction.

Task 1 (P2) (M2) (D2)

Research and record available materials and techniques that are appropriate for your bag design. From this research, produce a range of preliminary designs exploring style, scale, texture, materials and construction techniques.

Task 2 (P1) (M1) (D1)

Produce research on bags. Look at examples from different countries, cultures, environments and ages, both historical and modern. You can also research work on artists or designers that use recycled materials and found objects in their work. Include any notes you have on professional craft-workers. Look at the 3D making techniques they have used.

Task 3 (P1) (P2) (M1) (M2) (D2) (D3)

Generate ideas from your preliminary sketches and research work. Explore and develop ideas in 3D design showing experimentation with materials and techniques. All findings need to be recorded and presented in your sketchbook with clear annotation.

Task 4 (P1) (P2) (P3) (M1) (M2) (M3) (D1) (D2) (D3)

Construct your bag, explaining how you have used formal elements. Aim to be as creative and inventive as possible. Evaluate the project, such as the working processes you have used, your selection of materials and techniques, suitability of function, use of visual elements such as form and **aesthetics**.

These are the materials you will need:

- A4–A2 paper
- wet and dry drawing materials
- painting media
- mixed media materials
- hand tools
- library and Internet access
- handouts and books in studio
- sketchbooks.

Here are some useful sources to help you with your research:

Alistair Faud-Luke (2005), *The Eco-Design Handbook: A Complete Sourcebook for the Home and Office*, 2nd Rev. Ed., London: Thames & Hudson ISBN-13: 978 0 500285 21 3

Holly Harrison (2003) *Altered Books, Collaborative Journals and Other Adventures in Bookmaking*, Gloucester, MA: Rockport Publishers Inc. ISBN-13: 978 1 564969 95 8

Rice Freeman-Zachery (2004), *Creative Clothes and Accessories: New Ideas and Techniques for Transforming Your Wardrobe,* London: Apple Press ISBN-13: 978 1 840924 64 0

BTEC Assessment activity 3.7: Recycled bag design (cont.)

Grading tips

To work on the activity you will need an awareness of the possibilities of recycling materials. Practise using these and seeing if they can be used to 'match' or represent formal elements – i.e. wire can represent line, and so on. Record all of your experimentations and evaluate the work you do.

To achieve **P1** you will need to use the techniques and materials safely. To achieve **M1** you will need to be consistent in all the stages you work on and use the techniques effectively. To reach **D1** you really need to be imaginative in using the techniques independently.

To achieve **P2** you need to show that your work meets the brief and communicates your ideas. To reach **M2** think about how you can consistently communicate your ideas and how effective they are. Seek opinions from other people – your peers and tutors – to help reach this level. **D2** means being imaginative and independent in communicating your ideas and meeting the brief. This will mean considering many ideas and avoiding more obvious solutions.

P3 involves using the formal elements we looked at earlier. To achieve **M3** you need to explain your use of formal elements and how they meet the brief. To reach **D3** you need to analyse your use of formal elements and consider their strengths and weaknesses in more detail. Using notes and an ongoing work journal will help with this.

Bag designs and details by art and design students

form
colour
line
character
structure
texture
scale
materials
cutting
carving
joining
assembling
stitching
embroidery

The photos show examples of bag designs by art and design students. You can see how the learners have combined different making techniques, such as gluing, joining, collaging and embroidery. They have also used decorative techniques to make the surfaces more interesting. Although one bag is made from soft fabric, it still has a shape that the learner needed to consider. Their sketchbook work also demonstrated their understanding in communicating 3D design ideas, in this case with a craft or accessory bias.

Marc Friend
Designer, friend associates limited

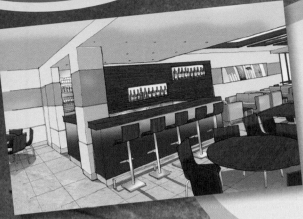

Our brief was to redesign an existing restaurant into a contemporary Italian restaurant (100 covers) offering high-quality homemade food. We were responsible for all stages from design concept through to the refit of the interior.

Timescale	
Design concept	4 weeks
Detailed drawing and specification package	6 weeks
Pricing	2 weeks
Building work	4 weeks
Interior fit-out	6 weeks

Concept stage

For the concept we created freehand drawings and put together mood and image boards. We also started to plan the overall space and look for the restaurant, in a very loose way.

Final designs

Once the existing space had been fully surveyed the final layout designs were developed in CAD (Vectorworks), and the final concept sketch visuals were created with colour applied in Photoshop. The final design stage was to produce a detailed drawing package which looked at all layouts including electrical, reflected ceiling, flooring etc. together with joinery construction details for the bar, seating, signage, doors and various key features.

Key design elements

The key design element of the scheme concept was a horizontal band and stripes to reflect a contemporary Italian style, this was complemented with a sophisticated colour scheme flag, together with highlights of walnut to key areas such as the bar, garden room wall and entrance frames. Wall coverings and black and white photography were also used to soften the spaces. The ceramic floor was sourced from Italy to ensure authenticity.

Implementation

During the implementation stages (demolition, building works and interior fit-out) we had weekly meetings to monitor the works and any variations to the design, timing or costs. We were responsible for producing and distributing written minutes to ensure that there was a detailed record of the project, in case of problems and to agree final costs.

Think about it!

- How do 2D and 3D visual communication techniques work together in projects like these?
- Why is planning and budgeting important when working for a client?

Just checking

Exploring materials: you can gain a lot of knowledge and understanding from looking at examples of 3D, but you will ultimately learn most from exploring the materials yourself.

1 Write a definition for each of these techniques and find an example of work that uses them:

- fusing • casting • slotting • forming

2 Write a short set of safety instructions for using a machine that you are familiar with.

3 List at least five 3D techniques that you can use to get across your design ideas.

4 Which of these materials are non-resistant and which are resistant?

- card • plywood • soft woods • paper • dry plaster
- wet plaster • clay • metals • plastic

edexcel :::

Assignment tips

3D visual communication is around us all the time. You worked through an exercise at the start of this section where you considered how many items you could find in your home that utilise 3D visual communication. You should be able to use your experience in this unit to become more aware of how much of our environment is affected by 3D visual communication. There is a wealth of examples in art, craft and design that have a real influence on our lives.

Using 3D visual communication

When you are working with 3D materials, techniques and processes you have to be aware of what the product is going to look like. It's easy to get bogged down in the technical aspects of a material or technique, and lose sight of the effect that you want to achieve. Regular and effective evaluation will help you overcome some of these difficulties.

The best sources of information

You may not get a chance to explore all the different ways of joining, cutting, fastening and so on mentioned in this unit. There are books and websites where you can see examples of what artists, designers and makers can achieve using 3D visual communication.

Websites

Support your work by taking time to look at the websites and information suggested.

- Design Nation
- Design Factory
- Eco Design
- Design Museum

- V&A Museum
- Tate
- Henry Moore Foundation

To see the examples on these websites go to Hotlinks.

4 Using ideas to explore, develop and produce art and design

Your specialist studies on this course will have introduced you to a wide world of art and design. As part of this you will have learned many ways of developing ideas and lots of techniques, and understood how to use a range of different processes and materials. This unit is intended to bring together all the things you have learned. You will apply your learning by working through an art and design project proposal that you have written based on a brief. This means that you can concentrate on working through your own ideas in your preferred pathway, such as fashion, 3D, graphics, photography or fine art.

Artists, craftspeople and designers use ways to explore, develop and process ideas all the time, especially when they work on specific briefs.

Some briefs are open-ended with an emphasis on materials, techniques and their applications. These briefs are often used by artists and some craftspeople who are exploring ideas and materials. Other design briefs meet the specific needs of the client.

For this unit you will have to develop a focused project within a given timescale. Your tutor will give the class a subject, theme or outcome to develop your ideas from.

The learning outcomes will take you through the four stages needed for this unit. You will be able to check the stages of your work by reading the Skills section units.

vocational
theme
final outcome
prototype

Learning outcomes

After completing this unit you should:

1 be able to research and record visual and other information from primary and secondary sources in response to the brief

2 be able to develop ideas that meet the requirements of the brief, through the use of specialist materials, equipment and techniques

3 be able to present and communicate developmental work and final outcomes

4 know the strengths and weaknesses of developmental work.

Assessment and grading criteria

This table shows you what you must do in order to achieve a pass, merit or distinction, and where you can find activities in this book to help you.

To achieve a **pass** grade the evidence must show that the learner is able to:	To achieve a **merit** grade the evidence must show that, in addition to the pass criteria, the learner is able to:	To achieve a **distinction** grade the evidence must show that, in addition to the pass and merit criteria, the learner is able to:
P1 research and record visual and other information from primary and secondary sources in response to the brief **Assessment activity 4.1 Task 1 Page 83**	**M1** research and record a variety of visual and other information from primary and secondary sources in response to the brief **Assessment activity 4.1 Task 1 Page 83**	**D1** research and record diverse visual and other information from primary and secondary sources in response to the brief **Assessment activity 4.1 Task 1 Page 83**
P2 develop ideas that meet the requirements of the brief, through the use of materials, techniques and processess **Assessment activity 4.1 Task 2 Page 83**	**M2** develop alternative ideas that meet the requirements of the brief, using a range of materials, techniques and processes **Assessment activity 4.1 Task 2 Page 83**	**D2** develop selected alternative ideas, imaginatively meeting the requirements of the brief with the use of specialist materials, techniques and processes **Assessment activity 4.1 Task 2 Page 83**
P3 present and communicate developmental work and final outcomes to meet the brief **Assessment activity 4.2 Task 1 Page 84**	**M3** present and communicate coherent developmental work and final outcomes effectively **Assessment activity 4.2 Task 1 Page 84**	**D3** present and communicate diverse developmental work and final outcomes imaginatively **Assessment activity 4.2 Task 1 Page 84**
P4 identify the strengths and weaknesses of the work in terms of meeting the requirements of the brief using appropriate technical terms **Assessment activity 4.2 Task 2 Page 84**	**M4** explain the strengths and weaknesses of the work in terms of meeting the brief requirements, using technical terms consistently and accurately **Assessment activity 4.2 Task 2 Page 84**	**D4** analyse the strengths and weaknesses of the work in terms of meeting the requirements of the brief **Assessment activity 4.2 Task 2 Page 84**

How you will be assessed

Your project proposal will be the basis of the final assessment along with all the practical work, including the planning, research, development of ideas and the final design idea.

Your practical work will be completed in ten hours under controlled conditions. This will allow for adequate access to specialist workshops, tutors, technicians and materials.

Your assessment might be a presentation to your group, an end of year show or a portfolio of work.

Greta Staron

Assignment: Design a fashion outfit by exploring different ways of developing ideas.

I decided to use ideas from textile samples as a starting point for my fashion ideas. Here are some of the ways that I tried to work out my fashion designs by using collage.

I made a rectangle using a glue gun with lines across the rectangle in one direction. Then I cut fabrics into long slim strips, which I wove in the opposite direction into my glue sample to show a range of colours.

Finally, I turned my glue and fabric sample into a drawing for a fashion design. After scanning the drawing, I cropped it into the shape I wanted, and then traced round the outline using the **polygonal lasso tool** and cut away the pixels. I really liked my design but next time I need to use a different sample of my product, because in some places it doesn't look good.

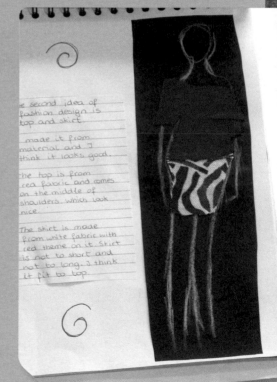

The second idea for a fashion design is a top and skirt, which I made from material scraps. The top is from red fabric and sits on the middle of the shoulders which looks nice. The skirt is made from white fabric with a red theme on it. I think the skirt works well with the top.

For my third idea I used a plastic bag and material. I made the top from dark blue material and on top of the material I put a plastic bag. I really like this T-shirt because the sleeve comes just to the elbow. The trousers are made from light blue material and come just to the knees.

Key term

Polygonal lasso tool – creates polygonal selections in Photoshop and allows you to cut away shapes.

1. Be able to research and record visual and other information from primary and secondary sources in response to the brief

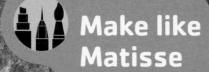 Make like Matisse

Henri Matisse (1869–1954) was best known as a painter, but he was also a brilliant draughtsman, printmaker and sculptor. As Matisse grew old he also found it hard to be mobile and spent much of his time in a wheelchair. His helpers painted papers in different colours which Matisse then cut into shapes, using scissors to 'draw' with. The paper cuts were arranged to make patterns inspired by different topics like the Matisse-styled image below.

Use Matisse's technique and develop an idea based on a theme such as 'summer' or 'the figure'

1.1 Writing your project proposal brief

When you write your project proposal brief you are expected to indicate how you can achieve this outcome. Here are some reminders of what you will need to do.

Primary and secondary resources will vary depending on your subject specialisms and the brief you have written, so choose your sources carefully. It is essential that you investigate historical and contemporary references to support your ideas. The research needs to be sufficient to support the aim and objectives of your brief.

Primary sources

Make your visual research from objects, places, people, galleries, exhibitions and museums that you have seen first-hand.

Secondary sources

Get your information from digital technology, paper-based and online publications, commercial products and audio visual sources.

Record

Use different methods to record what you have found through your research. You might take photographs, make mood boards, sketch in pencil and paint and write notes. You might also use video to record information.

What other methods have you learned to record information?

Respond

Although you will have written your own brief, be clear about what you intend to do. Identify all the information needed to develop your work. Include limitations and constraints, the needs of a client, users or audience. Think about the technical skills you need for realising ideas. Do not embark on anything that you cannot do. It's fine to improve your skills in this unit but you shouldn't try to do anything you haven't learned. This unit is intended to showcase what you have learned during the course.

Planning your time

Plan your work carefully and refer to the Skills section on planning for extra suggestions. Remind yourself about the importance of keeping to time and meeting the hand-in deadline. Make yourself a weekly calendar and write down milestones of when you aim to complete tasks that you have identified.

- **What tasks have you identified?**

- **What are the limitations and constraints – such as, have you allowed for kiln firing and cooling time or screens to dry?**

What do you need to consider when planning a visit to a gallery?

73

Case study: The Graphics Design Team, Marketing Department, Southampton Solent University

The Graphics Design Team from the marketing department at Southampton Solent University gives an insight into this stage.

'Designing for us is all about teamwork. For most jobs we are given a brief. We research first. For us this means **competitive analysis** – where we find out what's already out there. We need to know:

- how we can do it better

- the market for our products (usually 16 to 21 year-olds)

- who else is pitching out there, so we research the audience, the market and what other universities are doing.

The research unit at the university holds focus groups in schools and talks to pupils about what they like. This is how we "keep our ear to the ground", by talking to schools and members of staff.

We have to know what the **graphic trends** are within the industry – we need to know what's trendy and what's not. We look for trends and see how we can get them into our work. Our ideas always need to be fresh.'

1. What competitive analysis might you do before you start your project? Write a short report on what competitive analysis would you carry out.

2. Identify recent fashions and trends that might influence your designs. Carry out research using secondary sources such as design magazines, books and the Internet.

Dora Carrington used oil, ink, silver foil and mixed media on glass for *Bon Voyage*. It sold at auction for over £9000 in 2008.

Sometimes artists' ideas are born out of poverty or the need to make something different to sell.

Many painters such as Vincent van Gogh (1853–1890) and Gwen John (1876–1939) were very poor, and painted self-portraits or used their friends as models to save what little money they had.

Dora Carrington (1893–1932) used oils on glass to paint a variety of subjects such as flowers and galleons. Carrington left gaps in the paint which she filled with tin foil from chocolate wrappers. These shiny pictures were sold in a London bookshop.

2. Be able to develop ideas that meet the requirements of the brief, through the use of specialist materials, equipment and techniques

2.1 Requirements of the brief

Although you are responsible for writing the brief you now need to go through all the stages you have learned on your course to analyse a brief. This should link back to the timescale on your action plan – have you missed anything?

2.2 Developing ideas

You have lots of ideas to start you off so you now start to 'think on paper', to work them out. Review some research that you have done for one of your projects and go through the planning cycle (see Planning skills unit).

- Is your research relevant to the brief?
- Do you need to refer back to any contextual information? Look back at all the case studies in this book and see how much information the artists, designers and craftspeople needed to develop their ideas. Do you have enough yourself?

Start developing your ideas that respond to the brief requirements.

You will need to produce 2D and/or 3D prototypes, models, mock-ups, samples and test pieces to support the development of ideas and ensure that they will work in practice.

Let your ideas flow, keeping the aim of the brief in mind at all times. This helps ideas remain appropriate **P2**. To work towards **M2**, your ideas need to lead from one to another. To do this you need to think how you can improve your work each time. You might realise that things aren't working out as you intended, or you could be faced with something that you don't have the skills to do. Make sure you note down your thoughts and feelings to help explain why and how your ideas change. As you improve on each idea, work out how they can change for the better. If, for example, you are designing a seat, think about different materials, heights for the seat back and so on, to help develop alternative ideas **M2**. To develop selected alternative ideas **D2**, you need to bring out your creativity and originality. If you have backed this unit up with a wide variety of research that looks at the work of others, you should be able take what you have learned and apply it to new situations.

Remember

Keep all your notes, drawings, research, thumbnails – anything that can show the thought processes you have used to develop ideas.

Case study: Nicki Williams, textile artist

This case study looks at the work of an artist to understand how ideas are developed.

What have you made recently?

I have been making commercial pieces for sale through galleries and craft markets. I have recently made papier maché bowls, stitched jewellery using dissolvable fabrics, purses stitched with appliqué and 3D stitched vessels. I have also made mixed-media paintings for myself which give me an opportunity to explore materials and techniques.

Can you give an example of how you explore and develop your ideas?

When I was studying for a BA (Hons) in Textiles/Fashion Design at Loughborough, a fascination for puppets and theatrical inanimate characters began, providing the inspiration for much of my early work. My pieces continue to be theatrical, reflecting influences of the puppet theatre. Dramatic colours, shapes, structures and patterns are evident throughout my work – from hangings to jewellery, with delicate stitched textures and dramatic colours of manipulated silks, taffetas, lamés and organza.

I use photography as a starting point to explore ideas, and capture my inspiration on film. One example was using photographs I took of Worthing Pier. I focused on the rust, barnacles, seaweed and other debris hanging off the metal and wooden structures. The colours and textures were absolutely beautiful. I used iridescent threads and fabrics in rusty colours, golds, purples and oranges to explore ideas in fabric, stitch and dye. The colours were like corroded metals, especially the blue-greens which have a powdery effect. I explored with fabrics stitching different combinations and layers. It was essential to have my visual materials, the photographs, as my starting point. As a textile artist I tend to develop my ideas by using fabrics and dyes very early in the process.

I developed ideas from this experience to create precious vessels incorporating mixed media. The vessels could be opened, and inside hung 'little urchins' that resembled bits of seaweed (see below). The urchins were three-dimensional like seedpods hanging down, with beads as seeds mixed with stitched fabrics. The vessels are about 15 cm high. These pieces are exquisite and I can imagine them in the V&A under a glass case.

What other sources of inspiration have you used recently?

I like visiting the south coast and have used photographs of boats on the shore at Hastings. I'm inspired by old boats with peeling paint, looking at the textures, the layers of revealed paint and the abstraction that appears. From this I have recorded my thoughts in mixed-media collages which will develop into something else. To make these collages I painted papers, made marks, tore all the papers up and then layered the pieces over each other. These formed bigger collages. I enjoy exploring through piecing together, constructing and layering.

1 Where does Nicki get her ideas from?

2 What has inspired her choice of colours?

2.3 Developing through experimentation

Jessica Ryles gives some examples of experimental paper making and mixed-media work to support her ideas. Jessica set herself the task of using the lyrics of a song to inspire her work. She wanted to develop a textile piece based on 'Carpal Tunnel of Love' by Fall Out Boy. Jessica Ryles described how she made these artworks:

'I made this out of pulp (mushed up paper), feathers and my lyrics. I used a wire-mesh sheet and dipped it into the mushed-up paper and pulled it back out again to make sure there was enough pulp. I then put another layer of pulp on top. I also stuck down some feathers. For one of my samples I used string to give a rippled effect.'

Jessica then investigated other methods where she could incorporate the lyrics. This one is embedding lyrics in plastic. The example on the right shows lyrics embedded in weaving.

Examples of Jessica Ryles' work using pulp, feathers and lyrics

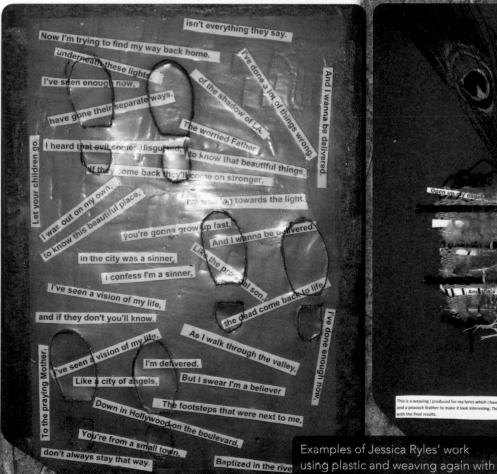

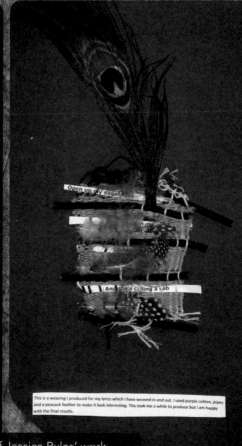

Examples of Jessica Ryles' work using plastic and weaving again with feathers and lyrics

2.4 Reviewing and evaluating ideas in progress

It is important that you review and develop your ideas. Consider what works and what doesn't. Evaluate and refine the most appropriate ideas and produce several versions until a final design idea has been reached. Keep these versions small as you refine and change them. This contributes towards learning outcomes 2 and 4.

Even though artists and designers specialise in different subject areas, they all use a range of techniques to work through their ideas. You might see all of these methods being used in the studio. A selection of methods is shown below.

layout pads   **story boards**
maquettes   **experimental samples**
contact sheets   **thumbnail sketches**

What will you use?

The Graphics Design Team at Southampton Solent University commented on this stage:

'We bounce ideas around as a group. Lots of ideas are scribbles which turn into thumbnails and these we sketch out and develop more. Then we pick the ideas that might work and knock them into something cohesive.'

2.5 Specialist materials, equipment and techniques

Specialist materials, equipment and techniques will vary depending on your specialism. Whichever specialism you follow, you will need to indicate early ideas as a result of the mind maps, mood boards and other ways that you have gathered your thoughts together. Before you start your project it is essential to check on the materials you have available before you write them into your brief.

- **Are you proposing to use materials that are available?**
- **If not, where will you get them from? How much do they cost? Will you be able to get them within the time allowed to resolve your ideas? Who is going to pay for any extra materials?**
- **Have you got alternative ideas if you can't get the materials you want?**

Remember

Develop ideas and techniques that keep building on the previous ones – take the best bit of a piece of work and use it again and improve it **M2**. Be imaginative and try out unusual ideas **D2**.

Case study: Alexander Elliot Welch

Alex was asked how he wrote his project proposal and developed his ideas. Alex set himself the brief of designing and making a large arm puppet.

What gave you the idea for your project proposal?

I had seen lots of puppets on TV and liked the idea of being a puppeteer.

How do you plan you ideas and work?

I looked at other people's puppets such as *Spitting Image*. I made a list of puppeteers, Paul Fisco for example – he is responsible for Alf. I also like the work of Warwick Danes who did Ewok for *Star Wars*.

I decided to make my puppet a rabbit because rabbits are popular in the spring, which is when I decided on my project.

What did you do next?

I did lots of drawings about rabbit puppet ideas. I changed my ideas every time I redrew the puppet. I thought about the ideas quite hard on the page and eventually decided on one that I could use to make my final idea.

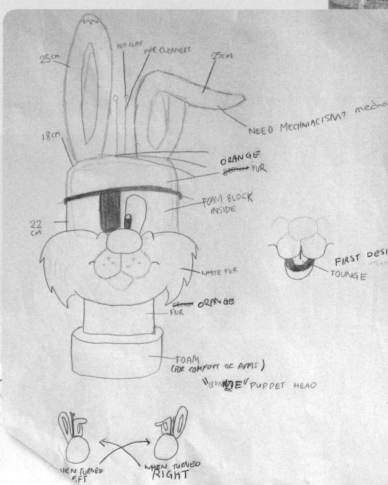

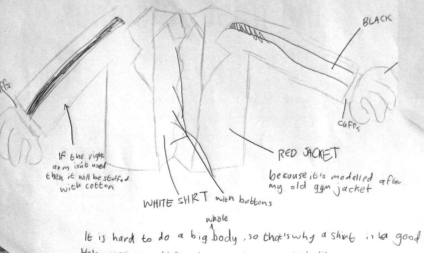

Activity: New art from old

Throughout his life Picasso researched the work of other artists and produced his own work in response to theirs. For example, he did a series of paintings in response to works by the old masters; each one was a development of the other. The final images had some resemblance to the original painting in the way that people and objects were placed, but Picasso made them contemporary and his own.

Research an artist that you like. How could you develop your ideas in response to theirs and make a new piece of art?

How is this linocut by Pablo Picasso (*Portrait of a Woman after Cranach the Younger*) a response to the original painting *Portrait of a Woman* by Cranach the Younger?

3. Be able to present and communicate developmental work and final outcomes

3.1 Presenting work

This means you have to show how your work has progressed from initial research and design ideas through to final design. You must present the stages in realising the final design. It's often difficult to decide how many sheets of ideas and other evidence you have to go through to come up with your design. Think back on how you have been taught to do this during the course. You need to show how your ideas changed from one idea to the other, even if only small changes were recorded. The important thing here is to annotate your work so that you can clearly show how your ideas developed and changed.

What does annotate mean?

This means making short notes on your work to explain what things are and what you are thinking about. Look back at Alex's work (page 79) – he annotated his drawings. Greta wrote notes alongside her work as it was stuck in a sketchbook (page 71). Both ways are examples of annotation. When you present your work, make sure that you are selecting techniques appropriate for the work and presentation format. For example, you might be making an exhibition display or presenting your work in a portfolio. Get advice from a teacher as to the most appropriate method. At the most basic level it should be in a neat and tidy order. You do not need to mount up everything – that isn't always appropriate. You could mount:

- the final drawing that expresses your design

- photographs of your final outcome.

Choose to give special treatment to the final pieces. If you have designed a 3D item, this might be a sculpture, a fashion drawing or an accessory. If you are displaying your 3D piece as part of the presentation in a display, you need to show it off to its best advantage. Could a garment go on a dressmaker's dummy? Could a small 3D piece go on a plinth?

Make sure you present all of your work. Learners need to show their thought processes in the experimental pieces.

Nicki Williams, textile artist, describes how she presented her 'Little Urchins' work (shown here and on page 76):

'The boxes were suspended on painted sticks reminiscent of the stilts that support the pier. It was interesting to elevate the pieces.

I usually recycle my sample ideas and experimental pieces into other bigger pieces of art. They are frequently incorporated into new ideas.'

Remember

If you are mounting work, do ask for help. Keep your work clean as you mount it up.

Can you think of unusual ways of presenting your work?

4. Know the strengths and weaknesses of developmental work

For this learning outcome you will need to produce an evaluation of the final piece(s) of project work and all the development work you made in response to the brief. You must use the correct technical terms.

4.1 Developmental work

Development work means all your thought processes, alternative solutions and experiments that you went through to work out your ideas. You also need to think about how you have communicated this work to others.

4.2 Strengths and weaknesses

Annotations are a useful way to record your opinions on the strengths and weaknesses of your work. To make an ongoing review of your work, add comments that say what you think about your ideas. For example:

I really like this idea but it was hard to do and really fiddly so I might not use it.

or

I like the colours and textures of this idea so will develop them further.

Keep your ongoing evaluations brief and put them in your visual diary, in sketchbooks or on design sheets. You might even try a blog about this unit.

When you have completed the project you must produce a final evaluation. To do this, you need to look back at the original project proposal and the way you worked through your ideas. You need to say if your project worked and what you might have done better. Ask yourself these questions:

- **Were the sources you used and the reasons behind the proposal enough to achieve your aims?**

- **Did your initial ideas help you take different directions, or did you stick with ideas you felt safe with?**

- **What was your inspiration and what were the successes?**

- **What did you learn from your rejected ideas, the problems you faced and the solutions you came up with? These might include initial ideas, familiarity, unfamiliarity, taking different directions, creative risks, knowledge of processes; final outcome.**

Nicki Williams describes how she evaluates her work:

'I like to use the opinions of others to see if they think the pieces have worked. It is difficult to know sometimes and useful to hear comments. When I make the mixed-media bowls, I evaluate their shape and the balance of the fabric and stitching with the papier maché. This helps me assess if the pieces work visually.'

 Functional skills

Maths

As you develop your ideas you might be scaling models and maquettes, timing as in developing dyebaths, using exposure times, measuring as in using perspective. Sometimes you can use maths without thinking, so annotate your sketchbook or workbook to say what you are doing.

What was the scale?
How long was the exposure?
Where else can you use maths?

IT

You might also be using software packages for design development, especially in fashion, graphics, textiles, 3D.

The Skills section will remind you what you need to include in your evaluation. If you aren't sure about the strengths and weaknesses of your ideas, remember to ask someone else for their opinion. Ask a variety of people of different ages from your family and friends so that comments are balanced.

Finally, review your final outcome.

- **Has it worked out how you expected?**
- **Are you pleased with the final outcome?**
- **Could you have changed anything to improve on your work?**

Include the presentation of your work in this review.

 Functional skills

English
Speaking and listening is used when you are presenting work in discussions with your teachers and peers. You will be reading as you research and analysing information throughout the unit. You will be writing as you write up research work, perhaps as a result of gallery visits; or producing an evaluation of the final outcome in relation to the project proposal. To improve your English always check your spellings.

IT
IT skills improve when you use the Internet to help research and then write your project proposal.

 ## Assessment activity 4.1: Writing a project proposal brief, part 1

Task 1

- Decide on the specialist area you want to explore.
- If you are interested in more than one area can you combine them?
- Decide what you will work towards producing. To do this, set yourself a task to achieve. This is called the AIM.
- Write a rationale. Set the scene and give a reason for doing your project.
- Say what your general research will be. For an example see Aim in the Key terms box on page 84.
- Then state what historical and contemporary artists' work you will look at to help shape your ideas. If you are designing a chair, you would look at historical and contemporary chair designs and note down who designed them.
- List some of the books and websites you intend to use for your research.
- Do you intend to visit anywhere for visual research? You might plan to go to a local museum, an aquarium or a special location. Write down your intentions.

Task 2

- Then write down how you are going to develop your ideas. These are the OBJECTIVES.
- What is the point of your research? Why are you doing it and where are you going with it? Keep it relevant.
- What materials, techniques and processes will you use to make your idea?
- What is the timescale and is it achievable? Write an action plan of what tasks you think you should do each week.

Assessment activity 4.2: Writing a project proposal brief, part 2

Task 1

After completing Assessment activity 4.1 consider how you are going to present your work and the final outcome.

Task 2

Make sure you include ongoing evaluation in your proposal. This includes a work journal, annotated sketchbook or a reflective diary.

When you have completed your proposal your tutor will review what you have written and give you feedback. This will either agree your project, or you might be asked to look at it again. You may be asked to increase your research or re-think your timescale, or to include more techniques.

Grading tips

Make sure your research is relevant, appropriate **M1** and diverse. Remember to use different sources **D1**, including primary and secondary research sources.

 PLTS

Independent enquirers

Planning and carrying out research relevant to theme and art, design or craft proposal will evidence your independent enquiry skills.

Creative thinkers

Generating ideas and exploring possibilities relevant to the project proposal will evidence your creative thinking skills.

Reflective learners

Revisiting what you are doing, examining your work and how you can improve it will evidence your reflective learning skills.

Key terms

Aim

I am going to design a ceramic wall plaque/design a mural for a children's ward in a hospital/paint a portrait of my grandma in the style of an artist/produce a portfolio of prints based on 'decay'/design a magazine cover.

Objectives

This is where you explain how you are going to develop your ideas. Mention what you are going to research, what materials you are going to use, which techniques you will use.

Evaluation

The example below includes self and peer evaluation. What other types of evaluation could you use?

The top will be designed for a teenager, so I shall ask my art group what they think of my design ideas. This will help me work through my ideas so that I can design a top that teenagers will like and I am able to make. I will write a final evaluation and consider what improvements I could make.

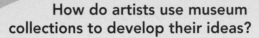

Ann Wise

Museum curator

How do artists use museum collections to develop their ideas?

Collections are used as an inspiration that stimulates someone to explore the history or the manufacture of objects. This in turn generates ideas for new work which might be textiles, ceramics or jewellery. Or an object might be investigated as a starting point, with ideas coming from observation of the texture, shape or colour.

Give me an example of an unusual starting point?

Archaeology collections have inspired people. The Highdown Goblet (at Worthing Museum) is a rare piece of Egyptian glass found on Highdown hill, and a motif on the glass has been used as a starting point.

Artists and designers have developed work from industrial archive pieces using the actual ledgers with their worn out leather spines as a starting point.

What other starting points might they use?

Many artists and designers are inspired by old photographs of people. Photographs of spinners and weavers have inspired stitched textiles, and one artist made an embroidered hanging mobile inspired by a flywheel.

How do commercial designers use archives and collections?

Commercial textile and surface decoration firms license designs. This means they pay a fee to copy complete designs or motifs from old designs that belong to industrial archives. These archives could be owned by a museum or a private collector.

Commercial firms will make a direct copy and just reproduce the work in a different colour way and this will be an expensive licence. Commercial firms may just reproduce a motif they've seen on archive materials and pay to copy the motif and put it in a new design.

Think about it!

- Find out about the collections that are local to you. How might you use them in your work?
- How would you make sure that you got the most out of a visit to a museum collection – what if you only had an hour to spare?

85

Just checking

1 Create a spider diagram of different sources that you can use for researching.

2 Write down six ways of how you can develop your ideas.

3 List the materials, techniques and processes that you can use with confidence.

4 How can you make your presentation different?

5 What makes a good evaluation?

Assignment tips

To help extend your primary research you could:

Collect objects together and set up a still life, and from this make small studies in pencil and paint. This is something that you could do at home to supplement work you are doing in college. Perhaps you could set up a small still life in the corner of your bedroom?

Use this work to add to the things you do in class. **P1 M1 D1**

Record

As you research your information make sure you record what you've done. Keep to the brief you have set yourself and don't waste time researching things you don't need. However, if your research gives you ideas that you hadn't considered, you can usually change your mind about the outcome. Check with your teacher first, but this shows that you have reflected and developed on your ideas. **P1 M1 D1**

To aim for **D1** make sure that your research is diverse. Look at the Planning skills unit for more information about how to do this.

Talk the Talk

Learn the correct vocational terms for the things you use and do. As your ideas develop think about the materials and techniques you can use. What are their correct names? **P2 M2 D2**

For **M2 D2** the key word is *alternative*. This could mean that you consider the size and scale of what you are doing. You might consider different colour ways or techniques.

Portfolios

If you intend to continue with art and design at Level 3, now is the time to consider investing in an A1 or A2 portfolio that opens out flat and has a zip all the way round. These portfolios help keep your work together and can be easily opened up to be assessed.

Present your work appropriately, effectively, imaginatively. Make sure all your research and developmental work is easy to understand and that ideas can be followed. **P3 M3 D3**

5 Building an art and design portfolio

In the art and design industry your portfolio will be an important factor in your career development. It is the vehicle that you will use to showcase your talents and abilities. It's what you use to show potential clients, galleries, other practitioners and the public what you have achieved so far. It also points the way to what you are capable of – it shows your potential.

In this unit you will work through tasks that are essential for producing and presenting a portfolio. These tasks are:

- evaluating your own work
- selecting work for the portfolio
- presenting the work to its full potential
- explaining your work.

You will research examples of art, craft and design portfolios in different formats, as they are used in the industry. You will need to explain their **purpose**, looking for themes and identifying the choices practitioners make and why. This will be presented in a format that you and your tutor will agree, and on which you will be assessed. You will then work through building your own art and design portfolio, using knowledge you have gained at the different stages, such as selecting or mounting work.

career development
talent
potential clients
galleries
portfolio

Learning outcomes

After completing this unit you should:

1 understand the purpose of an art and design portfolio

2 be able to present an art and design portfolio.

Assessment and grading criteria

This table shows you what you must do in order to achieve a pass, merit or distinction, and where you can find activities in this book to help you.

To achieve a **pass** grade the evidence must show that the learner is able to:	To achieve a **merit** grade the evidence must show that, in addition to the pass criteria, the learner is able to:	To achieve a **distinction** grade the evidence must show that, in addition to the pass and merit criteria, the learner is able to:
P1 describe how artists and designers use portfolios **Assessment activity 5.1 Page 92**	**M1** explain how artists and designers use portfolios, reaching consistent conclusions **Assessment activity 5.1 Page 92**	**D1** independently describe how artists and designers use portfolios, reaching informed and in-depth conclusions **Assessment activity 5.1 Page 92**
P2 present an art and design portfolio **Assessment activity 5.3 Page 94** **Assessment activity 5.4 Page 97** **Assessment activity 5.5 Page 98**	**M2** competently select and present examples of their work to produce an effective art and design portfolio **Assessment activity 5.3 Page 94** **Assessment activity 5.4 Page 97** **Assessment activity 5.5 Page 98**	**D2** independently select and present examples of their work to produce an exciting art and design portfolio **Assessment activity 5.3 Page 94** **Assessment activity 5.4 Page 97** **Assessment activity 5.5 Page 98**
P3 justify reasons for selecting work for an art and design portfolio **Assessment activity 5.1 Page 92** **Assessment activity 5.2 Page 93** **Assessment activity 5.3 Page 94** **Assessment activity 5.4 Page 97** **Assessment activity 5.6 Page 100**	**M3** consistently and effectively explain their reasons for selecting work for an art and design portfolio **Assessment activity 5.1 Page 92** **Assessment activity 5.2 Page 93** **Assessment activity 5.3 Page 94** **Assessment activity 5.4 Page 97** **Assessment activity 5.6 Page 100**	**D3** independently and fluently explain their reasons for selecting work for an art and design portfolio **Assessment activity 5.1 Page 92** **Assessment activity 5.2 Page 93** **Assessment activity 5.3 Page 94** **Assessment activity 5.4 Page 97** **Assessment activity 5.6 Page 100**

How you will be assessed

You will be given assignments by your tutor, which will focus on researching existing portfolios and then producing your own. You will present your portfolio at the close of the unit, and you'll be assessed on your performance in:

- researching and reaching conclusions
- selecting and presenting your portfolio
- explaining and justifying your reasons for selecting work.

Ellie Simkins

I want to apply to college to carry on studying art and design, this time at Level 3. I really want to get a job in graphics, and my tutor has recommended I do a Level 3 course to get a good portfolio of graphics together. After that I might try to go to university or get a job. My tutor has given me some guidelines to work to when selecting my work.

I am going to put my strongest pieces first, which in my case is the graphics work. I have three graphics projects so I'm going to select work from each of them. This can be tricky, because I want to put everything in and I have far too much. I agreed with my tutor that a complete project would be useful to explain the way I have worked. I'm quite good at researching, so I am keen to show off my sketchbook work as well.

I'm going to show the range of things I've done on Level 2 First Diploma, so I'll include drawing, painting and 3D, selected for the strongest. I made a piece of motion graphics as well so I'm taking my laptop to the interview. My tutor said not to take a memory stick or disk, as it might not work. I'm going to get notes together to help me explain my work, as I know it's really important to present my work well.

- **Think about the work you have produced so far. Which pieces would you select for your portfolio?**

Selecting work

Selecting work is an important part of building a portfolio. Take a recent project you have done. Get the work together – research, design or ideas development, visuals and final outcome. Arrange them so you can see them all. Now select the strongest piece of work from each part of the project:

- one page from a sketchbook or work journal (research)
- one page of ideas development
- one rough version
- one final outcome.

Can you explain why you chose these? Do they summarise the project?

1. Understand the purpose of an art and design portfolio

This section looks at why portfolios are used in the industry and at how different materials and technologies can be used in the making of a portfolio.

1.1 Making the portfolio work

All practitioners need to show examples of their work. The reasons for this vary, depending on the scenario. Practitioners might create a portfolio to:
- support an application for a job
- highlight their work for an agency
- provide potential clients with a past history of their work
- highlight specialist skills in particular fields
- show how they have met specific briefs
- highlight strengths in their work.

1.2 Different types of portfolios

The form the portfolios take can also be varied, and may be any combination of:
- paper-based art and design work
- photographs supported by statements
- material samples
- DVD, video or web-based
- animated sequences
- show-reels
- IT presentations.

specialist skills
pedigree
of work
design briefs
published
examples
client base
recording
exhibitions
demonstrate
abilities

Paper-based portfolios of art and design work are still used in face-to-face interviews. Many clients also still prefer to see actual artwork as examples, rather than reproductions. This is fine if you have an interview opportunity, but what if you don't?

There are useful links about portfolios and presentations on the Creative Pool UK website. To view the Creative Pool UK website go to Hotlinks. Now let's look at it from the other perspective. You are the creative director of a small design company specialising in graphic communication. You have a range of well-known clients who respect you for delivering quality outcomes to deadline. You have recently begun to develop leads into larger advertising campaigns, and are keen to develop new ideas for existing campaigns to win new contracts. You have advertised for junior designers who you want to bring exciting new dynamics to the team.

What do you think the creative director will be looking for? What kind of characteristics would he or she be hoping to see in portfolios?

It's useful to think like this before an interview. You can always contact the company before and ask them point blank what they want to see – they might tell you there and then. It would help you plan the portfolio order and contents.

Functional skills

IT

Using the Internet and online sources to investigate different areas in art and design, and developing, presenting and communicating information in ways that are fit for purpose and the audience will evidence your ICT skills.

PLTS

Independent enquirers

Researching different portfolio formats and looking at areas within the art and design industry will evidence your independent enquiry skills.

Activity: Portfolios for different purposes

Work though the activity in the table below. The column on the left has a series of potential scenarios where you might use a portfolio – your task is to fill in, in the right-hand column, the type of portfolio that would best fit the purpose. You can have more than one type of portfolio, but you should put them in order of preference. To do this, you will need to research examples of portfolios.

Scenario	Portfolio
An interview for a job as a junior designer in a specialist field	
An interview for a job as a junior designer in a general field	
Advertising your work to the professionals and agencies in the industry	
Highlighting the range of work you have produced over the years	
Pitching for a commission	
Using a mailout to a broad range of companies/professionals	
An assessment of a recent brief	
An interim presentation of 'ideas so far' to a client	

Table 5.1: Think about the different ways you can present your work. What are the advantages and disadvantages of each?

Assessment activity 5.1: Purpose and content

You have gained a placement with an interior designer. You work in his or her studio for two days per week. The designer has been awarded a commission to re-design a bar and restaurant area in your local town. He/she has just completed the preliminary stage of the design work, and is meeting the clients to show the ideas developed so far to meet the brief. The designer has asked you to come up with ideas on the content of the portfolio and presentation format.

• What is the purpose of the portfolio and presentation?

• What formats for portfolio and presentation do you think would be most beneficial to the designer?

• What do you think the clients would like to see?

• What would you include?

• What would you leave out?

Grading tip

In this activity you will need to research how interior designers use portfolios and presentations. The more in-depth your research into portfolios, the higher your grade is likely to be. Use the research to reach consistent and informed conclusions, supported by the examples.

 PLTS

Independent enquirers and creative thinkers

Raising questions, analysing information and generating ideas about your portfolio will evidence your independent enquiry and creative thinking skills.

2. Be able to present an art and design portfolio

This section focuses on you learning the skills and strategies needed to work through the tasks shown above – evaluating, selecting, presenting and explaining.

When you are building your art and design portfolio it's a good idea to have a plan. This will help you target what you include, and how you present it. The plan could contain any of the features listed below.

> purpose   checklist of work   complete projects
> developmental work   sketchbooks
>   written statements   IT-based work
> photographic requirements, i.e. 3D work
>   amount of work

Assessment activity 5.2: Evaluating work – what to put in and what to leave out?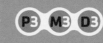

You are applying for jobs in design-related industries. Your work has strong elements of graphics and 3D Design. You also have examples showing creative treatments of surface pattern and consistent drawing skills. You want to get your portfolio ready, and to represent what you believe are your all-round skills. Develop a written plan for your portfolio, showing:

- what you want to put in
- what you want to leave out
- how you are going to justify your selection
- how your selection will highlight your skill range.

Grading tips

Look at the grading grid. The criteria tells you how tutors will need to categorise your work – use this to help you select and explain your selection processes. Where criteria mention *effectively* **M3**, *consistently* **M3**, and *fluently* **D3**, write a description of the meanings in your own words, to help you demonstrate the characteristics of these criteria – you can call this your 'grading grid taxonomy' and refer back to it.

Jason Noble has worked as a tutor advising learners at all levels on their portfolios. In particular, he advises learners at higher level who are compiling portfolios to secure jobs and placements in the fine art field. He says:

'It's really important that students research the job or course interview they are going for. Many interviewers like to see things such as transferable skills – presentation techniques, communication skills and so on. If you are going for a job where the employer finds these things important, then you need to demonstrate them. Also, get other people to look through your work; what you think is the best doesn't always sell your all-round abilities as well as you think. And get everything neat, clean and well mounted where appropriate; there's nothing worse than scruffily mounted or presented work.'

Functional skills

ICT and English

Writing documents, including extended writing pieces, communicating information, ideas and opinions effectively and persuasively will evidence your ICT and English skills. Deciding what order to put your work in and what presentation techniques to use will evidence your ICT skills.

Figure 5.1: Think about the different ways you can present your work. What are the advantages and disadvantages of each?

Let's clarify and summarise the skills you need to apply before you begin your own portfolio building:

- **evaluating** – identify the purpose of your portfolio; define your goal; consider strengths and weaknesses

- **selecting** – decide the criteria for inclusion of work; edit examples; use feedback from others to help you decide

- **presenting** – cleaning, mounting and preparing art and design work; taking photographic records; using IT if required; using show-reels or DVDs; producing written statements to support your work

- **explaining** – justifying your reasons for selection and rejection of work; explaining your work in terms of subject matter and production methods; articulating the meaning or **rationale** of your work.

Functional skills

ICT and English

Speaking and listening – making a range of contributions to discussions and effective presentations in a wide range of contexts, explaining and justifying your choices and listening to feedback will evidence your ICT and English skills.

PLTS

Reflective learners

Reviewing your practical work, identifying strengths and weaknesses and listening to feedback from your peers and tutors will evidence your reflective learning.

Self-managers

Organising your time and resources for presentation and other purposes will evidence your self-management skills.

BTEC Assessment activity 5.3: Selecting work

Work in teams of four. Take your favourite project from the course so far. Get all the work you have done for this together, and display it. Make your selection of which pieces from the project you would include in your portfolio and which you would reject. Each person in the team should work through the same process with a project. When you have all completed the task, take turns to present your selection to the remaining three members of the team. You should explain your reasons for selecting the work, and how you would present it in the portfolio. Ask the team for feedback.

- Did they agree with your selection?

- Did they raise any points about work you rejected that made you think again and reconsider your choices?

- Did they agree with your choices of presentation methods?

- Do you agree with their choices?

It would be useful to record the results of this activity in your sketchbook or work journal.

Grading tip

Learn to explain your reasons as *consistently* and *effectively* **M3** as possible. As you practise this process see if you can *independently* **D3** apply these skills to explain your selection of work. Use correct terminology and relate your choices to the overall purpose of the portfolio.

2.1 Presenting work

There are different ways to present yourself and your work. A selection of these presentation methods is shown below.

> **mounting paper-based work**   **framing**   **photographing work**
> **using film and animation**   **using IT, i.e. PowerPoint**   **producing**
> **a DVD**   **producing a written statement**   **producing a CV**

Let's look at some examples of portfolio work.

This is a large-scale painting (120 x 92 cm). It was photographed for inclusion in a portfolio. This is a method you can use to include work that might be difficult to transport to an interview. You can also use photographs in an online web-based portfolio, or in a PowerPoint or IT-based presentation.

Detail from the painting opposite

Mounting paper-based work

This is a mounted silkscreen print and collage. The print has been **window mounted**, which means it is mounted behind a thick piece of mountboard, with the hole or aperture cut at 45 degrees. You need to use a **mount cutter** to do this.

Remember

Take photographs of details as well as the main picture – these can provide information on production techniques – in this case the detail in the painting or surface qualities.

Remember

Practise cutting window mounts on scrap pieces of card before you use the card you have bought. It's easier to make mistakes and using a mount cutter requires practice.

Did you know?

The bottom area of the mount should be slightly wider than the top area. This gives the mount more 'weight' at the bottom, and makes it look right. If there is too much space at the top area it can look top-heavy. Try this out by looking at artworks displayed when you next visit a gallery, museum, art shop or dentist's waiting room.

If you are unsure of where to position things like photographs (especially if you are mounting more than one on a sheet of card) you can position them on the top of the sheet and move them into different positions before you start cutting, to get the 'look' of the mounted sheet correct. This is called 'working by eye'; you can then use measurements to finalise the positions.

Examples of multi-work mounts

You can mount more than one picture per sheet.

This example was mounted so viewers could see the drawing and photograph that were used in the project. Without them the gouache paintings shown would not have had the same impact. It also helped the learner explain the work in a group critique.

Work by eye to position photographs on a mount

An example of mounting photographic work to support a project on 'light'. This mount has 10 standard-sized photographic images. These images have been surface mounted using Spraymount

Assessment activity 5.4: Presenting work

Get together some small preparatory work and images from a project. Make a selection of the best, and explore arranging the pieces on sheets of card. You could also include photographic examples of the final piece/s to place the developmental work into context.

Grading tips

To meet the Pass level criteria for **P2** and **P3** you need to work through the task, present your work and justify your reasons for selecting what you have. To reach **M2** you have to competently select the examples and make an effective display – this will be more considered than work assessed at **P2**. To meet **M3** you have to consistently and effectively explain your reasoning – you'll need to go into more detail about the choices, and be able to explain why you feel they are the best examples to choose and why you left some things out. Don't worry – working out what to leave out is a real skill, so the more you practise the better you will get.

To meet **D2** you need to make the selection on your own, without guidance from tutors. And to meet **D3** you need to explain your reasoning independently, coming up with points that you can relate directly to the examples you have chosen, using correct terms and language.

Figure 5.3: See Assessment activity 5.5 for more information on how to set up a photographic shoot

How you photograph work is important. If the shots are poor it will affect how people see the pieces. You can use a basic set-up for this, shown in the diagram above.

Assessment activity 5.5: Presenting 3D work

Get your 3D work together. Arrange the two lights as in the diagram shown on page 97. They should be at 45 degrees to the work, and the camera should be on a tripod, facing the work square. Put one of the lights slightly nearer the work – this will act as the **key light**. The second light will add detail to the shadows. If you only have one light, you can still reflect light into the shadows by putting a reflective surface at an angle and out of shot. This will reflect some of the light back into the shadows. If you don't have a pull-down backdrop, bend a sheet of clean white paper and arrange it behind the work, so that it forms a curved surface.

Take photographs of your work and experiment with close-ups of the surfaces.

Grading tips

When you are working through this kind of activity you need to balance two things: working safely to a high technical standard and working creatively. Make sure you know how the camera and lights operate to get technically sound pictures – this will meet **P2**. To reach **M2**, you need to show that you can manage the technical process and get strong shots consistently. This will make for an effective set of photographs. To reach **D2** you can also explore creative approaches, such as camera angles, using just one light for some of the shots, details and so on, as well as making sure you have a consistent and effective set of photographs.

Two studio shots of a learner's 3D work

PLTS

Self-managers

Working towards goals, organising time, resources and photo shoots, transporting work, setting up equipment, using lights and camera, downloading and processing images will all evidence your self-management skills.

This is a large-scale maquette for a project on enlarging, shot at two different angles – the learner took a basic two-chambered pencil sharpener and scaled it up. Maquettes and models were made in cardboard to keep costs down and because it is an inexpensive and recyclable material.

There isn't much colour in the card model, so the learner experimented with the second light and reflectors to inject detail into the shadows, yet still had enough contrast to make the form visible. Note the use of a plinth, also white, to act as a stand. You will probably have some of these in your centre. If not, they are relatively easy to make.

Explaining

You can use your portfolio to explain things about you and your work. These could include:

- your interests
- what materials you use
- your skills profile
- how you manage your time on projects
- how you work within a team
- any skills you have in working with employers.

Sometimes, you might use your portfolio at an interview and get the chance to talk through it. At other times you may be placing your portfolio online or on disks, so you will need to think about a written statement and CV to support it. When giving a presentation about your portfolio, you can use prompt cards to remind you of the main points that you want to get across.

CVs

You will need to produce one! This will allow you to demonstrate skills and produce evidence for writing skills and communicating information, ideas and opinions effectively and persuasively.

Look at examples of CVs to see what they contain. Your CV should have a skills section related directly to what you feel you are able to bring to a course or job, and will also need to highlight specific skills relating to art and design.

Did you know?

You don't always need to use a really high megapixel rated digital camera; if you are printing up to A3 maximum, then around 6 megapixels will be fine. If you are printing larger than that then you may need a larger rating.

Functional skills

English

Speaking and listening, contributing to discussions, making effective presentations in a wide range of contexts, and discussing your and others' portfolios will evidence your English skills.

PLTS

Teamwork

Collaborating with peers, making presentations and listening to others will evidence your teamwork skills.

 BTEC Assessment activity 5.6: Explaining work   P3 M3 D3

In small groups of three, take turns to present your portfolio and at the same time explain the reasoning behind the work you have chosen. Try to explain how the selection illustrates your skills and attributes. Your peers, acting as the 'interviewers', should feed back their responses to you following your portfolio presentation.

Portfolio presentation

These are the likely terms and phrases you will need to know in developing and presenting your portfolio.

Key terms	Meaning and context
Purpose	The aim of your portfolio. Can vary according to type of scenario where portfolio is used.
Preliminary work	Work that is important to show as it highlights the developmental stages of your work. Highlights how you think. Can show clients different approaches to let them choose the one they prefer.
Mount cutter	Specialist device used to cut window mounts. Used in exhibition mounting.
Foam board	Stiff lightweight sandwich board used for model making and mounting work.
Window mounting	Cutting of an aperture or window, behind which the work is taped. Creates a neat viewing window.
Key light	The main light used in photographing artwork.
Compression	Method of making digital files smaller and easier to access from web-based or DVD/disk presentations.
Rationale	Statement that explains your reasons for doing something. Used as a statement in project proposals.
Running order	Denotes the order that you put your work in. Important as it can determine the 'hook people in' factor if strong work shown at the beginning.

Table 5.2: Key terms for portfolios

I am a textile and graphic artist and designer based in New York. It's taken a while to develop my career, but my portfolio has been really important all the way through.

I studied First Diploma in Art and Design in the early 1990s, and then went on to do a national diploma and a BA. I had set my sights on studying an MA in textiles at the Royal College of Art in London, and put together a portfolio specifically for this interview, which needed to show creativity, potential to develop and an understanding of visual language. They weren't planning to look at my work at interview, but I insisted on going through my portfolio – it paid off, as I got a place.

After graduating, I worked in England for a year and then decided to re-locate to New York. I applied for a job at Calvin Klein designing print-based patterns for their garments. For this I needed to show an understanding of commercial product, which I didn't have much experience in, so my portfolio was important in demonstrating my diversity and creativity. After four years I left to set up my own company, which I am in the process of doing now. I am collaborating with my cousin Lee Copperwheat, and we are launching a range of printed menswear at New York Fashion Week this year, 2009.

I also have my own portfolio website which provides examples of what I have done, whom I have worked with and where my design work has been used. (To view Ben's portfolio go to Hotlinks.) Setting it up was much harder than I expected. People will be viewing it without me present, so it needs to be very clear and simple. I put in drawings and examples of fabrics, but not sketchbooks as these are too abstract for the workplace. It's a really important resource and expresses my work and vision.

It's always a challenge knowing what to put in a portfolio, but it's imperative to include work you believe in 100 per cent. Your career development really does depend on how your portfolio sells you.

Think about it!

- What criteria are important for a website-based portfolio?
- What skills can a portfolio show?

Just checking

Portfolio checklist

- **The context.** Think about what your portfolio needs to achieve and how it will be viewed. There are many formats for portfolios. What examples of artists' and designers' portfolios can you remember?

- **Stage 1** – evaluating your work and understanding your strengths is really important. Make regular notes in your work journal or sketchbook **P3**, **M3**, and **D3**.

- **Stage 2** – selecting work. This is based on the results of the first stage and the purpose of the portfolio. Make sure that your strongest work is highlighted in your portfolio early. You don't always need as much as you think. Editing the work down can make your portfolio stronger and more accessible. Make notes as you do this.

- **Stage 3** – presenting your work. Work through the presentation methods that are best suited to the purpose of the portfolio and the nature of the work. Can you remember which methods you might be able to use?

- **Stage 4** – explaining your portfolio and work. Use the notes and observations you have recorded throughout the process to help you. Don't rely on making it up at a presentation or interview. Ask yourself the following:

  - What work have you done?

  - What have you learned about yourself and your work?

  - What are your strengths?

  - Can you improve your weaker areas?

- **Look for support and advice** from peers and tutors. It's easy to think, 'I'm not very good at this' or, 'I don't have that much good work', but remember that your portfolio is just a snapshot of what you have achieved so far.

edexcel

Assignment tips

Portfolios change: As you produce more work you will want to include newer work in your presentations.

Create a portfolio for a purpose: If you are applying for an all-round job you might want to include different examples of work. If you are applying for a specialist field, your all-round skills are not as important.

Do the groundwork first: If you are placing a portfolio with an agency, research the examples they already have and see how to make yours different.

Stand out from the crowd: Think about how your portfolio can make a strong impression and really sell you and your skills.

Planning skills

Planning is an important skill. All artists and designers have to plan their work. Here are some examples of why planning is important for artists and designers:

- they may have more than one job on the go
- they will have deadlines to meet, such as providing goods to a client or work for an exhibition
- work has to be kept within budgets
- meetings with clients will have to be organised
- materials will need to be ordered or found
- other people may be involved, such as in a project group or a foundry, which might be casting a sculpture as a team.

Can you add to this list of reasons why planning is important?

When you read the artist case studies throughout this book you will see how much planning is involved. Often an artist may obtain work because he or she has submitted a proposal for a project. The artist might not know for some time if the proposal has been successful, and will need to plan for both getting and not getting the work.

Planning is also an important part of how you work out what you are going to do to answer an assignment, and involves the following stages:

1 researching a topic
2 getting ideas from your research
3 recording ideas for the development stage
4 further research as your ideas expand and you reflect on what you've done.

Whatever you plan to do for an assignment must be achievable within the timescale given to you by your tutor. There are hidden planning terms used in the Assessment and grading criteria. Have a look at a few examples here.

communicate ideas
select appropriate materials and processes
develop ideas   **produce   identify**   describe

Jade Grant

Assignment: Working in your favourite medium, design and make an item or items for a celebrity

I'm thinking about being an interior designer so I decided to make an item for a celebrity's interior. I knew I was setting myself an unusual task to represent my ideas about a celebrity in an object for their home.

This is how I planned to tackle the assignment:

1   List things that I can do well, e.g.: printmaking, papier maché, batik, glass mosaic, ceramics.

2   Brainstorm favourite celebrities to work out their tastes. This was hard so I started to include their personalities.

3   I decided to make something for a television weather presenter. Her personality is always sunny whatever the weather. I drew spider diagrams to help think through ideas of images and colours that could help me.

4   I worked out artists to research who used inspiring patterns and bright and cheerful colours. I researched Kaffe Fassett, the interior and knitwear designer, and Matisse the painter. I also researched colours and shapes that I had seen on holiday in Tunisia.

5   I worked on my ideas again and worked out that I could design and make a glass mosaic frame for a mirror based on my artists' research in the time given for the assignment.

6   My action plan helped me work out what was achievable in the timescale. I listed when I would need to develop skills and where I would be challenged.

Having planned my work I felt confident about the development stage.

- **What's your attitude towards planning? Do you plan ahead or jump straight in?**

My final idea was inspired by a door I had photographed in Tunisia

Ideas to go

Inspirations come from no end of surprising places. Architecture – both historical and contemporary buildings – and the natural world, such as flowers, birds and sea life, will all kick-start ideas. Artists also get ideas from materials such as fabrics, old bits of plastic or broken jewellery.

Create a spider diagram with 'travel' as your starting point to see how far your ideas might go.

Did you think of ways of travelling or what you might find when you get somewhere?

Researching, getting ideas and recording

To start your planning there are a number of things that will need careful consideration before starting an assignment.

- Work out what the assignment is asking you to do.
- Who is the target audience and who is the final outcome for? This information is essential as it will help you work towards an appropriate outcome.
- Look carefully at the pass criteria as you must cover all the requirements.
- What is the timescale? You are usually given a hand-in date on the assignment brief.

From this, work out how many hours you can reasonably give to the work and check how much time you are supposed to give each assignment. Each unit is meant to cover 100 hours of study, which includes teaching input and time spent in the studio with staff. Contact with tutors and technical staff is usually about 60 hours, which means that you are expected to do 40 hours work on your own. If you have an assignment that is assessed against more than one unit, or more than one assignment per unit, make sure that you talk to your tutors to find out how many hours of work they expect you to give to an assignment.

How do you actually plan? – unpicking the skills.

Researching a topic

At the start of the project brief you might have a discussion about different approaches to working on an assignment, and your tutor may show you useful contextual examples or objects.

Your assignment will be open or closed. If it's open, you will probably be asked to explore a theme, such as music or decay, a historical art theme such as Art Deco, or a cultural theme such as Mexico, and produce your own work in response to your investigations. A closed assignment might be to design a piece of art (such as a fabric or chair in the style of an artist or movement). A closed assignment will give you parameters in which to work, while a more open assignment will give you wider areas.

Ways of gathering ideas

You may be taken on a day visit so that you can research visually to kick-start your assignment. Visits are normally organised to reflect a brief. It might be that you are expected to develop your ideas after a visual studies trip.

You might start your ideas by creating a spider diagram. This is a process that helps generate lots of ideas. You can either work in a group or on your own. Record your thoughts as a list or mind map.

Functional skills

ICT and English

This activity requires you to research on the Internet and read information you find. You also have to write your ideas down as you work. This will evidence your ICT and English skills.

Mind mapping

Alia Thomas created a spider diagram of her ideas for her 'Who am I?' project. Alia used images of things she liked to inspire her.

Alia Thomas was given the title 'Tropical' for another assignment. She started her thinking and planning with a mind map.

What is the difference between these two examples?

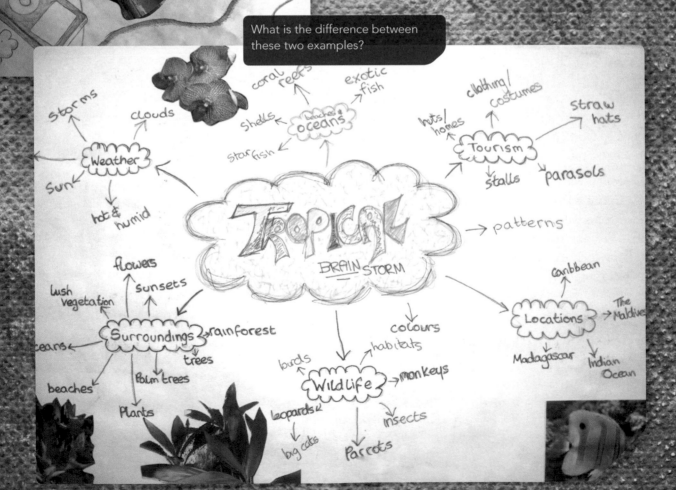

Mood boards

Another way of thinking through ideas is to make a mood board. A mood board helps you clearly visualise a theme. Try making a mood board on an A3 sheet and aim to cover all of the background paper. You might use your own small sketches, postcards, magazine pictures, photographs, bits of coloured paper, ephemera, found items such as threads, feathers and other embellishments.

Another way of making a mood board is to get a small cork pin board and pin things on to it. Designers use mood boards to get ideas started, present to clients and give a sense of the theme, colours and images running through the designer's mind. It's much easier to see these things than to just rely on a description. A mood board gives visual clarity to thoughts.

Alia Thomas designed a mood board on a 'Tropical' theme and used it on the front of her project file. She took the photos of the flowers and the green leaves herself. The other pictures came from the Internet.

Below is another example of a mood board looking at styles of fashion related to a tropical theme.

Why was it important to look at current styles?

Activity: Time to think

For the next project you and a friend are asked to brainstorm ideas to take forward, mind mapping ideas as you work. Next, work independently to see how much further you can take you ideas on your own.

Here's an example based on the topic 'The fairground'.

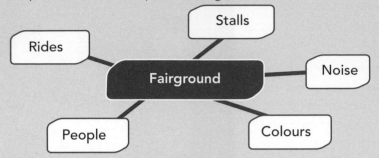

Try to work out how you can use this information to create a mind map and expand it to include: caravans, fluffy toys, screams, travelling, horses and candy floss.

It's quite hard to find out if any artists in the past used fairgrounds to inspire their artwork.

British artist Mark Gertler painted a merry-go-round in 1916 inspired by the madness of the First World War. Important members of the armed forces are seated on the horses going round in endless circles. To see Mark Gertler's painting go to Hotlinks.

Type 'fairground + artist' into a search engine and see who you can find.

Other ways of gathering ideas for initial research

1. Take your own photographs on a theme.
2. Make your own drawings from observing objects, people or places.
3. Research and gather imagery of others artists' work to see how they have explored the theme, from magazines, journals and websites. Look at the shapes, patterns and colours they use. You may like to look at:

- fashion
- textiles
- graphics
- 3D
- sculpture
- fine art
- photography.

Question: Which type of research are points 1, 2 and 3 above?

Answer:

1. is primary research because you are taking the photographs.
2. is primary research because you are drawing from real life.
3. could be primary research if you visit galleries and museums to look at the work of others, or secondary research if you use books, magazines and websites.

You might use one or two or all of the above ways of researching to help get your ideas together. You might make a mood board after you have researched the work of others, made a collection of visual studies or taken photographs. The mood board is intended to help you focus your ideas.

Where else can you get ideas from?

words in a pop song **children's books** **science and nature books**
travel books and magazines
information about other countries and cultures
holidays, a day out or a party with family or friends

A graphics student might collect lettering from different sources. If you are interested in buildings and architecture then your visual diary might contain line drawings of buildings that you are interested in. It might also have detailed drawings of special features such as ornate chimney pots.

Getting ideas from your initial research

Look at your initial research and decide which images and ideas you like the best.

Read the brief again and, focusing on your research, jot down ideas that you can develop further.

Analyse these two fashion labels. What is effective about each one and why?

Remember

Explore materials in your visual diary. Annotate – squeeze a few handwritten words, such as thoughts or comments, on to each page.

Make your visuals work for you and try to relate them to your specialism.

PLTS

Independent enquirers, creative thinkers and self-managers

Using these planning techniques will evidence your independent enquiry, creative thinking and self-management skills.

Activity: Keep a visual diary

Buy a small pocket sketchbook. Collect bits and pieces that represent or remind you of things you do during the week and glue them in. Keep a tiny packet of crayons with the sketchbook and make sketches of what you see or do. Write a few words to record your thoughts, feelings and ideas.

Use your visual diary as a starting point for an assignment.

What sorts of bits and pieces?

Keep and use: sugar packets, bus and train tickets, tickets to gigs and shows, photos, postcards of places you've visited. The term for bits and pieces like this is 'ephemera'. A fashion student might collect labels from garments.

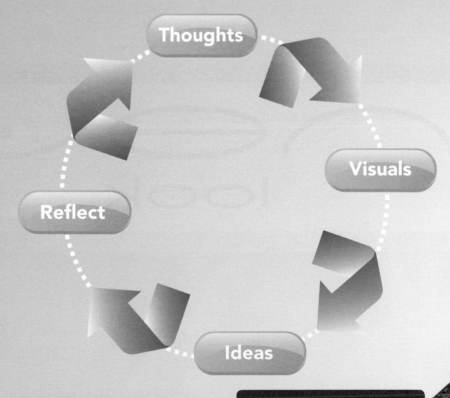

Figure 1: Researching and developing ideas is a cycle

Recording ideas for the development stage

Produce a study sheet or workbook which gives you the opportunity to think your thoughts through. Work on the sheet could be quick thumbnail sketches or experimental samples. Keep looking at the brief to make sure that you are linking your ideas with what you've been asked to do.

Research further as your ideas expand and you reflect on what you've done.

What did Alia Thomas do next?

Alia Thomas explored paper-cut ideas that had a tropical feel to them after being inspired by the paper-cuts of Matisse. Alia kept on refining her ideas but kept to the 'Tropical' theme. She also began to look at the work of other artists and at the idea of tropical jungles. An example of this work can be seen in Unit 1. This shows that she reflected on her initial ideas and then found further information for her theme.

What further information do you need?

- the work of others

- make more drawings

- explore other starting points

- take more photographs

- help from your tutor about what might be successful

- develop and extend your mood board.

Cut Paper Collage

I created this picture by using Matisses' technique of *cut paper collaging. The picture is of bamboo and flowers. I really like the piece of bamboo on the left. The leaves are good, and you can easily tell what it is. I also like the flower, with its large Petals.

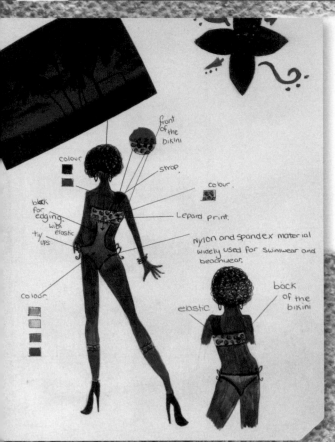

What did Bernie do?

This is the work of Level 2 BTEC learner Bernie Grant. Bernie chose the fabric she wanted to make a swimsuit from after looking at a selection of suitable swimwear fabrics. She researched lots of fabrics and explored their suitability through a series of tests. She then started designing different ideas for swimwear using the chosen leopard skin print somewhere on the design.

Bernie recorded different swimsuit ideas by drawing. She used the same model but varied the design, and continued to looked at the idyllic picture from her mood board to keep her mind focused.

Activity: How busy are you?

Did you know that there are 168 hours in a week? Understanding how to manage your time will help you plan your work schedule effectively.

Make a timetable.

Apart from the sleep section which represents 7 hours, each section on the table counts as one hour. Be realistic – do you have a job? Where do you fit in socialising? Suddenly the week looks busy, so plan your time sensibly to allow space for your art and design assignments.

Figure 2: How much time do you waste each week?

Time	Activities
00.00	Sleep
01.00	
02.00	
03.00	
04.00	
05.00	
06.00	
07.00	Get up/breakfast
08.00	Go to School/College
09.00	Lesson
10.00	Lesson
11.00	Study time
12.00	Lunch
13.00	Lesson
14.00	Lesson
15.00	Travel home
16:00	?
17:00	
18:00	Dinner
19:00	
20:00	?
21:00	
22:00	
23:00	Sleep

Read the case study about Nicki Williams, textile artist, in Unit 4. Nicki talks about how she uses materials, techniques and processes creatively. She even recycles experimental work into new pieces of art. However creative you feel, don't recycle your experiments at the moment as they all need to be evaluated and presented for assessment.

Apart from embroidery, what other mixed media do you think Nicki Williams has used to create this bowl?

What might Nicki's inspiration have been for her mixed-media drawing, *Angel*?

113

Case study: Mark Gaynor, performance artist

The performance artist Mark Gaynor tells an unusual story about planning, involving group work. Performance artists use themselves as the artwork.

'A recent project, called 'Rules and Regs', was for a site-specific performance in the medieval vaults in Southampton. The project was for artists working in Live Art, where they made work in response to rules devised by a curator. The idea was to create a work around pre-defined rules and regulations. All the artists had two weeks from meeting each other to plan and develop their performance.

There were already regulations about the site, what you could and couldn't do. I discovered that the vaults used to be at street level, but the pavements had been built up over hundreds of years so the ground floor gradually became the cellar. My grandfather had been a roadworker, so the piece became partly autobiographical.

In the final performance I stretched a roll of drawing paper across the floor and placed a pile of coal on one end. As I delivered the **narrative** I dragged the coal and spread it out along the paper. I then scooped the coal back up into a pile. It was very

dusty work. I ended up with a drawing made by the coal marks on the paper, which became a document of the event. However, not all the audience were clear about the link with the pavements being built and the vault being underground.'

1 **List the things Mark had to plan to do in order to realise his performance.**

2 **Look at the evaluation for the assignment you've just completed. How can you improve on your planning skills for your next assignment?**

To find out more about Mark's project, 'Rules and Regs' go to Hotlinks.

Mark in the medieval vault in which his performance art took place. What factors would you need to take into account when working in an environment like this?

Key terms

Synopsis – a short (brief) outline version of (for example) a story, an article, a film or a television programme.

Secondary illustrations – drawings made to help form initial ideas.

Narrative – the story.

Using planning skills

The table below shows the units and the relevant learning outcomes where planning is central to the tasks involved.

The key words are: **research**, **record**, **select**, **produce**, **make**.

To meet these criteria as indicated by these key words you have to **plan**.

Sometimes the planning words are hidden, so look for other words that mean you have to plan in order to achieve something.

Unit	Assessment and grading criteria	Tips and activities
Unit 1 Contextual references in art and design	**P2** use contextual research to support the development of own response	Use the planning cycle to point you to what you need to research at each stage.
Unit 2 2D visual communication	**P2** communicate design ideas using 2D visual communication techniques	Plan which techniques will look best by researching examples of the work of others.
Unit 3 3D visual communication	**P2** communicate design ideas using 3D visual communication techniques	Plan to perfect a few techniques rather than be poor at many.
Unit 4 Using ideas to explore, develop and produce art and design	**P1** research and record visual and other information from primary and secondary sources in response to the brief	Make sure you plan to use other information which means something you've read or heard.
Unit 5 Building an art and design portfolio	**P1** describe how artists and designers use portfolios	Plan on a visit to an open day at a higher level art course to see some portfolios.
Unit 6 Working in the art and design industry	**P1** identify how organisations operate in the art and design industry	Plan your research carefully and look for a wide range of organisations. Spider diagrams and mind maps will help and so will visits to galleries where you can pick up leaflets about art organisations.
Unit 7 Working with graphic design briefs	**P3** research and record primary and secondary sources in response to a pre-defined brief	In a pre-defined brief you are given an imaginary client, so you have to plan your research in a way that will provide the client with what they want.
Unit 8 Working with photography briefs	**P3** select appropriate materials and processes to meet photography briefs	Plan the equipment you will use and the content of your pictures.

Unit 9 Working with fashion briefs	**P4** select appropriate materials, techniques and processes to meet fashion design briefs	Plan the fabrics you will use to make the best of your designs.
Unit 10 Working with textiles briefs	**P2** develop ideas and outcomes to meet textiles briefs	Plan to collect sweet wrappers, beads and buttons to use in your experiments.
Unit 11 Working with 3D design briefs	**P3** develop ideas and outcomes to meet 3D design briefs	Make sure you plan to make some maquettes.
Unit 12 Working with interactive media briefs	**P4** produce an interactive media product with integration of images, text and sound	This tells you what you have to make, so you need to plan the steps that will get you there.
Unit 13 Working with visual arts briefs	**P1** research and record from primary and secondary sources in response to visual arts briefs	Planning the steps you take through your research and what to research is essential here.
Unit 14 Working with 3D design crafts briefs	**P1** research and record primary and secondary sources in response to 3D design crafts briefs	Include research about the work of others. See what has been done already and use it to inspire you.
Unit 15 Working with digital art and design briefs	**P2** plan and develop ideas and outcomes for a digital art and design project	This tells you to plan your ideas. The planning stage has to be very clear so that you can pass these criteria.
Unit 16 Working with accessory briefs	**P1** research and develop designs for accessories **P2** make maquettes to meet design requirements	Make sure that as part of **P1** you make scaled-down maquettes as part of the design development stage. This will give you an idea of what works and what doesn't work to achieve **P2** .
Unit 17 Working with moving image briefs	**P2** plan and develop ideas and outcomes for a moving image brief	Mind mapping is a great way to plan. Make thumbnail sketches to put your ideas into a visual form.
Unit 18 Working with site-specific briefs	**P2** develop effective ideas and outcomes for site-specific briefs	Plan time to visit the site and think about suitable sizes for your work. Forward plan and take a sketchbook and camera with you.

Tim illustrates children's stories. The main characters are based on drawings of a grey knitted toy elephant and a pink beanbag pig.

I happened to buy a knitted toy elephant at a church bazaar. I picked it up and it began to cast shadows on the wall which were really interesting. To do my work I get inside the characters of the elephant and the pig. I imagine them and what they're like. By playing around with ideas using the characters the stories evolve.

When planning my ideas I think of a theme, a **synopsis** of a story. If it's winter I might plan to write a story about snow or a windy day. I speak the story aloud to my wife and friends, often several times, who will give suggestions about the story or what to draw. Once I've written the story and know which bits to illustrate I sketch out **secondary illustrations** before the final illustrations.

I like to be able to draw the toys doing what they do, and have built them a small house which I furnished. The roof comes off so I can look down into their world and draw the toys in the correct place. The drawings are set in an idyllic and calm time around the 1950s, before mass-media culture.

I do all the drawings at once so there is a consistency of style. I have 10 to 12 sheets of paper stretched all around so I can work on them simultaneously. If I did just one drawing at a time, by the time I reached the end the style would be different.

Think about it!

- List the five most important things that Tim had to plan.
- Think about your own planning for your current assignment. Which aspects of your planning could you improve on?
- It might help to think about the feedback you have had from tutors in previous assignments.

Just checking

How can you improve your grades with careful planning?

The Assessment and grading criteria tends to have similar words throughout the units, so an understanding of what these words mean will help you work towards achieving a grade.

Independent: This means that you have planned your work well and that early discussions with tutors show that you are able to develop your work on your own. Ideas that come to you as you research will spark off other ideas and lead you to new discoveries. Discussion with tutors will help you explore and clarify your ideas, but you won't be asking them for ideas.

Appropriate: You've brainstormed your ideas in a group and have a good idea of where to focus your research. For example, you have been asked to develop an assignment around 'the natural world'. Your brainstorming leads you to concentrate exploration around roundish forms such as curled up animals, seed heads, flowers, fruit, shells and ammonites. *Appropriate* in this context means that you present research on these items. If your research wasn't appropriate you might spend time drawing lots of ideas to do with the natural world that don't have any links, which would indicate that you haven't thought through ideas in relation to the assignment. However, if you can link disparate work then that will help make sense of preparation.

Diverse materials: This means using more than one method or material. Make sure that you plan to do this. If you are basing your assignment on the figure, use a variety of wet and dry materials, such as pencil crayons, pastels, paint, wire, ceramics, papier maché, collage and so on.

Diverse techniques and processes: This means that you explore different techniques and processes. An easy example is in ceramics where you might present different glazes, patterns and ways of making items, such as coiled, thrown or moulded.

Creatively: This means that you have learned how to use materials, techniques and processes with skill and have worked out new ways to work.

Preparing and making skills

The skill of preparing and making is an essential part of every artist's and designer's job and because of this it is covered within all 18 units. It includes being able to develop new ideas, make use of specialist techniques and processes and experiment with media.

Developing ideas is completed at the beginning of assignments. It's about taking a given starting point on a design journey in order to come up with a range of ideas. Many small changes are made to the original idea along the journey in order to end up with lots of alternatives. It is often a good idea to work quickly at this stage so that you have more ideas to select from rather than less!

Experimenting could involve exploring different colour combinations, or working at different scales, or working with different media, techniques or processes. Artists and designers develop their ideas in different ways in order to produce an original design. A selection of the elements that can be changed and altered are listed on the right.

Selected ideas will need to be refined and the final piece needs to be made carefully and accurately.

This section you give you ideas and examples of how to meet the pass, merit and distinction criteria in Units 1–5 and suggest ways to further develop and extend your ideas.

colour palettes
styles of lettering
materials
scale and proportion
composition
media
placement of imagery
patterns
surfaces

Hope Talbot

My favourite thing is generating ideas. I never used to think about producing loads of ideas for a project, but I now realise it's better to come up with different ideas so that I can combine them together and mix media. This makes my designs more exciting and fun!

I usually produce my first idea worksheets in pencil. In a recent project to advertise an exhibition called 'Home Sweet Home' we produced first ideas, and then discussed these in groups to develop and improve them before realising them on the computer. I found this really useful and it helped improve my work.

I enjoy experimenting on the computer using different tools in Photoshop. It can take a while to get something that looks good, but gradually you learn something useful. I usually start by scanning in my drawings and then alter the colours, arrangement and scale of each part of the pattern. I save all the layers so that I can print out all my ideas. Within graphics projects I have begun to use text and link this with my drawings.

Hope's idea generation sheet evidences her wide range of designs

Observational drawings of a mushroom exploring a range of media and mark-making

This design development sheet contains a range of imaginative pattern ideas which explore scale, colour and a range of media and would meet the distinction criteria

101 mugs

Think about how you could develop design ideas for a mug inspired by geometric shapes. Remember to work quickly and produce as many ideas as possible! Aim for 101 – it doesn't matter how unusual and impractical they are!

Activity: Developing ideas

Start by drawing a basic mug shape. Now list all the geometric shapes you can think of, such as a circle, square, triangle, rectangle, hexagon, etc.

Next, produce a sequence of designs altering one element each time, so that you gradually start to involve the geometric shapes. You may wish to work through the following list:

- change the height – your mug could be taller, thinner, smaller

- change the handle – your mug could have lots of handles, or different shaped ones

- change the surface – your mug could be smooth, rough, textured, patterned

- change the colour – think about who it is for: children, a shop?

Have fun and aim to make your designs as inventive and unusual as possible!

Developing ideas

Throughout every assignment you will need to demonstrate that you can develop your ideas. You will do this in a number of different ways at different stages throughout your project work. The first ideas will need to be quick – the more you produce at this stage the better, so that you have lots to select from in order to develop something original and exciting. Depending on your project these first ideas could be 2D or 3D.

Many practising designers work in groups for this first stage of a project so that they can discuss and share ideas in order to produce a range of designs more quickly. First ideas can be written or drawn or made. These are then evaluated and the best ones are selected to be experimented with further.

Initial ideas for a graphic design logo. Practise developing your ideas by producing first ideas as quickly as you can

Here's how one learner has developed a range of ideas to illustrate the line of a nonsense poem: 'If a butterfly courted a bee'

Think back to your 101 mug ideas and see if you can develop them further. Begin by reviewing the mugs you have designed and select your favourite. Evaluate your choice and consider carefully why you like it.

Produce a second sequence of designs with this as your starting point and create alternatives of your design. If you have selected a mug with stripes then experiment with the width and colours of the stripes, their direction or where they are – the stripes could be on the outside or the inside or on the handle.

Finally, select your favourite three mug designs and illustrate these on a final presentation sheet. Aim to include colour notes and technical information about the media and processes you would use to construct it.

Using sketchbooks

First ideas are often very 'rough' and 'sketchy', with written notes to explain and expand upon the visuals. It's a good idea to get used to writing and drawing in the same media so that your ideas and thoughts can flow quickly and easily. At this stage you shouldn't worry about spelling or how accurate your design drawing is. You could begin with a mind map so that you write or draw your starting point in the middle of the page and then think of lots of alternatives leading from this.

Figure 1: This mind map demonstrates how you could start to generate a range of ideas for your assignments

Sometimes it can be very useful to do this in groups so that you all take turns to add one idea at a time. You often get more ideas working like this, and you will find that each student adds something new which you may not have thought of. This is often the way graphic and fashion design teams work in industry to come up with new concepts and branding ideas.

Activity: Mind maps for winter coats

Try producing a mind map to generate first ideas for a winter coat. Start by writing this word in the middle of the page and then write or draw all the design features you need to consider around the outside. Aim to get as many ideas recorded as possible, and don't worry at this stage about how impractical they may be.

To help you get started try answering the following questions on your mind map:

- How long should it be?

- How thick should it be?

- Does it need sleeves?

- Does it need a hood?

- How will it fasten?

- What colour should it be?

- Who is it for?

Stop after 10 minutes and have a look through what you have produced. Select your favourite ideas to develop further on a new mind map. This time, take each idea on a design journey so that you produce several alternatives. Try to get into the habit of drawing one idea and then listing all the possible alternatives as bullet points alongside it. This will evidence your thinking skills and help you produce more ideas.

BTEC Grading tips

You need to produce a range of alternative and imaginative ideas to meet the merit and distinction criteria. So the more you produce at this stage the better!

PLTS

Creative thinkers
Generating ideas for the given brief through exploring, adapting, selecting and refining finished ideas evidences your creative thinking skills.

Many artists and designers choose to work in sketchbooks for these first thoughts. A fashion designer would carry around a small sketchbook to record silhouette ideas, colour selections and swatches of fabrics when gathering research and first ideas for a collection. This could include prices of fabrics, fastenings and trims in addition to drawings of possible patterns to be printed onto the fabrics.

A graphic designer would produce lots of quick visuals or 'scamps' when investigating first ideas for a logo. These would often be produced in pencil or thin black pens for speed of working. The best ideas would be developed on the computer to a professional standard for the client.

An artist may experiment with colour mixing or different ways to apply the paint, and draw selected objects in different compositions to find the best one.

Some artists' and designers' sketchbooks include all sorts of found imagery, from packaging to postcards, labels, photographs and found objects, such as feathers, leaves and shells, which could be used as starting points for future projects. These are often referred to again and again in their work. Matisse collected patterned fabrics and would use the same fabric numerous times in portraits and still-life paintings throughout his life.

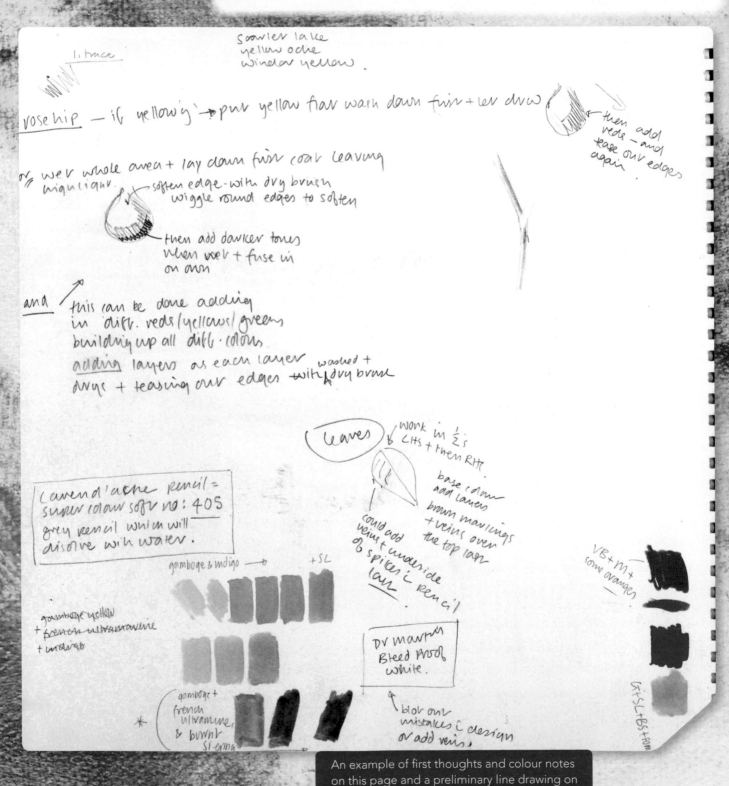

An example of first thoughts and colour notes on this page and a preliminary line drawing on the next page. The artist can make use of these when completing the final painting.

Sketchbooks come in a variety of sizes and can be very easy to carry around with you, so that you can add to your ideas all the time. You can draw, write notes, stick in photographs or pages from magazines as starting points, research artists, stick in leaflets or postcards from exhibitions and so on.

Sketchbooks can become very individual and an exciting record of each assignment. It is a good idea to use the front and back of sketchbook pages and really cram in as many ideas as possible.

Activity: Sketchbooks

Use your sketchbook to gather information and record the 3D shape and structure of a jug. This is a great way to work in a sketchbook as you can build up lots of facts and information to take into a finished piece later. Try to draw all key details, paying particular attention to the front, back and sides so that you can work only from your drawings and produce a replica of the jug.

Use a double-page spread in your sketchbook so that your drawings can flow, and start in the top left corner by writing down the characteristics to identify what you need to draw. The list below is the 'menu' of design features that you will need to work through.

When you start to draw work quickly it is better to produce lots of drawings than one, so don't worry if they are not very accurate to start with. Turn the jug around and draw it from different viewpoints to get an understanding of its form. Look at the scale and shape of the handle and how it is positioned opposite the spout. Pay attention to how the handle and spout join on to the jug and to any pattern or details that go around the outside.

Enjoy this process of finding out about the jug. As you draw, think about which parts you like the best – is it the shape of the handle? Or the decoration around the surface? Focus on these sections and redraw to ensure you have captured detailed information.

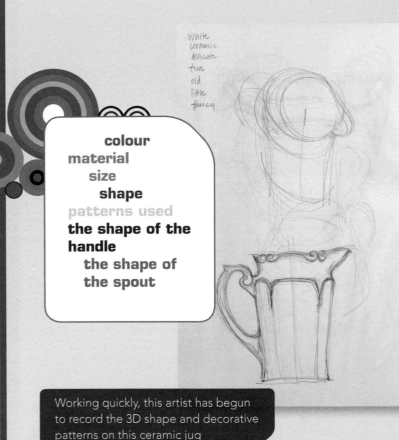

colour
material
size
shape
patterns used
the shape of the handle
the shape of the spout

Working quickly, this artist has begun to record the 3D shape and decorative patterns on this ceramic jug

Grading tips

In order to meet the merit and distinction criteria, you will need to record all the key details found on the jug so that you can demonstrate you have fully explored its structure, independently selected elements to focus on and produced further detailed studies. You could do this by remembering to write about, as well as draw, the key details and by working in a range of media.

Experimenting

When you have produced your first ideas and selected the best to take forward, you will need to start experimenting with a range of materials, techniques and processes. The range and variety of work you produce will give you more choice for the final product. Again, it is a good idea to work quickly and produce lots of samples, mock-ups and prototypes so that you have more to select from for your final piece. At this stage of your assignment it is best if you can avoid having a set idea about your final outcome, so try to keep an open mind and explore every option thoroughly. This way you are more likely to come up with something new and individual.

Who are you aiming at?

Within industry, designers often need to think about their target market and what would appeal to the person they are designing for, as well as the cost of the materials they use in their work. But there are still lots of possibilities to produce something new and different. When designing patterns for T-shirts, textile designers would be given a colour palette by their client that fits the season they are designing for. They can then experiment with the scale and positioning of the pattern. Shapes can be printed on the front, back and sleeves and around the hem or neckline. Patterns can be tiny and repeated in stripes, or huge as one single shape.

PLTS

Independent enquirers and creative thinkers

Selecting what to draw and write about your jug, and producing these observations in a range of drawing styles and media, evidences independent enquiry and creative thinking skills.

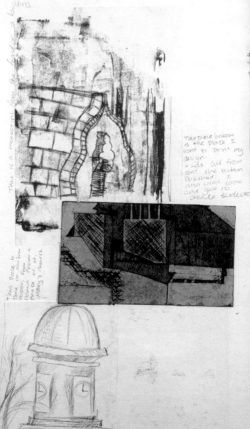

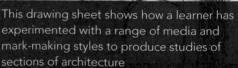
This drawing sheet shows how a learner has experimented with a range of media and mark-making styles to produce studies of sections of architecture

Grading tips

Select one type of media. Then produce lots of ideas using this media, combined with others in different ways, to demonstrate that you have fully explored its potential to begin to meet the merit and distinction criteria. The more inventive and experimental the better!

Activity: Through the window

Cut a square hole in the middle of a piece of paper so that it becomes a window to look through. Place this window over drawings you have already produced in your sketchbook and find some interesting patterns. It doesn't matter if you select parts of an object or the whole thing – this is just the starting point.

Draw your favourite pattern and then experiment with it. Produce lots of examples by experimenting with different media and colour combinations to create a range of surface pattern ideas which can be used for wrapping paper and greeting cards.

The more experiments you produce the better! Experiment with how you can use different media and which media you can layer and combine together to get interesting and original results. Aim to be as inventive as possible. To help you get started you could work through the list below.

First, cut a stencil of your pattern to print through – try using a sponge with paint, spray paint, or a toothbrush. Then you could:

- Reduce your pattern using a photocopier and rearrange in different patterns.

- Enlarge your pattern on a photocopier and use a section.

- Paint your pattern onto different surfaces – white paper, coloured paper, patterned paper.

- Cut out the shapes of your pattern and stick them down – try using tissue paper, fabrics, wallpapers.

Begin to make more complicated patterns and layer media such as:

- ink and charcoal
- wire and oil pastels
- tissue paper and chalk pastels
- fabrics and paint.

Select your favourite three experiments and present on a finished sheet.

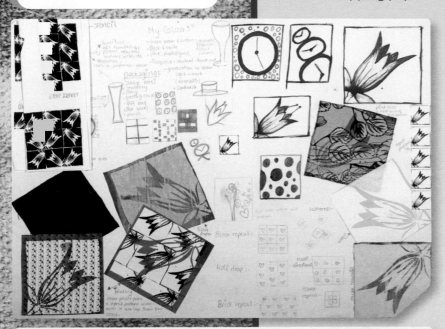

Here's how one learner has developed her initial surface pattern ideas, experimented with colour, pattern and media and selected the most successful as final pieces

PLTS

Independent enquirers and creative thinkers

Experimenting with media, materials, techniques and processes to generate and explore ideas will demonstrate independent enquiry and creative thinking skills.

Where to find ideas

In industry, artists and designers often make use of the world around them and work produced by others to inform their own experimentation and development of ideas. They do this in different ways. Some look back at and take inspiration from history, such as fashion designers re-using elements from historical garments and adding a modern twist.

Some designers draw and use objects in their designs, such as when textile designers draw objects for fashion or interior fabrics.

Other designers have drawn objects, such as cakes, or cups and saucers for greeting cards and wrapping papers. Some artists and designers look for inspiration from within their own specialism, so graphic designers might get ideas from other graphic designers or artists from other fine artists. Some look to other specialisms, such as jewellery designers getting ideas from fashion designers or vice versa.

Taking ideas and techniques from a range of starting points is a great way to extend your own experiments with media and processes to help you design something new and original. Many artists and designers keep research files which they make use of when they start new projects or collections. A research file might be a box or ring file filled with magazine pictures, exhibition reviews, photocopies from books, found imagery, photographs – anything that appeals to them!

Some designers would use these as mood/inspiration boards at the start of their work, such as when fashion designers put together a theme for a new collection, or a graphic designer gathers background imagery for a new branding idea. Many designers will group this research together, so that particular techniques and processes are linked and easily referenced in their experimentation.

Here's how a learner has made use of a wide range of media and mark-making on a design development sheet

PLTS

Independent enquirers, creative thinkers and reflective learners

Carrying out research into practising artists' and designers' work, and then adapting and making use of this to inform your own experimentation, will evidence independent enquiry, creative thinking and reflective practice.

Activity: Research file

Produce a research file to help you experiment further with a range of media, techniques and processes. Divide this into four sections so that you collect information from:

- historical sources
- contemporary sources
- your own specialist area
- other specialist areas.

You should aim to collect this information from a range of sources, including books, magazines, the Internet, shops, galleries, museums. Remember to highlight passages in the text that mention how different media, techniques and processes have been used, so that you can use this in your experimental work.

Grading tips

In order to meet the merit and distinction criteria you will need to research a diverse range of materials, techniques and processes and then make use of these creatively in your own work. So, the broader your research the better, because this will give you more to combine and mix to enable you to produce imaginative and original work.

Technical skills and techniques

As you experiment with media and processes to develop your ideas, you will begin to make use of a range of techniques and technical skills. These will be introduced at the beginning of assignments through workshop inductions and demonstrations, and also be developed throughout your course during each assignment. Research into practising artists and designers and visits to galleries, museums and shops will also develop your knowledge, skills and understanding of the specialist processes and technical skills required within specific areas of art and design.

Health and Safety

All inductions to workshops will start with a health and safety briefing. It is important that you keep these notes to refer to throughout your course. Knowledge of technical skills is very useful when working as an artist or designer, although not all have jobs that require you to be competent at every process. For example, within fashion design a team of people would be employed – some would focus on menswear and others on womenswear, design, making patterns and constructing the garment. However, the more knowledge you have of all the skills required the more you will understand the characteristics of materials and realise what they will and won't do so that you can create original designs.

Keeping up with technical terms

As you progress through your course you will develop a glossary of art and design equipment used and terms related to technical skills. You may find it useful to record all of these at the back of your sketchbook so that you can use them within your written evaluations.

Activity: Keeping tabs on equipment

Construct a table to record the names and characteristics of all your drawing equipment. Begin by listing what you use down the left-hand side and then next to each one write key bullet points to explain what they do, and finally list what you use them for. Aim to include technical names of processes and as much detail as possible, such as:

- Pencil – linear, light and dark tone (depends on pencil grade), sketching first ideas.

Try this activity when working in different workshops. So for printed textiles you might have:

- squeegee – wooden handle with rubber end, used for pushing dye through the screen onto fabric

- screen – wooden or metal frame with mesh to print through onto fabric or used with stencils

- pigment dye – fabric printing ink, translucent in natural state or concentrate colour mixed with binder

- opaque white paste – can be added to pigment dye so that the colour becomes opaque and can be printed onto a dark ground.

Grading tips

In order to achieve merit and distinction grades you will need to evidence that you have explored a diverse range of specialist techniques and processes. Technical notes will support this process.

PLTS

Self-managers and team workers

Working individually and in groups to use of a range of technical processes, materials and equipment evidences your ability to be team workers and self-managers.

Using your preparing and making skills

Where does preparing and making occur in the units on the BTEC Level 2 First Diploma in Art and Design? The table on page 132 shows the units and relevant learning outcomes where preparing and making is central to the tasks involved.

Unit:	Learning outcome number:
Unit 1 Contextual references in art and design	**2** be able to use historical and contemporary references to support research and development of own response **3** be able to present information about the work studied in an appropriate format
Unit 2 2D visual communication	**1** be able to use 2D mark-making techniques **2** be able to communicate design ideas using 2D visual communication techniques **3** be able to use formal elements in 2D visual communication
Unit 3 3D visual communication	**1** be able to use 3D making techniques **2** be able to communicate design ideas using 3D visual communication techniques **3** be able to use formal elements in 3D visual communication
Unit 4 Using ideas to explore, develop and produce art and design	**2** be able to develop ideas that meet the requirements of the brief, through the use of specialist materials, equipment and techniques
Unit 5 Building an art and design portfolio	**2** be able to present an art and design portfolio
Unit 6 Working in the art and design industry	**2** know about job roles in the art and design industry
Unit 7 Working with graphic design briefs	**1** be able to use appropriate graphics materials, equipment and techniques **3** be able to develop ideas and produce a final product in response to a pre-defined graphic design brief
Unit 8 Working with photography briefs	**1** be able to use photographic processes **2** be able to develop ideas to meet photographic briefs
Unit 9 Working with fashion design briefs	**1** be able to use pattern drafting techniques and processes **2** be able to use construction techniques and processes **3** be able to develop ideas to meet fashion design briefs
Unit 10 Working with textiles briefs	**1** able to use textiles materials, techniques and processes **2** be able to develop work to meet textiles briefs
Unit 11 Working with 3D design briefs	**1** be able to use 3D design materials, techniques and processes **2** be able to develop ideas to meet 3D design briefs
Unit 12 Working with interactive media briefs	**1** be able to develop ideas and outcomes to meet interactive media briefs **3** be able to use digital techniques and technology
Unit 13 Working with visual arts briefs	**1** be able to research and record from primary and secondary sources in response to visual arts briefs **2** be able to use visual arts materials, techniques and processes **3** be able to develop ideas and outcomes to meet visual arts brief
Unit 14 Working with 3D design crafts briefs	**1** be able to research and record primary and secondary sources in response to design crafts briefs **2** be able to explore and develop ideas to meet design crafts briefs **3** be able to use 3D design crafts materials, techniques and processes
Unit 15 Working with digital art and design briefs	**1** be able to create visual material using digital technology **2** be able to plan and develop ideas for a digital art and design brief
Unit 16 Working with accessory briefs	**1** be able to develop ideas to meet accessory briefs **2** be able to produce outcomes to meet accessory briefs
Unit 17 Working with moving image briefs	**1** be able to use materials, techniques and technology for moving image briefs **2** be able to plan and develop ideas for digital art and design briefs
Unit 18 Working with site-specific briefs	**1** be able to use site-specific materials, techniques and technology for site-specific briefs **2** be able to plan and develop ideas for a site specific brief

Sally Moret
Freelance footwear and card designer

I studied BA (Hons) Fashion and Textile Design at De Montfort University in Leicester, and specialised in footwear design. After graduating, I got a job in London and worked in the footwear industry for a range of high street companies, such as Mothercare, Next, Monsoon and ASDA.

These companies would commission shoes to be designed to complement their range of clothes and would often provide me with a sample of a shoe they liked and ask me to adapt to fit in with their colours, price point and branding style. I would begin the design journey by gathering research about new and existing shoes to link colours to next year's predication palettes of colours and styling details.

I would often be working one year ahead. I would produce an initial collection of designs on paper using a black pen outline and marker pens. I tended to use photocopying paper, which is a cheaper alternative to layout paper, and just as see-through. These would be shown to the client on large presentation sheets of foam board and as a booklet of 20 to 30 images.

Usually about five would be selected and these would be made up as one-off samples in the factory. This sample would go back and forth until by about the fourth sample it would be right, and finally approved by the client! A specification sheet would be put together with swatches of all fabrics, trims and precise colours to be used. The shoe would be made in a range of sizes, and fit tests would be carried out to ensure the shoes were a good width and fit all around.

I have recently retrained as a teacher and returned to my love of pattern and textile design designing a collection of illustrations to be used as greeting cards, textiles and book illustrations. I love the work of artists such as Gustav Klimt, Antonio Gaudi and the Art Nouveau and Art Deco artists and it's great to be able to draw, paint and experiment with media for a variety of different end results.

I have put together a website of my work and have aimed to demonstrate many different styles and techniques in order to appeal to different companies. I have particularly enjoyed using acrylic paint and also acrylic inks which I like to mix with white so that they become 'flatter' and more opaque.

Think about it!

- How does Sally gather her ideas together?
- Where does she draw some of her inspiration from?
- What techniques does Sally use that would be helpful in your work?

Just checking

Research

Use elements from other artists' and designers' work to extend your ideas. Select colours, shapes or lettering styles to include in your own drawings or photographs, or experiment with techniques artists have used in a different material or scale, or for a different end result.

Talk

Try talking through your ideas with your friends and family. Get them to ask you questions so that you have to explain all the details of each idea. This will help you think through an idea fully.

Photograph

Remember to photograph all stages of your work so that you can evidence the design journey. These photographs can be printed and displayed as a sequence in your sketchbook, with written notes alongside describing the materials, techniques and processes.

Time

Set yourself time limits for each stage. You will need a short amount of time for first ideas and a longer amount to make the final piece. Remember also to allocate time to reviewing and selecting, so that you can reflect upon what you have produced and select which is the best to take forward.

Experiment

Experiment with different styles of working to further develop your ideas. Make a list to refer to whenever you get stuck for ideas, such as:

- black and white media – transparent, opaque, drawn, painted, collaged

- different colour combinations – use paint charts or postcards of artists' paintings

- scale – thin, tiny and huge, and everything in between

- media – 3D, 2D, low relief, mixed, layered.

Technical notes

Include as much technical detail as possible in your written notes to develop your specialist knowledge, such as materials, measurements, weights and timings, and evidence this in your evaluations.

Websites

There are many museums and websites devoted to contemporary design. To view some of these go to Hotlinks and click on the following examples:

- Design Museum – for historical and contemporary designers such as: Ron Arad, Saul Bass, Hussein Chalayan, Terence Conran, Richard Rogers, Timorous Beasties, Philip Treacy

- Contemporary Applied Arts Gallery – ceramics, glass, metals, textiles, jewellery, wood

- Victoria and Albert Museum – architecture, ceramics, fashion, jewellery, accessories, furniture, glass, metals, painting and drawing, photography, printmaking, sculpture and textiles

- Tate: Tate Britain, Tate Modern, Tate Liverpool, Tate St. Ives

Evaluating skills

To evaluate means to assess something. There are tasks that use evaluating skills in all of the first units in art and design. In this section you will find out ways to use evaluation in your work.

The process of evaluating can be broken down into four areas shown in Figure 1 below.

Communicating

is important because you need to explain what you have found out through your analysis. To do this effectively and reach higher grades in your work you will need to understand and use specialist language.

Analysing

means to examine something methodically and in detail in order to explain or interpret it.

Presenting

will involve you in producing your evaluation in ways that best show your analyses and communicate clearly your conclusions. You can present your findings and ideas in different ways, and we will look at some of these later.

Critiquing

means to evaluate in a detailed and analytical way. It works hand in hand with analysing. There are methods you can use to help structure your analysis, and these are shown later in this section.

Figure 1: You will use all of these four skills when you are evaluating

Matthew Cooper

Matthew's work journal: Evaluation of design in domestic environments

I find evaluating really difficult sometimes, because I don't know how to express my views or ideas clearly. We were asked to bring in examples of domestic design from home. Each person brought in an object, evaluated it and presented to the group.

I chose a modern corkscrew. I said that I thought it was a good piece of design because it worked really well, and was good to hold and use. I also said that it was well made and looked bright and modern, as it was all silver. Luckily my dad had an old corkscrew that I used to compare it with, and this helped me to explain the differences. The old one was really lightweight and looked like it wouldn't work – in fact my dad said they were rubbish and used to break the corks. The tutor said I had done well, and could have made the presentation better by using 'formal language' and talking about the 'aesthetic qualities' more. I did make notes to help me but I ended up just talking about the corkscrews without really looking at the notes I had made. I want to get better at doing this.

What formal language would you use to evaluate this design?

* **How might you decide between two products? What criteria would you use?**

Evaluating everyday designs

When designers are working on a brief to redesign an object, they will begin by evaluating what already exists, to see how they can improve on it.

Think back to something you have had in the past, like a phone or MP3 player that you have upgraded. Now ask yourself:

* **How have the designers improved the earlier version?**

* **How is it 'fit for purpose'?**

* **Write your evaluation down; what does it tell you about the product?**

Evaluating

Matthew was evaluating the corkscrews by analysing how well they functioned: when you look at something – an object or design – think about why it was made and what it does.

Activity: Is it fit for purpose?

Look at these three different types of corkscrew. Try evaluating the three examples using fitness for purpose as your main line of enquiry. Allow yourself ten minutes to do this.

Here are some of the points you might have written.

The wooden-handled corkscrew: This is a simple two-piece design, with a basic wooden handle that is easy to grip. It can be made easily at a low cost, so is cheap to buy. But to use it you need to have a degree of strength, in order to wind the corkscrew down into the cork and then pull the whole thing up. This might be difficult for some people, and there can be problems with the corkscrew if it isn't correctly located in the middle of the cork, which can split.

The winged corkscrew: This is a much more effective piece of design. It has a round profile so will fit over the top of the bottle, and locates the corkscrew in the correct position. The 'handle' at the top then twists the corkscrew into the cork, and when it is fully positioned the two arms can be pulled down to ease the cork up. It is robust and easier to use, but as a more complex design will cost more than the other two.

The metal corkscrew: This example could be quite awkward to use. It's a combination piece, including a basic can opener and bottle opener. To get a cork out, you have to work hard to position the corkscrew correctly, and it doesn't have a comfortable wooden handle to pull on.

- **How do these points match what you have written?**

- **Do you agree with the points made?**

- **Which corkscrew would you buy?**

You can try this with other objects around the house, and practise your skills in evaluating fitness for purpose.

describing
mechanisms
looking at
the work of
others
describing
your working
practices
which
materials?
improving an
earlier design
clients'
needs
customer views
audience
reaction
rough sketches
annotating
drawings
presenting ideas

Activity: Evaluating and recording

See if you can get two or three of the same items, such as cameras, tools etc. You might need to ask around, as it would be useful to get items that have been produced at different times. For example, you could get a film camera or SLR Single Lens reflex camera from the 1970s or 1980s, a compact camera from the same time, and a digital camera from today (or maybe even use your mobile phone camera as one of the items).

Work through the same exercise as Matthew did – compare and contrast the items. When you do this you will be working through the skills shown in the introduction: analysing, critiquing when you think about how easy or user-friendly the items are, and communicating and presenting when you write up your notes – include drawings as well if you want to, or photographs of the items. Using these skills is something you can keep practising – talk to your relatives about cars and how these have changed over the years, and so on.

Analysing

What materials has the artist used?
How have the colours been arranged?
What types of composition work best and why?

When you analyse something you really have to study it closely, whatever it is. If it's an object, you might look at the components that make it up; if it's a painting, you might look at the kinds of colours that have been used, or the way the artist has applied them. This analysis is important because it gives you the information you need to start critiquing the work. It's like having the building blocks you need; if you have these blocks then you can avoid that feeling of 'I don't know what I'm looking for' or 'What am I supposed to be researching?'.

Activity: Compare and contrast

Allow yourself 15 minutes to analyse the three drawings – five minutes for each one. Remember you are analysing, so you need to be looking at the way the drawings were made, what the subjects are, what materials were used and so on. Don't worry too much about which one works best or any meaning in them. Just record the information in note form.

line drawing

full colour drawing

tonal drawing

Your observations

So what did you observe in the Activity above, compare and contrast? You might have something like this:

Line drawing:

- line drawing of clothed figure, male
- made with colour pencils
- uses short, sketchy lines, overlapping colours
- lots of white paper showing
- not solid or filled in
- energetic
- scale or sizes of lines varies according to parts of the drawing
- small lines on face, bigger lines or dashes on jacket, very light lines on background.

Functional skills

English

Making notes is an important writing skill. You can use your notes as a prompt to help you communicate your ideas and opinions when you are making presentations.

View clear image

Full colour drawing:

- colour pencil drawing of life model, female
- solid drawing, figure filled in
- emphasises skin colour
- reminiscent of classical painting
- full-figure
- light and dark contrast as well as colour contrast, i.e. warm and cold colours
- figure cut off at top and bottom of picture, emphasises composition.

Tonal drawing:

- black and white (monochrome) Conté drawing of two casts (figures)
- full figures, one white, one black
- treatment of surfaces reflects the hard nature of materials used, e.g. plaster
- full surface of paper treated – background as well
- figures slightly cut-off by edge of page – emphasises composition
- strong light and dark contrast, emphasised by full shading.

These are only guideline points – you might have some very different ones. As long as you are analysing the images that's fine.

In this example we have looked at analysing using words to describe what you see. There are other ways to analyse, such as drawing. Here is an example:

In this example the learner is using drawing to analyse the different parts of the bike. This is work made right at the start of the project, and is 'getting to know' the parts that make up the bike. When you draw something closely you have to study it and it helps you to understand how it works. These drawings show the learner analysing it, using a mixture of drawings, annotations or notes linked to the drawings.

You can also use analysis to help you make decisions about your work and ideas. When you do this you are also involved in critiquing. A learner is going to use the urban shot of a biker as a basis for a print. Before the printmaking process could begin the learner decided to analyse the photograph to see how it could be cropped to make the composition more interesting.

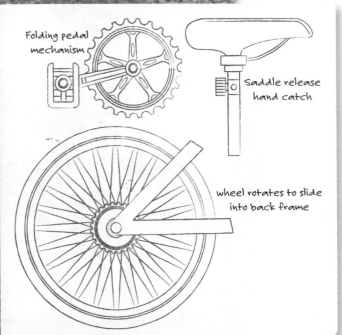

Figure 1: When analysing an object for your project try this kind of analytic drawing

Folding pedal mechanism

Saddle release hand catch

wheel rotates to slide into back frame

Activity: Cropping and composing

Now try this way of analysing. Source a photograph that you like. Get some card and cut into strips about 20 cm long and 3 cm wide. Take your photograph and arrange two of the strips either side of the photograph (left and right-hand outside edge) and the other two strips at the top and bottom of the photograph – a bit like a frame. Now play around with the composition by moving the pieces of card in towards the middle of the picture – do this gradually and see how this cropping changes the effect of the photograph, through altering its composition. Explore different options – leave one strip near the edge, and move its opposite one in towards the middle of the picture. Make sure you maintain some kind of frame as you do this on all four sides of the photograph. It's like moving a viewfinder over the image and selecting the best composition.

Creative thinkers

You will be developing your creative thinking skills when you generate ideas and explore different possibilities.

Reflective learners

Evaluating both your work and the work of others will help you improve as a reflective learner.

Grading tips

The more times you explore this, the better your work will be placed towards meeting the merit or distinction criteria, especially if you can explain the different effects on the image clearly, effectively and imaginatively.

Once you have made notes about this process, you can start critiquing the different versions, by asking questions such as 'which is the most interesting composition, and why?'.

You might have ended up with images similar to these – think about how the composition changes the feel or meaning of the image.

Figure 3: How many different ways can you crop a photo?

Critiquing

What is the intention?
Why was it made?
Which materials work best in describing the form?
Which version best meets the artist's aims?
How could the pieces be developed further?

Let's return to the drawings in the earlier activity. You are going to critique these, using your analysis to help you. If you can do this effectively you will be working towards a merit grade – effectively means conducting a more in-depth analysis and reaching clearer conclusions that are well thought through. If you can do this independently, you will be working towards a distinction grade.

A good way of critiquing art, craft or design work is to ask questions – this helps you move beyond the 'like it/don't like it' way of describing works, which is not really effective evaluation.

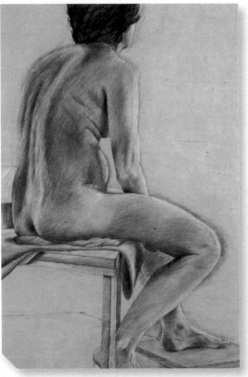

When you are looking at art, craft or design work, there are some general questions that you can ask before you get down to specifics. Some of these are listed below.

> **What is/are the subject/s?** What materials were used?
> **Who or what is the target audience?**
> When were the items made?
> **Is there an obvious message?** **What's the purpose?**
> What's the scale?

This is not a definitive list – you can build on this list to make some of your own questions. In critiquing you have to ask questions that make you think about the successes and weaknesses in the work; this could be your own or others'. Ultimately, you have to be able to justify your decisions.

Being able to critique is an important skill in the workplace. For example, a senior designer in a graphics company needs to look at design ideas produced by a team of juniors to select those that will go forward to production. He or she would have to justify or explain the reasoning behind the choice, especially if the work is for a client. This will involve evaluating – critiquing – the designs, in this case against fitness for purpose. The designer might also consider the designs in the light of their potential to grab the public's attention.

Activity: Critiquing questions

Critique the three drawings using the general questions above, and then move on to the questions specific to these drawings.

Use the specific critique questions below to critique the three drawings, allowing 15 minutes to make notes.

*   Compare the three drawings and the materials used to make them – which best fits the traditional idea of a life drawing, and why?

*   Which drawing is the most difficult to look at – in other words, which drawing requires the most effort from the viewer to make it work?

*   Why is this?

*   What do the drawings tell you about the figures drawn, if anything?

*   Which materials work best in describing the form of the figures?

*   Why is this?

*   What emotions or messages do the drawings give you, if any?

*   Which compositions work best, and why?

PLTS

Effective participators
Supporting conclusions, using reasoned arguments and evidence will demonstrate your ability to participate in discussions effectively.

talking
using words
explaining ideas
discussing views
what works best
technical terms
aesthetics
composition
fitness for purpose

Communicating

When you are evaluating you need to be able to communicate your conclusions. This will involve you using words, and possibly drawings, or other imagery. It's often easier to work with notes and develop these if you are required to. Many of your tutors will accept notes as part of the submission of your work – discuss this with them. What will be important is to use clear guidelines when setting out your conclusions so you can communicate clearly.

Checklist for communication:

- Think about your audience: who are they, what do they know, why are they going to listen?
- Use appropriate language.
- Use correct technical terms.
- Be clear on what you want to say.
- Be prepared to support what you want to say with examples or supporting materials.
- Think about what you want to say and stick to it.

Some approaches to communicating can be seen in the examples of learner work shown in the following pages.

Activity: Photographing everyday objects

Scenario: A photographer has been commissioned to produce a series of images of everyday objects shot in unusual ways. To achieve this he or she has experimented with photographing games and brightly coloured plastic toys from unexpected angles. The photographer has to decide which versions to submit for publication. The publisher has asked for the images to be ranked in order of preference. You are the photographer and have narrowed the images down to the three below, which you are going to rank in order of preference.

Allow 15 minutes to evaluate the three images, putting them in order of preference. Explain the reasons for ranking them in the order you have. Analyse the images and critique them in terms of interest and how well they fit the brief of everyday objects from unusual viewpoints.

Presenting

Let's not forget how important communicating is in the industries. Artists have to communicate with galleries, agents, public bodies, funding agencies and arts officers all the time, if they are going to mount a successful career. Designers also have to communicate their intentions to clients, sometimes changing ideas and re-drawing designs with the clients present.

There are different types of presentations and presentation techniques, and you can present your work for different forums. These are listed below:

using sketchbooks
presentation boards
mood boards
                   exhibitions
using IT
       framing work

Presentations

- written
- verbal
- pitch to clients
- private viewing of your work
- outlining your plans for a project
- explaining your work – mid-project critique
- explaining your work – end of project critique.

Presentation techniques

- displays of sketchbook
- displays of preliminary work/ finished work
- external exhibitions
- mounting techniques, e.g. card, window mounting
- framing techniques
- PowerPoint
- notes at a presentation
- handouts.

Using these skills will enable you to approach evaluating with confidence. There is a knowledge check at the end of this section that will help you to summarise and remember what you need to do.

Functional skills

When producing verbal presentations – contributions to discussions and presentations in a wide range of contexts – you are providing evidence for speaking and listening skills.

Activity: Presenting work

Select a piece of work that you really like. Think about how you could present it; if it's a painting, you could frame it and mount the preparatory works. Now practise talking about the work, communicating:

- your subject

- choice of materials

- what you wanted to say in the work

- whether you feel you were successful in this

- what you would do to improve future work

- what you have learned through doing the work.

You can extend this to other pieces of work. You don't need to present and communicate to whole groups of learners or tutors – you can practise this at home with your family or relatives. The more you do it, the easier it will become to communicate your thoughts and ideas about your work.

Case study: Examples of evaluation by learners

How might an evaluation look? Let's look at some examples produced by learners.

In these examples the learner is evaluating or assessing the standard 13-amp plug and socket, looking at a brief history and the **use of materials**. He or she is also beginning to plan the making of a large model of a plug, so is using evaluation to help plan the design work. Sketchbooks are being used as the basis for

presenting ideas, and written language is used to communicate conclusions.

In this example the learner has evaluated the letterforms that have been developed and used in a final piece. Notes explain the reasons for choosing certain fonts or typefaces to develop ideas from, and why these are thought to be successful.

Evaluation process

Looking at fitness for purpose is just one way of evaluating. Some of these relate to looking at things in the real world, like the household objects discussed earlier; sometimes it involves evaluating or assessing your own design work or final pieces. Sometimes it can mean looking at materials you have chosen, or the techniques and processes you have used. At other times you have to evaluate the work of others in a specific discipline or area. Evaluations can be recorded in sketchbooks, work journals, on design sheets, or used in verbal presentations or critiques. Some of the key terms are shown in the table below:

Key terms	Meaning and context
Fitness for purpose	Evaluating design work by others. Evaluating own design work.
Aesthetic qualities	Evaluating use of shapes, scale, materials, colour and finish in work of others, and in own work.
Formal elements	Evaluating use of colour, contrast, scale, shape, texture, line, pattern, etc. in work by others, and in own work.
Use of materials	Evaluating how you have used materials in art and design work, and how others have used them.
Use of techniques and processes	Evaluating use of specific techniques and processes in own work and work of others.
Intention or intended message	Evaluating how well you have communicated your idea, or got across what you wanted to say, and how well others have communicated their ideas or message.
Research	Evaluating source material you have researched for projects.

Table 1: Evaluation criteria

The table below shows the units and the relevant leaning outcomes where evaluating skills are central to the tasks involved.

Unit	Learning outcome and title
Unit 1 Contextual references in Art and Design	1 know the influences of historical and contemporary art and design developments 2 be able to use historical and contemporary references to support research and development of own response 3 be able to present information about the work studied in an appropriate format.
Unit 2 2D visual communication	3 be able to use formal elements in 2D visual communication
Unit 3 3D visual communication	3 be able to use formal elements in 3D visual communication
Unit 4 Using ideas to explore, develop and produce art and design	1 be able to research and record visual and other information from primary and secondary sources in response to the brief 4 know the strengths and weaknesses of developmental work.
Unit 5 Building an art and design portfolio	1 understand the purpose of an art and design portfolio 2 be able to present an art and design portfolio

Unit 6 Working in the art and design industry	1 know about organisations in the art and design industry 2 know about job roles in the art and design industry
Unit 7 Working with graphic design briefs	4 understand the successful characteristics and quality of graphic design work
Unit 8 Working with photography briefs	2 be able to develop ideas to meet photography briefs 3 understand the successful characteristics and quality of photographic work
Unit 9 Working with fashion design briefs	3 be able to develop ideas to meet fashion design briefs 4 understand the successful characteristics and quality of fashion design work
Unit 10 Working with textiles briefs	2 be able to develop work to meet textiles briefs 3 understand the successful characteristics and quality of textiles work
Unit 11 Working with 3D design briefs	2 be able to develop ideas to meet 3D design briefs 3 understand the successful characteristics and quality of 3D design work
Unit 12 Working with interactive media briefs	2 be able to explore the use of interactive media products 4 be able to review interactive media production work
Unit 13 Working with visual arts briefs	4 understand the successful characteristics and quality of visual arts work
Unit 14 Working with 3D design crafts briefs	4 understand the successful characteristics and quality of 3D design crafts work
Unit 15 Working with digital art and design briefs	3 understand the successful characteristics and quality of digital art and design work
Unit 16 Working with accessory briefs	3 understand the successful characteristics and quality of accessory briefs work
Unit 17 Working with moving image briefs	3 understand the successful characteristics and quality of moving image work
Unit 18 Working with site-specific briefs	2 be able to plan and develop ideas for a site-specific brief 3 understand the successful characteristics and quality of work for site-specific briefs

Table 2: Units that require evaluation skills

Marc Friend
Designer, friend associates limited

Why do you think it's important to use evaluation?

In the design industry, it's really about meeting the brief and ensuring the client or clients are happy with all the aspects of your ideas, for example about ethos, materials to be used, budget and time constraints.

The design ideas (what kinds of materials, colour and so on to be used) can be developed from a very tight client brief, where they know exactly the kind of feel and look they want. They will sometimes list the materials and where they will be sourced.

At other times you might have more freedom, but you still have to work within the constraints of the job.

Whatever you do, you have to meet the brief. So it's just as important to evaluate the brief at the start of a project, by concentrating on what the client is really looking for and picking out any key themes or tricky topics, as it is to know what criteria your work will be judged against at the end of the work.

What are the key factors that influence your evaluation of your work?

It's really important to the success of a job that the brief is met. If the client wants changes made to a design then this has to be discussed and agreed, and the changes made, before the actual work starts. It's a lot more expensive to do this once contractors or manufacturers are involved.

For example, on any job, it is important that we meet the clients on a regular basis to make sure that everything is moving smoothly. We usually have to ensure that minutes are produced and we document everything that is discussed and conclusions noted. These are really important documents. The key factors in most jobs are the clients' views, suggested modifications, and bringing out any key themes in the work.

Think about it!

- What criteria would you use to evaluate one of your pieces? What might someone else say about it?
- How can you test that your work is successful?

Just checking

There are stages to evaluating, and it's worth remembering these as you plan and work through the process.

Stage 1 – get your resources together. Whatever it is you are evaluating, you need examples in front of you, so you have to source or find them. It's much better to have more than one image or one type of the same object, so you can work through the 'compare and contrast' exercise.

Stage 2 – decide what you are looking for. This is not as easy as it sounds, so you need to be clear about this. There are no rigid rules, but there are guidelines. For example, in design disciplines a piece that is designed is meant to have a function – it is meant to perform a task or serve a purpose. This is the 'fitness for purpose' that we have looked at earlier.

Stage 3 – look at it. This sounds simple, but you need to really look hard at the objects or images. For example, factors like fitness for purpose are not always that obvious at first.

Stage 4 – make notes as you are evaluating. When you are making your observations, write the information down. Work to headings like 'fitness for purpose', 'cost' (if you can find out), 'target audience', 'materials used' and so on.

Stage 5 – try to make conclusions about the objects. Which objects work best, which don't and why? Write up your conclusions. Remember, this doesn't have to be in long sentences or an essay, unless the assignment specifically asks for this. You can use notes, bullet points and diagrams or drawings to help you make your point. If you do this well, you can also use it as a basis for doing the kind of presentation that Matthew Cooper (the learner at the beginning of this section) had to do.

To recap, you can use evaluation to assess your own work – as you are doing it (called 'ongoing evaluation') and at the end of the assignment. Using these techniques will help make your work stronger.

You can use evaluation to assess your **research** for projects, and to analyse the work of others.

Remember key terms like **fitness for purpose**, ideas generation, outcomes, design process, formal language, presentation methods, and so on.

Now you have looked at evaluation in more detail, how do you think Matthew managed the process of evaluating his corkscrew? How could you do it better?

6 Working in the art and design industry

In this section you will learn what it's like to work in the art and design industry. Each of the units provides a case study that gives a great insight into the working lives of artists and designers. The case studies also provide examples of how industry professionals respond to different types of briefs and how they work with clients and organisations. This will give you the opportunity to think about where your art and design skills can be used and help you identify a specialism and possible area of future employment.

By reading the case studies and completing the activities in this section, you will learn about different organisations in the creative industries and find out about the broad range of job roles available.

fine art galleries   fashion houses
advertising agencies   magazines
theatres   interior design companies
animation companies   arts centres

Learning outcomes

After completing this unit you should:

1 know about organisations in the art and design industry

2 know about job roles in the art and design industry.

Assessment and grading criteria

This table shows you what you must do in order to achieve a pass, merit or distinction, and where you can find activities in this book to help you.

To achieve a **pass** grade the evidence must show that the learner is able to:	To achieve a **merit** grade the evidence must show that, in addition to the pass criteria, the learner is able to:	To achieve a **distinction** grade the evidence must show that, in addition to the pass and merit criteria, the learner is able to:
P1 identify how organisations operate in the art and design industry **Assessment activity 6.1** **Page 154**	**M1** explain how organisations operate in the art and design industry **Assessment activity 6.2** **Page 155**	**D1** independently and fluently analyse how diverse organisations operate in the art and design industry, reaching informed conclusions **Assessment activity 6.2** **Page 155**
P2 list job roles within the art and design industry **Assessment activity 6.1** **Page 154**	**M2** explain the characteristics of job roles within the art and design industry **Assessment activity 6.2** **Page 155**	**D2** independently and fluently explain the characteristics of diverse job roles within the art and design industry, reaching informed conclusions **Assessment activity 6.2** **Page 155**
P3 describe the characteristics of job roles within the art and design industry **Assessment activity 6.1** **Page 154**		

How you will be assessed

You will be assessed on the findings from your research, which should cover a variety of organisations and jobs in the art and design industry. Make sure that you present information in your own words – you could include diagrams and charts to present information in different ways.

Your evidence for assessment could be in the form of:

- a research portfolio with notes and posters

- records of presentations

- records of discussions that include your contributions and findings.

You will be encouraged to research a range of organisations and gather information about how they operate. This could include organisations such as: fine art galleries, fashion houses, advertising agencies, magazines, theatres, interior design companies, animation companies and arts centres. You should investigate the different types of jobs within the organisation and what each job includes. You may find the same jobs in different organisations or particular specialist roles in some companies. It is useful to find out the details of each job to see if you would be interested in doing this in the future.

You may be able to visit organisations which are based in your town, or your tutors may arrange for artists and designers to visit you and talk about what they do. Further information can be gathered from using the Internet, magazines and specialist journals or by visiting or writing to the company. Many organisations have excellent websites which include information about roles within their company and any job vacancies.

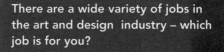

There are a wide variety of jobs in the art and design industry – which job is for you?

Assessment activity 6.1: Organisations and opportunities

Think about the area of art and design you are interested in – fashion design? interior design? graphic design? jewellery design?

List the range of jobs you think would be involved within that organisation.

Now, extend your first ideas by finding a real organisation linked to the area you are interested in and collect information about the work they produce and the range of jobs within their company. If you type into a search engine such as Google, the area of art and design you are interested in, you will find a wide range of organisations listed – some large and some small. Some good ones to get you started, including magazines, which list jobs, vacancies and the skills required, are listed below. To view some of the websites go to Hotlinks.

- **Aardman Animations** – film and animation
- **Designers Guild** – textile design
- **The National Theatre**
- **The Artist's Newsletter**
- **The Arts Council**
- **Design Nation**
- **Connexions Direct**
- **Visual Arts Career Guide**

Organise the information you have found and use it to list each job and its key characteristics.

BTEC

Assessment activity 6.2: Research and investigation

 **M1 M2 D1 D2**

Select three further companies to research. Gather similar information about them, so that you begin to build up a picture of the range of art and design organisations and job possibilities within them that you may be interested in. Search out companies who are working within the same speciality (i.e. three jewellery companies or three interior design companies) and investigate what the companies produce and how they operate in addition to how each job fits within the organisation.

Take some time to evaluate what you find, and think about how you can evidence and present this to best represent the specialist area of art and design. See below for different ways to present your research.

Finally, share your findings with your peer group and tutor as a visual, verbal or written presentation.

a database
a visual report
a PowerPoint presentation
visual examples of artwork produced
a sketchbook of information
a recorded interview with the artist or designer
printed information from the Internet

 PLTS

Independent enquirers

Gathering research about art and design organisations will evidence your independent enquiry skills.

Team workers

Working in pairs or small groups to investigate and collate your findings about an organisation will evidence your team-working skills

Creative thinkers and reflective learners

Considering your own art and design skills and how they might be relevant to job roles that you have investigated, and thinking of ways to present your findings creatively, will evidence your reflective learning and creative thinking skills.

 Functional skills

ICT and English

Using the Internet to undertake research and presenting your findings will evidence your ICT skills.

Creating a database of job roles and collating and presenting your findings will also evidence your ICT skills.

Using books and journals, interviewing artists and designers, contributing to discussions and presenting your information will evidence your English skills.

Just checking

Be prepared

Buy a ring file, plastic sleeves, page dividers and Post-It notes so that all research information can be easily kept, filed according to speciality and labelled as you collect it.

Highlight

Read the information you find and use a highlighter pen to identify the key points. Number and list these points on a separate sheet of paper. This is a great way to quickly summarise lots of written information.

Use local, national and international companies

You will be able to find lots of information on the Internet, in magazines and books about national and international companies. To see websites that will help you get started go to Hotlinks.

- Creative & Cultural Skills: The Sector Skills Council for Advertising, Crafts, Cultural Heritage, Design, Literature, Music, Performing and Visual Arts

- Creative Choices: A service to support people interested in careers in the arts, media and design

- Skillset: The Sector Skills Council for Creative Media

- Skillfast-UK: The Sector Skills Council for Fashion and Textiles

Aim to search out local companies as well so that you can contact key employees directly and perhaps visit and interview them. This is a great way of finding out about the local job market and really investigating what each job entails. If you do manage to visit you may want to think about finding out the following information from an interview:

- name of the organisation

- a brief outline of the type of work they produce

- name of the employee you interview

- name of their job role

- their education and training

- the media(s) they use

- the style(s) of mark-making they use

- the techniques and processes they use.

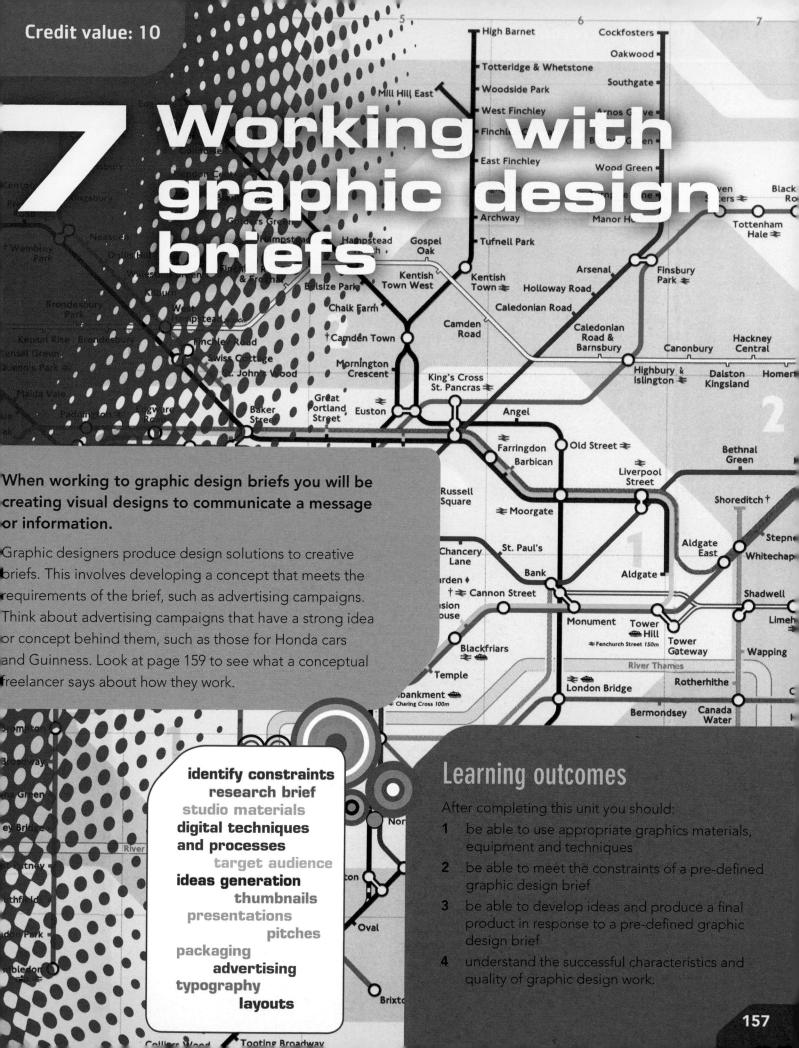

7 Working with graphic design briefs

When working to graphic design briefs you will be creating visual designs to communicate a message or information.

Graphic designers produce design solutions to creative briefs. This involves developing a concept that meets the requirements of the brief, such as advertising campaigns. Think about advertising campaigns that have a strong idea or concept behind them, such as those for Honda cars and Guinness. Look at page 159 to see what a conceptual freelancer says about how they work.

identify constraints
research brief
studio materials
digital techniques and processes
target audience
ideas generation
thumbnails
presentations
pitches
packaging
advertising
typography
layouts

Learning outcomes

After completing this unit you should:

1 be able to use appropriate graphics materials, equipment and techniques

2 be able to meet the constraints of a pre-defined graphic design brief

3 be able to develop ideas and produce a final product in response to a pre-defined graphic design brief

4 understand the successful characteristics and quality of graphic design work.

Assessment and grading criteria

This table shows you what you must do in order to achieve a pass, merit or distinction, and where you can find activities in this book to help you.

To achieve a **pass** grade the evidence must show that the learner is able to:	To achieve a **merit** grade the evidence must show that, in addition to the pass criteria, the learner is able to:	To achieve a **distinction** grade the evidence must show that, in addition to the pass and merit criteria, the learner is able to:
P1 use materials, equipment and techniques safely **Assessment activity 7.2 Page 163**	**M1** explore materials and techniques effectively **Assessment activity 7.2 Page 163**	**D1** integrate materials and techniques creatively and independently **Assessment activity 7.2 Page 163**
P2 use graphic design processes **Assessment activity 7.2 Page 163**	**M2** explore graphic design processes effectively **Assessment activity 7.2 Page 163**	**D2** integrate graphic design techniques and processes creatively and independently **Assessment activity 7.2 Page 163**
P3 research and record primary and secondary sources in response to a pre-defined brief **Assessment activity 7.2 Page 163**	**M3** conduct competent research and record appropriate visual and other information from primary and secondary sources in response to a pre-defined brief **Assessment activity 7.2 Page 163**	**D3** conduct independent research and record appropriate visual and other information from primary and secondary sources **Assessment activity 7.2 Page 163**
P4 produce developmental work and a final product in response to a brief **Assessment activity 7.2 Page 163**	**M4** produce effective and varied developmental work and a final product to meet a brief **Assessment activity 7.2 Page 163**	**D4** produce imaginative and varied developmental work and final product to meet a brief **Assessment activity 7.2 Page 163**
P5 discuss successful graphic design work **Assessment activity 7.1 Page 162 Assessment activity 7.2 Page 163**	**M5** compare and contrast experimental, development and final creative works **Assessment activity 7.2 Page 163**	**D5** evaluate experimental, development and final creative works **Assessment activity 7.2 Page 163**

How you will be assessed

You will be given a brief to work to. Because graphic design is about communicating, you will need to identify the constraints and purpose of the brief and know what to communicate. You will use graphic design processes and research from primary and secondary sources to generate ideas and final outcomes to meet the brief. Once you have completed the brief you will get the chance to evaluate your work and explain your ideas.

Case study: Danny Stijelja, freelance conceptual consultant

Danny Stijelja is a freelance conceptual consultant in the advertising and creative industries, working across a wide range of graphic communication projects. He also teaches graphic design at HND level at his local college.

What is your main role in the industry?

I work as an ideas generator, an advertising and promotional campaign strategist and as a tutor to HND Graphic Design learners at my local college.

Are you employed directly, or as a freelance artist/designer?

I am employed as a freelancer by creative agencies, often acting as a creative catalyst across a wide variety of graphic communication projects.

What do you think inspired this graphic design work by Neville Brody?

Can you describe some of your recent projects and how you approach the work?

No two projects are the same. A typical day will involve my being briefed on a project by the creative director. He or she will provide some background information on the client and outline the scope of the project – its objectives, requirements and deadlines. Depending on the job, I either work on my own or as part of a team to brainstorm initial ideas. The strongest would then be developed as a number of separate routes and worked up as visuals, backed by a rationale of the concepts before being presented to the client.

How do you find your work?

My work is specialised and based on working with big brand names, but like most freelancers I have to find the work myself. This can be done by placing ads, asking friends and contacts about opportunities, approaching creative agencies directly, or registering with a specialist agency. I work mainly with a small group of regular clients, who know they can rely on me to deliver, as I rely on them to keep giving me work.

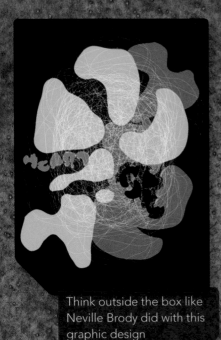

Think outside the box like Neville Brody did with this graphic design

What graphics equipment and materials do you use?

The things I use are very basic, usually a layout pad, pencil, black fibre-tipped pens and a selection of markers for scamps and visuals. I also use a Mac for research, writing copy and putting together artwork and presentations. Ideas and rough visuals are always done on paper – I never use a Mac for design until I have all my ideas roughed out on paper first.

What skills do you need for the different roles you carry out?

An enquiring mind, a fertile imagination and an ability to listen and absorb everything around you. It also helps be able to take criticism on the chin, as long as it's constructive. Once you have these 'human skills', you can then learn the basic technical skills and techniques.

Do you have strategies for developing ideas for a brief?

Sometimes I write down words or phrases associated with the brief. Research into the market is also important because it provides a context for ideas. After getting as many ideas down as possible, I evaluate them until I end up with the strongest starting point for visual development.

What other skills are important in your job role, such as communication?

In an industry built around communication it is imperative to be a communicator yourself – speak clearly, listen and express thoughts and reasoning intelligently. People skills, such as tact and working in a team are also important, as well as having a head for business.

What things do you enjoy about your work?

I enjoy everything – working with colleagues, being my own boss, being flexible, having a good work/life balance, the variety of the projects, being respected for my craft, coming up with ideas and seeing them work, but most of all I love using creativity to solve problems.

How would you sum up your experience in the industry?

My experience has allowed me to express myself. It has been a rollercoaster ride, but it has also provided me with some of the best highs of my life.

What advice would you give to anyone thinking of going into the industry?

The business can be difficult and there is no substitute for hard work, but if you put in the effort you will always find a way. The answer is always in the brief. Believe in yourself and others will too. If you cannot get excited about your work then don't be surprised if no one else does!

Here are some of the key terms and issues that you may encounter when working with graphic design briefs.

Key terms	Meaning and context
thumbnail sketches	• small, quick drawings, made without correction, normally in line/pencil/pen • used to explore ideas visually in an abbreviated manner
roughs	• visuals produced normally to the intended size • communicates more information than thumbnail
letterforms	• study of individual letters
typography	• study of groups of letterforms or typefaces/type families
target audience	• who or which group your project is aimed at
ideas generation	• process of developing ideas for a brief • essential part of the design process

application of brief	• what the products are used for, i.e.
	  o packaging
	  o signposting
	  o advertising
	  o promotion
	  o typography
	  o corporate identity
	  o layout
	  o logos
	  o titles
	  o idents

constraints	• factors that need to be considered when working on brief, i.e.
	  o budget
	  o target audience
	  o message
	  o timescale
	  o materials
	  o health and safety
	  o ethics

What do think might have been the starting points for the designs of these branding logos?

Remember

Take time out when you are with your friends or in your studio to look at your peers. How many of them are wearing an item or carrying a product that has a distinctive logo? List them.

Did you know?

There are often clear symbolic ideas behind apparently simple logos.

Take the Hyundai logo: the name Hyundai was chosen for its meaning, which in English translates to 'modern'. The oval Hyundai logo is symbolic of the company's desire to expand, while the stylised 'H' represents two people (the company and customer) shaking hands.

Hyundai logo

 Assessment activity 7.1: Information graphics

Evaluate examples of information graphics. Go to your local gallery, arts centre and tourist information centre and collect examples of leaflets and information graphics. Display them in your studio or at home and describe the characteristics of successful examples. Define the success criteria before you begin. If you are working in your studio, this can be performed as a group task.

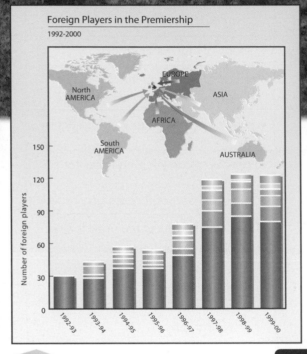

What are the strengths and weaknesses of these examples of information graphics?

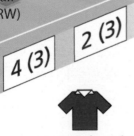

BTEC Assessment activity 7.2: Developing advertising ideas

P1 P2 P3 P4 P5
M1 M2 M3 M4 M5
D1 D2 D3 D4 D5

How could you develop ideas for advertising a new brand of phone? Work though ideas generation and visual development of your ideas into design work.

What kinds of things do you need to be aware of?

The target audience is age 12 to 18.

The design reflects youth branding – heavy music and multimedia content, download capability, brightly coloured finishes.

What else should you research?

I am all the boys
I've kissed
and the ones I will.

search online for 'I am'

What do you think of this advertising idea?

Assignment tips

Remember to look at the grading criteria. The differences between the pass, merit and distinction are often explained as your work having purpose, being effective or independently produced, and creatively meeting the brief. Take risks in your work – avoid producing obvious solutions (who would have thought a gorilla – or a person wearing a gorilla suit – miming the drums to a Phil Collins song could be used to advertise chocolate?)

Develop different strategies for coming up with ideas – some learners find this the most difficult part of their projects, especially at the beginning. Writers have cut up sentences and rearranged them to make new, random, sentences that they then use as starting points; designers play games with words to see if this can suggest new ideas or approaches. Avoid coming up with a single idea and sticking to it – you won't reach the higher grades unless you can demonstrate the ability to evaluate different approaches to graphic communication techniques, or explain a variety of graphic solutions.

Look at typography as well as image. The uses of certain type families have associations. What are they and how do they work? Do these associations influence the readers in choosing them?

Take risks when exploring your ideas. Sometimes an idea can come out of the blue – don't dismiss it, just record it – you never know whether you might use it. Beware judging examples that look simple – strong graphics that look simple are often the result of an extensive design process.

Websites

There are a number of websites that will help you. To view these go to Hotlinks.

- Creative & Cultural skills
- Creative Choices
- TED
- Design Council.

How does the audience of a magazine or newspaper determine the typeface used?

8 Working with photography briefs

The ability to take a good photograph is a wonderful skill. It is an exciting process area and great fun to see your initial ideas realised in print. You can use your camera to gather research ideas, document project work as it develops or as an art form in its own right.

There are a great many techniques and processes that you can explore and experiment with and lots of opportunities to see other photographers' work in galleries, magazines, newspapers, and on their individual websites. From traditional 35 mm cameras to digital cameras, and from black and white processing and printing to making use of Photoshop, the possibilities are endless!

This unit introduces you to the range of equipment you can make use of and some of the materials, techniques and processes you can explore.

Turn to page 167 to read about Donald MacLellan. He is a freelance editorial photographer with 20 years' experience. He works for national and international magazines, design companies and advertising agencies.

techniques
35 mm camera
colour
digital SLR
contrast
black and white
Photoshop
special effects

Learning outcomes

After completing this unit you should:

1 be able to use photographic processes
2 be able to develop ideas to meet photography briefs
3 understand the successful characteristics and quality of photographic work.

Assessment and grading criteria

This table shows you what you must do in order to achieve a pass, merit or distinction, and where you can find activities in this book to help you.

To achieve a **pass** grade the evidence must show that the learner is able to:	To achieve a **merit** grade the evidence must show that, in addition to the pass criteria, the learner is able to:	To achieve a **distinction** grade the evidence must show that, in addition to the pass and merit criteria, the learner is able to:
P1 use photographic techniques **Assessment activity 8.1** **Page 169** **Assessment activity 8.2** **Page 170**	**M1** explore photographic materials and processes effectively **Assessment activity 8.1** **Page 169** **Assessment activity 8.2** **Page 170**	**D1** integrate diverse photographic materials and processes imaginatively **Assessment activity 8.1** **Page 169** **Assessment activity 8.2** **Page 170**
P2 use photographic equipment safely **Assessment activity 8.1** **Page 169** **Assessment activity 8.2** **Page 170**	**M2** develop effective, coherent ideas and outcomes to meet photography briefs **Assessment activity 8.1** **Page 169** **Assessment activity 8.2** **Page 170**	**D2** develop innovative, imaginative ideas and outcomes to meet photography briefs **Assessment activity 8.1** **Page 169** **Assessment activity 8.2** **Page 170**
P3 select appropriate materials and processes to meet photography briefs **Assessment activity 8.1** **Page 169** **Assessment activity 8.2** **Page 170**	**M3** compare and contrast experimental, development and final creative works **Assessment activity 8.1** **Page 169** **Assessment activity 8.2** **Page 170**	**D3** evaluate experimental, development and final creative works **Assessment activity 8.1** **Page 169** **Assessment activity 8.2** **Page 170**
P4 develop ideas and outcomes to meet photography briefs **Assessment activity 8.1** **Page 169** **Assessment activity 8.2** **Page 170**		
P5 discuss successful photographic work **Assessment activity 8.1** **Page 169** **Assessment activity 8.2** **Page 170**		

How you will be assessed

You will be assessed on your ability to use photographic equipment and techniques, as well as on the ideas you develop in response to the briefs that you are given. As you work, you will be choosing and using different materials, techniques and processes.

Your evidence for assessment may take different forms, but you will need to demonstrate that you have covered all of the grading criteria. You could do this through:

- observation records from your tutor or work placement that show how you have worked

- presentations

- annotated log books or worksheets

- written or visual reports.

Case study: Donald MacLellan, freelance editorial photographer

Donald is a photographer with 20 years' experience working for national and international magazines, design companies and advertising agencies. He has exhibited at the National Portrait Gallery in London and at the Scottish National Portrait Gallery in Edinburgh. His work has appeared as covers and features in many leading magazines and publications including the *Sunday Times* magazine, *The Independent* magazine, *Radio Times*, *Empire*, and *The New York Times* magazine.

Can you tell me about a recent job that you've done?

I was commissioned to take a photograph of Jenny Pitman for the *New Review* magazine within the *Independent on Sunday* newspaper. They cover this type of story on the 'Living' page each week so the format has to stay the same. The picture needed to be a 'mid-shot' (from the middle of the body up to the head) and fill the space, and there had to be room in the photograph for written information to run down the side of the page.

What did you have to consider first in order to meet the demands of this brief?

I knew I would have to photograph Miss Pitman 'portrait' and not 'landscape' format so it would fit the page, and I had to make sure that the writing would be visible on top of the image, so I couldn't make the background too busy.

PLTS

Independent enquirers

Researching practising photographers and making use of these findings to develop a series of ideas will evidence your independent enquiry skills.

Creative thinkers

Exploring processes and techniques and trying out different options for each image will evidence your creative thinking skills.

Reflective learners

Reviewing your work, making changes, adapting and producing further ideas will evidence your reflective learning skills.

Team workers

Working with each other, offering support and suggestions, helping each other with developing and printing will support your team-working skills.

Living

Jenny Pitman

I believe...

See how the text and photograph work together in this article

a full-length shot
a mid-length shot
head only
profile
sitting
standing
lying down
using props
using a particular
interior
using a plain
background
looking down on
the model
looking up at
the model
from the side
back lighting
low lighting
using torchlight

Which photographic processes did you decide to use?

All my work is digital photography now, which has caught up with the quality offered by traditional film and offers more range and information. Digital images can be sent immediately over the Internet, which suited this brief as the magazine was due to be printed the day after the shoot.

After the shoot I downloaded all the photographs and edited the most successful eight images to send as low-res jpegs for the picture editor to select from. The chosen shot would then need to be sent back as a high-res image.

How did you develop your first ideas for this brief?

I began by contacting Miss Pitman to discuss suitable locations for the photograph. We settled on a racing horse sanctuary, so that the photograph could link with information about her professional career.
On the day, I met her at her house and discussed ideas over a coffee. This 'relaxed' start is a very important – it helps me and the subject get to know each other.

Which photographic equipment did you take with you to use?

It varies according to the job, how much time I have and the brief. For this brief I took:

- 35 mm digital camera
- three lenses: 12 mm–24 mm, 28 mm–70 mm and 70 mm–200 mm
- hand-held flash to be used on my camera
- two-headed light kit, including two flash heads, two stands, cables and an extension cable
- tripod.

How did you develop your ideas and select appropriate processes on the day?

When we got to the sanctuary, we were directed to a training paddock to take the photographs. Miss Pitman has very white hair and this was lost in the strong light and sharp shadows. There is no avoiding this unless you choose to use artificial light, though I prefer to use natural light as the colours seem to be richer with more depth. I finally managed to move into the shadow of a building, where the light would be more flattering.

What's it like to be an editorial photographer?

I've been an editorial photographer for 15 years and have built up a group of magazines and newspapers that I work for. Picture editors keep changing so I have to keep promoting myself through my website, showing my portfolio and sending out e-cards to magazines and newspapers.

I work from home where I have a studio, computer and a printer. Jobs vary hugely depending on the budget and timescale. Success can often depend on how much time I get to photograph, which can be anything from 5 minutes to 5 hours. Some magazines have a distinctive style, and as a photographer I have to come up with the ideas to meet their brief. I usually get paid for a job within 3 to 6 weeks of sending in the invoice, although some magazines take much longer. When I invoice for a job I list charges for the following:

- time – a day rate or half-day rate
- digital services – the time in front of the computer touching up and making minor adjustments
- travel
- assistant (if required)
- stylist (if required)
- overnight stays (if required).

Can you see how being in shadow has made the image more flattering to Miss Pitman?

BTEC **Assessment activity 8.1: Landscape**

P1 P2 P3 P4 P5
M1 M2 M3
D1 D2 D3

Begin by researching photographers, such as Michael Kenna or Charlie Waite, and note the composition used in their work, in addition to the subject matter and techniques and processes explored.

Make quick compositional sketches of your chosen landscape before taking any photographs, exploring arrangement of shapes and cropping. Experiment with composition and how you divide the image making use of roads, rivers, railings or sky to lead your eye into and across the picture.

Take a series of landscapes using either a digital or traditional camera. Aim to keep vertical and horizontal lines true and explore light and shade within your series. You may find it useful to use a tripod so that your camera stays steady.

Having taken the photographs, experiment with the quality of paper that you print upon and how you can alter the image by cropping or adding sepia or colour tones to the developing process. Explore how you can manipulate and alter the images using Photoshop, by changing the contrasts, lighting and by darkening and using colour to retouch or change areas.

Remember to keep a small notebook with you to record all the technical details, so that you can make use of them in future projects.

 Functional skills

ICT, mathematics and English

Researching the work of others and developing your own photographs using Photoshop will evidence developing ICT skills.

Making use of and calculating the exposure, aperture and shutter speeds when taking photographs will evidence your developing mathematics skills.

Sharing and discussing your ideas and writing up research and technical notes will evidence your English skills.

Assessment activity 8.2: Portraits

Begin by researching photographers such as Sally Soames and Rankin and note their styles, how the models are lit and composed.

Take a series of portraits using either a digital or traditional camera trying to capture the characteristics of your model. Explore and experiment with composition, lighting and camera angles to produce a wide range of imaginative and inventive images.

Having taken the photographs experiment further with the final image by cropping and manipulating using Photoshop.

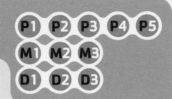

Assignment tips

- When taking a landscape image the best type of light is very early in the morning or evening. There are less shadows and less contrast which will give you more detail.

- Use a tripod for landscape photography to keep the camera steady.

- Be prepared – make sure you have all the equipment you need before you set out – check to make sure it is all working.

- When photographing people, begin with models you know so that you can experiment, take your time and try out lots of ideas. Take time to look for the models 'best side' and how the light falls across the contour of their face.

- Look at other peoples' work to get ideas – their websites and pictures in newspapers and magazines. It's a good idea to try to reproduce one of their shots, so that you work through how they would have composed the shot and the techniques and processes they used.

- Experiment with lighting – back light and top light, bedside lamps, TV light, reflectors, torches.

- Produce good quality contact sheets on different types of paper so you can clearly see all images and make a final selection.

9 Working with fashion design briefs

In this unit you will learn how to design and make a fashion garment. You will be taught the basics of designing a garment from a pattern block or by drape modelling on a stand, and how to make your own pattern in response to a brief. You will be taught how to make up the garment with the chance to learn construction techniques such as sample seams, facings, darts and zip insertions, which you will then be able to apply to make a garment that you have designed.

On page 173 there is a case study about Clare Allington who is a fashion designer. Clare explains how she designed a collection for her final university degree show. Clare is now working as a freelance designer.

Learning outcomes

After completing this unit you should:

1   be able to use pattern drafting techniques and processes
2   be able to use construction techniques and processes
3   be able to develop ideas to meet fashion design briefs
4   understand the successful characteristics and quality of fashion design work.

Assessment and grading criteria

This table shows you what you must do in order to achieve a pass, merit or distinction, and where you can find activities in this book to help you.

To achieve a **pass** grade the evidence must show that the learner is able to:	To achieve a **merit** grade the evidence must show that, in addition to the pass criteria, the learner is able to:	To achieve a **distinction** grade the evidence must show that, in addition to the pass and merit criteria, the learner is able to:
P1 use pattern drafting techniques and processes safely **Assessment activity 9.2 Page 175**	**M1** use a variety of pattern drafting techniques and processes effectively **Assessment activity 9.2 Page 175**	**D1** use diverse pattern drafting techniques and processes creatively and independently **Assessment activity 9.2 Page 175**
P2 use construction techniques and processes safely **Assessment activity 9.2 Page 175**	**M2** use construction techniques and appropriate materials, techniques and processess **Assessment activity 9.2 Page 175**	**D2** use diverse construction techniques, materials, techniques and processes creatively and independently **Assessment activity 9.2 Page 175**
P3 develop ideas and outcomes to meet fashion design briefs **Assessment activity 9.3 Page 175**	**M3** develop coherent ideas and outcomes to meet fashion design briefs **Assessment activity 9.3 Page 175**	**D3** develop imaginative ideas and outcomes to meet fashion design briefs **Assessment activity 9.3 Page 175**
P4 select appropriate materials, techniques and processes to meet fashion design briefs **Assessment activity 9.3 Page 175**	**M4** compare and contrast experimental, development and final creative works **Assessment activity 9.1 Page 175** **Assessment activity 9.3 Page 175**	**D4** evaluate and contrast experimental, development and final creative works **Assessment activity 9.1 Page 175** **Assessment activity 9.3 Page 175**
P5 discuss successful fashion design work **Assessment activity 9.1 Page 175** **Assessment activity 9.3 Page 175**		

How you will be assessed

You will be assessed by your tutor on presentation of a portfolio. This could include scale patterns with at least one full scale pattern correctly marked or a technical file showing construction samples. You could present a workbook with fashion design ideas translated into a pattern and then made up into a garment. Or, you could do an evaluation of your own work and that of other fashion designers.

Case study: Clare Allington, fashion designer

Can you tell me about a recent job that you've done?

I have recently completed my major project for the final year of my university fashion design course at Southampton Solent University. For my final project I created an avant-garde collection for the catwalk, and then replicated the collection on porcelain dolls to improve the status of the fashion doll within the industry.

What was your inspiration?

The starting inspiration came from the current media fascination with '**plastic fantastic**' and the increasing popularity with the cosmetic surgery industry. I wanted to create a collection that played on this, while replicating it on porcelain dolls to create an ironic element. From there, I then looked at 'Harajuku' in Japan for secondary inspiration. Harajuku refers to an area around Tokyo's Harajuku Station which is the centre of Japan's extreme teenage cultures and fashion styles. I became incredibly inspired by the eclectic and colourful mismatching combinations of garments.

For the silhouette inspiration I went back to the doll-like look and considered the shape of the Barbie Doll as the primary look. This led me to use a 1950s silhouette as this was when Barbie was originally created.

What did you consider first in order to meet the demands of the brief?

The brief was to design a collection for a catwalk show. First, I had to consider the market level and the customer to design for. The market level means making sure the fashions are what the customer will buy. I had to consider the right style, price and material. For this I had to work out a virtual customer and decide on her age and the types of shops she would visit.

How did you develop your first ideas?

My first ideas developed through researching Japanese street culture. I covered the walls in my flat with images of both men and women and then sat and stared at them for hours. I also worked all the images into my design roughs in my sketchbooks, on thin layout paper, one design on top of the other, to adapt and change ideas.

I created around 250 design roughs for the collection before choosing the initial line-up. This process was key for translating my inspiration into the designs.

Clare Allington poses here dressed like one of her dolls. How do other experimental designers get their inspiration?

Clare's work is very experimental – can you comment on her work? How do other experimental designers get their inspiration?

What are the advantages of using the 3D draping technique that Clare is using?

Which pattern cutting techniques did you use?

I used both traditional flat pattern cutting techniques as well as 3D draping on the stand. I cut my flat patterns using basic blocks, and then transferred the draped pattern ideas into flat patterns. I marked all the patterns to show the technical information, such as grain and darts. I then planned how to lay the patterns on to fabrics so I could estimate fabric quantity.

Which construction techniques did you use?

I used a wide variety of processes, including pinning, tacking, machine stitching darts and seams, inserting zips, making facings for collars, cuffs and button fastenings, hemming and finishing. I also laboriously made and sewed on ribbon bows. The collection contains around 10,000 ribbon bows, so this was one of the most crucial processes involved.

I used the following equipment:

- pattern cutting tables and body forms for the drape modelling
- pattern cutting paper
- domestic and industrial sewing machines
- overlockers
- general sewing equipment such as scissors, pin, needles and thread.

What is it like to be a fashion designer?

It's amazing seeing how your work progresses from the original ideas to when it all comes to life on the catwalk. Being able to see what the months of painstakingly hard work has been for makes the whole process worthwhile.

My goal is to start my own fashion brand, so I plan to teach for a few years and build up a customer base through freelance work.

Key terms

Pattern block – a basic body shape which is used as the starting point for garment design.

Drape modelling – designing a garment on a stand then translating this into a flat pattern.

Sample seams – practising machine stitching seams such as open seams, French seams or machine and fell seams which you find on jeans.

Facings – a finish, such as for an arm hole or neckline.

Zip insertions – practising putting in a zip.

Plastic fantastic – a model heavily made-up, to look like a doll.

Activity: Strengths and weaknesses

What are your strengths and weaknesses in fashion design and making? List your strengths and weaknesses:

- **What can you improve on your own?**
- **What do you need help to improve?**
- **Who can you ask for help?**

BTEC

Assessment activity 9.1: Inspiration

 M4 D4 P5

Sources of inspiration for fashion designers are unending. Architecture, travel and other artists are some of the subjects that can spark ideas for a collection. Research your favourite fashion designer and find out what has inspired his or her latest collection and a previous collection. You should research:

- their sources of inspiration
- key details from their collections
- fabrics/textures used
- colours.

Present your findings to the group. This could be as a design sheet, pages in your workbook or a PowerPoint presentation. Sum up your findings with an illustrated handout and bullet points.

BTEC

Assessment activity 9.2: Analysing

 P1 M1 D1 P2 M2 D2

1 Look at your favourite fashion garment.

2 Can you follow the shapes of each piece around and make pattern pieces?

3 Can you examine your garment and work out the direction of the grain and then transfer this to your pattern pieces?

4 Look at the garment and write a list of the techniques used such as darts, seams, zip.

5 Put the list in an order of how you think the garment would be made. What would you do first?

6 Take two of the processes that are new to you and work out how they have been done. For example, if the garment has an invisible zip and you haven't put one in before – try a sample now.

BTEC

Assessment activity 9.3: Experimenting

 P3 P4 P5 M3 M4 D3 D4

Look at other designers for inspiration and experiment by incorporating ideas from their designs into your next fashion design brief. You could be inspired by the way the designer has used fastenings, embellishments or manipulated fabrics.

Examine the way top designers work with materials – check out the latest *Vogue* or *Harpers Bazaar* and consider these questions:

- Which of the designer's ideas work well?
- Do the fabrics work well with the designs?
- Are the latest catwalk trends easy to adapt to the High Street? What ideas have you gained?

Incorporate the ideas you have gained through researching other designers and experimenting with those ideas into your next fashion design brief.

Assignment tips

Learn how to draft patterns well:

- Actively look at fashion garments to see how they are constructed.

- Measure and mark your patterns accurately.

- Adapt patterns from professional blocks.

- Use diverse techniques such as block drafting, drape modelling, pattern adaptation.

Use a variety of construction techniques and processes with increasing confidence:

- Perfect your making skills.

- Use the iron to press turnings and facings flat to improve presentation.

- Work with small, neat hand stitches.

- Learn how to make the most of a sewing machine.

- Learn how to use more than one method of doing something. How many different seams can you sew? How many ways are there of making pockets?

- Use your technical folder to show off your skills.

Evaluate your work as you go along: Look at the technical quality of your work; can you make any changes to improve the quality? Practise talking about your work so that your ideas are fluent and you can easily explain how and what you've done.

Websites

To view some useful websites for fashion design go to Hotlinks.

- Platt Hall Costume Gallery at Manchester Art Gallery – historical costumes

- Museum of Costume and Assembly Rooms, Bath

- Victoria and Albert Museum – stage costumes. You can also study the V&A online fashion collection by the century.

- Fashion and Textile Museum, London – created by Zandra Rhodes

- Vivienne Westwood

10 Working with textiles briefs

By following this unit you will learn how designs are applied to textiles. This might be through surface decoration where you add a pattern to a plain fabric. This could be through printing, painting, dyeing or hand and machine embroidery. Or it might be through learning how to construct a fabric through knitting, weaving or felting where the design is integral to the fabric.

Alison Willoughby is a textile designer who describes her work in the case study on page 180. Alison makes extraordinary skirts and these can be viewed as specialist textile art pieces which can also be worn. Many of the skirts are made as display pieces only.

Learning outcomes

After completing this unit you should:

1 be able to use textiles materials, techniques and processes
2 be able to develop work to meet textiles briefs
3 understand the successful characteristics and quality of textiles work.

Assessment and grading criteria

This table shows you what you must do in order to achieve a pass, merit or distinction, and where you can find activities in this book to help you.

To achieve a **pass** grade the evidence must show that the learner is able to:	To achieve a **merit** grade the evidence must show that, in addition to the pass criteria, the learner is able to:	To achieve a **distinction** grade the evidence must show that, in addition to the pass and merit criteria, the learner is able to:
P1 use textiles materials, techniques and processes safely **Assessment activity 10.1 Page 181** **Assessment activity 10.2 Page 181**	**M1** use materials, techniques and processes to meet the brief coherently and effectively **Assessment activity 10.1 Page 181**	**D1** use diverse materials, techniques and processes to meet the brief creatively and independently **Assessment Activity 10.1 Page 181**
P2 develop ideas and outcomes to meet textiles briefs **Assessment activity 10.3 Page 181**	**M2** develop effective ideas and outcomes to meet textiles briefs **Assessment activity 10.3 Page 181**	**D2** develop imaginative ideas and outcomes to meet textiles briefs **Assessment activity 10.3 Page 181**
P3 select appropriate materials, techniques and processes to meet textiles briefs **Assessment activity 10.1 Page 181**	**M3** compare and contrast experimental, development and final creative works **Assessment activity 10.1 Page 181**	**D3** evaluate and contrast experimental, development and final creative works **Assessment activity 10.1 Page 181**
P4 discuss successful textiles work **Assessment activity 10.1 Page 181**		

How you will be assessed

You will be assessed by your tutor on presentation of a portfolio of work. You might present the following:

- experimental samples showing a variety of textile techniques and processes presented with annotations on worksheets, in a work/sketchbook, in a technical file or in a box

- development work in response to a brief with a final outcome, which could be, for example, A1 textile designs for screen printing or knitted or woven examples

- an evaluation of your work and the work of other textile designers.

Jessica Ryles

Jessica, who featured in case studies in Unit 1, discusses here how she used textile design materials, techniques and processes to link with her historical and contextual studies:

I looked at the screen prints of Andy Warhol then produced my own design based on lips. These were screen printed onto fabric and then the lips were free machine embroidered with red thread and straight stitch.

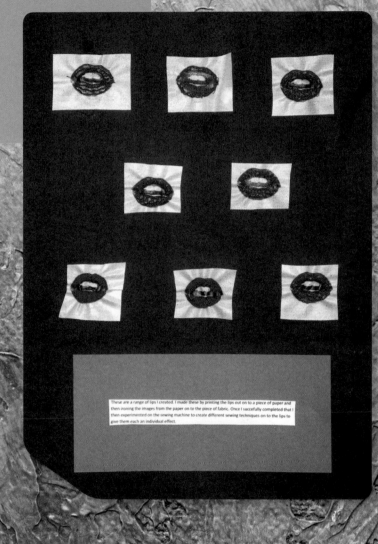

These are a range of lips I created. I made these by printing the lips out on to a piece of paper and then ironing the images from the paper on to the piece of fabric. Once I succefully completed that I then experimented on the sewing machine to create different sewing techniques on to the lips to give them each an individual effect.

Key terms

Surface decoration – applying a pattern to fabric through using print, paint, stitch or tiny objects like beads.

Printing – applying colour to cloth through a screen or directly with a stamp.

Painting – applying a design by hand with a paintbrush.

Dyeing – immersing cloth into a dye bath to infuse colour into fibres.

Hand and machine embroidery – applying threads in a pattern to cloth.

Knitting – making a fabric with yarn and needles, fingers or French knitting with a knitting dolly.

Weaving – making fabric using looms strung with the warp and threading a weft yarn across in a pattern.

Felting – traditionally, taking wool fibres and layering them on a flat surface before applying hot water and friction to help the fibres mat together to make a cloth.

Embellish – is to decorate something. In Assessment activity 10.1 it refers to the addition of beads, buttons, sequins, feathers and glittery things.

Case study: Alison Willoughby, textile designer

Alison is an established and innovative textile designer who studied printed and knitted textiles at Glasgow School of Art. She makes textile designs to commission and sells and exhibits internationally. Her clients include Selfridges, Liberty, The British Council, Habitat and Urban Outfitters, and her work is used for interior installations and specialist displays. She currently specialises in highly individual and intricate hand-constructed skirts, which are a vehicle for her textile designs. Some are for installations and others are to be worn.

Alison's materials include new and salvaged cotton, plastic, wood, metal, wool, linen, silk, ceramic, glass, leather and men's tie silks which have been manipulated into 'sushi rolls'. These are layered pieces of fabric, one on top of the other, with a circle cut out of them, which are then sewn down the middle and opened out to create a three-dimensional object. Other techniques she uses are silk-screen printing, foiling and mark-making, machine and hand embroidery, cording and material manipulation (ruffling, cut work, layering, looping and heating materials).

Much of the inspiration for her pieces comes from photographs, she has taken of streets, objects, architectural details, markets and people.

Why skirts?

A skirt is a very easy way of displaying a textile. It can become more than just a garment, it is a work of art in its own right.

Can you tell me about a recent job that you've done?

I have just had a solo show in Bonhoga Gallery, Shetland, called 'Skirt', which was 20 skirts hanging in a gallery.

What was your inspiration and how did you develop your ideas?

My inspiration came from everyday domestic photography, taken in India, America and the UK. I worked from my photographs and experimented with different textile techniques. When I was pleased with the results I made the skirts.

Which processes and equipment did you decide to use?

I had to make 20 skirts, so I used a lot of textile techniques – hand and machine embroidery, screen printing and fabric manipulation. I used an industrial Bernina sewing machine, silk-screen printing and general sewing equipment.

Skirt – painted, printed and embellished

Assessment activity 10.1: Embellishment

List all the things that Alison has **embellished** the skirt with.

1   What embellishments have you used in a recent project?

2   Did this work well or could it have been improved upon?

3   Can you think of other things that you could use as an embellishment for one of your pieces of work?

 Assessment activity 10.2: Working safely P1

To achieve P1 you must show that you can work safely.

What do you think this means?

- tidying away your coat and bag before you start work

- making sure your work place is kept clean and tidy as your work progresses

- checking all electrical equipment before use and making sure leads are positioned so they don't get in anyone's way

- not leaving irons on when not in use

- wearing protective clothing including face masks when necessary.

 Assessment activity 10.3: Textile design P2 M2 D2

The work of textile designers crops up in everyday and unusual places and forms: fashion, interiors, commercial markets, client commissions, or made as one-off pieces to sell in galleries and specialist shops.

Working in small groups, draw a mind map of fashion textile design or interior textile design. Identify:

- products

- designers (this will need extra research)

- types of textile design, such as printed, stitched and constructed.

How many legs and hubs has your spider got? When you've completed your mind map share your ideas.

 **Did you know?**

Textile designers specialise in surface decoration or fabric construction. This means that they either apply decoration to fabric through using print, dyes, paints, stitch and decorative items, or they make fabrics by knitting, weaving and felting. Designers will explore their ideas on paper and then experiment with textile samples. Many paper designs are sold to companies that print wrapping paper or wallpaper.

edexcel

Assignment tips

Look at the work of a variety of textile designers. Alison has told us what materials and techniques she uses, and Nicki Williams (see Unit 4) has also told us about her techniques and materials. By explaining aspects of their work they help us to understand processes.

Experiment with confidence

Be confident with your work; know when it does and doesn't work. Make small experimental pieces and stick them in your sketchbook/work book or technical file. Note down the processes, dyes, paints and stitches you use. This will help you to understand how to use a variety of materials, techniques and processes, just as the professional textile designers have described.

Developing ideas

Look at the work of contemporary designers and think about how you could find unusual starting points. The more you play around with paper and textile experiments the more likely that your work will be creative and imaginative.

Evaluating work

You have to describe successful textiles work. Our case studies are a good example. Do you think their ideas work well? Look at your work and make comments about whether or not your ideas worked and what you could have done differently. Then look at the work of other textile artists. Compare and contrast; write your ideas in a paragraph and try to explain the good points, what you think works well and perhaps what doesn't work for you.

What ideas do you think Nicki Williams is expressing in her embroidery *Madam Silverclang*?

- **Compare** means to make a list of the similarities between pieces of work.

- **Contrast** means to make a list of the differences.

Look at the Evaluating skills section to get extra hints and tips on how to evaluate well.

11 Working with 3D design briefs

When working with 3D design briefs you will be creating 3D visual solutions in direct response to a given brief. The type of work generated will address the needs of the brief and be fit for purpose. The area of 3D Design is extremely wide-ranging and has applications in many areas.

3D Design covers a wide range of applications. The furniture you work at, the homes you live in, the spaces you work in and the products you use are all part of the 3D design world. 3D designers also work in areas that are not so obvious, such as 3D computer modelling and film – there's an example on page 185.

3D animation
CAD
architecture
product design
industrial design
transport design
furniture
jewellery
ceramics
model making
3D typography
3D graphics
applications

spatial design
interiors
sculpture
special effects
design for film
set design
theatre design
exhibition design
retail displays
public art

Learning outcomes

After completing this unit you should:

1 be able to use 3D design materials, techniques and processes

2 be able to develop ideas to meet 3D design briefs

3 understand the successful characteristics and quality of 3D design work.

Assessment and grading criteria

This table shows you what you must do in order to achieve a pass, merit or distinction, and where you can find activities in this book to help you.

To achieve a **pass** grade the evidence must show that the learner is able to:	To achieve a **merit** grade the evidence must show that, in addition to the pass criteria, the learner is able to:	To achieve a **distinction** grade the evidence must show that, in addition to the pass and merit criteria, the learner is able to:
P1 use 3D design materials, techniques and processes safely **Assessment activity 11.1** **Page 187**	**M1** explore 3D design materials, techniques and processes effectively **Assessment activity 11.1** **Page 187**	**D1** integrate diverse 3D design materials, techniques and processes creatively and independently **Assessment activity 11.1** **Page 187**
P2 select appropriate materials, techniques and processes to meet 3D design briefs **Assessment activity 11.2** **Page 189**	**M2** develop effective, coherent ideas and outcomes to meet 3D design briefs **Assessment activity 11.2** **Page 189**	**D2** develop imaginative ideas and outcomes to meet 3D design briefs **Assessment activity 11.2** **Page 189**
P3 develop ideas and outcomes to meet 3D design briefs **Assessment activity 11.2** **Page 189**	**M3** compare and contrast experimental, development and final creative works **Assessment activity 11.2** **Page 189**	**D3** evaluate experimental, development and final creative works **Assessment activity 11.2** **page 189**
P4 discuss successful 3D design work **Assessment activity 11.3** **Page 189**		

How you will be assessed

You will be assessed through practical projects. You will use 3D design to meet the requirements of the briefs, and explore creative solutions to design issues. Your tutors will ask you to present your research, design development and final outcomes.

Case study: Joshua Ashmore, 3D designer

What kinds of things might a 3D designer for a film have to make?

Joshua Ashmore works as an art director's assistant. He works mainly in the film- and television-related industries, where he designs and makes props and sets for films or video productions.

What is your main job role in the industry?

I work as an art director's assistant for film and television.

Are you employed directly, or as a freelance designer?

My employment is usually on a fixed-term contract or freelance basis.

How do you find your work?

The Internet is my main source. There are sites that specifically list jobs in the production industry that I sign up to and check on a daily basis. A lot of work also comes through word of mouth from previous employers or contacts I have made on other jobs.

Can you describe a recent job?

A former employer approached me with an offer for a job as a sculptor and construction manager on a feature film. My day-to-day tasks in the pre-production stages of the film consisted of discussing the set, prop and sculpture designs with the designer and art director, reading through scripts and checking that all the design elements had received attention. Working with a budget, I then set about calculating and ordering all the necessary materials needed to construct the proposed sets and props. To set up a construction schedule, I organised and delegated jobs to the construction crew. I was also involved with building and dressing sets. Any sculpting I did myself.

What research did you do in response to this 3D design brief?

The film was fictional but involved a lot of Celtic and pagan symbols and imagery in the design, so I familiarised myself with these through reference to books and Internet searches. This helped when I had to sculpt a series of headstones for a cemetery scene. Knowing what symbols were authentic and what they meant helped with designing the detail.

How did you use primary and secondary sources for inspiration in the brief?

I made visual notes from the sources above, mainly reference books, and translated them into drawings. It was important to get the right visual information to begin with.

What 3D materials, techniques and processes did you use in the job?

Designing and constructing sets mainly consists of technical drawing, carpentry, painting and ageing techniques, poly-carving and dressing. However, each production is very different and you never know what may be required.

Was this job a success, and why?

For my part the job was a success – the sets were delivered to budget and on time, and the designer was happy with my sculpture work.

In general terms, what are the successful characteristics of 3D design work?

3D design work involves meeting the brief – it has to be fit for purpose. It also has to be visually interesting, but there are different criteria – a piece of 3D fine art has different constraints than a piece of 3D that is replicating something.

What skills do you need for your job role/s?

Creativity, a good eye for detail, practical skills and the ability to follow briefs and to work efficiently under pressure.

What other skills are important in your job, such as communication?

Time management, communication at all levels, budget handling and the ability to prioritise.

What things do you enjoy about your work?

I enjoy the creative atmosphere and the team spirit. The feeling of satisfaction when a shoot wraps successfully and your hard work has paid off makes it all worth it.

How would you sum up your experience in the industry?

I am still at the beginning of my career, but I have been fortunate in gaining the experience I have so far, and have worked hard to get it. When I stand in a replicated 17th-century London street that I have helped create, with the energy of the film crew around me, I know I am doing the right thing.

What advice would you give to anyone thinking of going into the industry?

Don't expect the work to come find you – you have to chase it – and don't take rejections too personally. Follow up leads and make use of contacts.

Assessment activity 11.1: Model making

Take a simple object such as one of the tools surrounding this Assessment activity. Make a series of quick sketches of the item, and see if you can take it apart – do this safely, and make sure your tutor is aware of what you are doing.

Make a model of the object or part of the object, at least double scale, using a 3D material and technique. Suitable materials might be modelling foam, card, clay and so on. This will introduce you to working with 3D materials. You can extend this task by exploring combinations of materials, especially if you can combine them to make the model reproduce the motion or action of the object, such as scissors that actually pivot etc.

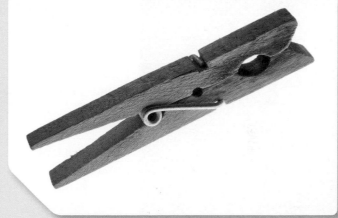

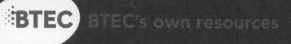

Here are some of the key terms and issues you will need to think about when working with 3D design briefs.

Key terms	Meaning and context
3D graphics applications	• software and animation techniques used to create 3D characters and environments for websites, games and interactive platforms (compare really early Sonic games with the more recent examples)
CAD/CAM	• stands for Computer Aided Design (CAD) and Computer Aided Manufacture (CAM) • used by designers to test, develop and create designs in computer technologies
target audience	• who or which group your project is aimed at
ideas generation	• process of developing ideas for a brief • essential part of the design process
fitness for purpose	• a way of gauging if your project is going to do what it was meant to do • often a key consideration in design work
Non-resistant materials	• plaster • card • paper • lightweight wood • string • soft wire • plastic sheet • glues • adhesives
Resistant materials	• glass • metals • wood • wood-based products • rigid plastics

Assessment activity 11.2: Recycling bins for schools

(P2) (M2) (D2) (P3) (M3) (D3)

Research and design recycling bins for two different ages groups in schools – the age groups are 5–10 years and 11–16 years old. The bins should in some way reflect the nature of the materials they are going to collect for recycling. Separate the bins for plastics, metals and paper. The shapes used should attract and encourage children to use them, as well as characterise the materials to be collected. To do this activity you need to:

- Research materials that are recycled (maybe produce statistics of volumes i.e. how many milk cartons, plastic drinks bottles, etc.).
- Collect some information about the shapes that the target groups might respond to (you can use direct questioning or short questionnaires, but you will need to seek permissions first – see your tutor for advice).
- Draw and design examples of shapes.
- Make a model of the finished outcome – can this be scaled down?
- Evaluate your final outcome model – was it successful?

Assessment activity 11.3: Evaluating

(P4)

Produce a display of the work produced for Assessment activity 11.2. Make a presentation to your peers or tutors, and explain how you produced your work. Develop your personal evaluation to describe the successes and weaknesses, and consider how you could improve them. Select one example of what you consider to be a strong piece of 3D design by another practitioner, and explain why you think it is successful. Use this to refer back to your own piece.

Assignment tips

When you are working with 3D materials, techniques and processes it is vital that you work safely **P1** . As you develop ideas to meet design briefs try to link the different parts of the design cycle – research, ideas generation, making and evaluating.

Aim to come up with ideas that are imaginative (this is used to define distinction level work); the more independently you can work the higher your grade will be, provided that you always make sure you meet the brief. The better you can understand these terms, the more likely it is you will achieve higher grades. Other key terms are effective, coherent ideas.

Websites

Below is a list of useful websites. To view these go to Hotlinks.

- Creative & Cultural Skills has information about careers in the design sector, including job descriptions.

- Creative Choices has links to design jobs, case studies and examples of contemporary work.

- TED has information about talks by designers, mainly from America.

- Design Council has links to case studies and examples of work.

12 Working with interactive media briefs

Working with interactive media briefs involves using technology and processes to create a device or system that people use, normally with sound, text and imagery. This can be related to areas such as software development and computer games. Interactivity means that people can interact with a product or system in some way – it enables them to make choices, decide how they want to do something and use it in a much more hands-on way.

Interactive media designers can work in a wide range of areas. These areas can cross over, so you might find such a designer working in animation-related industries, or in graphic communication. On page 193 is an example of what a freelance animator does.

CD-ROMs
computer games
interactive TV games
portable devices
websites
presentations

Learning outcomes

After completing this unit you should:

1 be able to develop ideas and outcomes to meet interactive media briefs
2 be able to explore the use of interactive media products
3 be able to use digital techniques and technology
4 be able to review interactive media production work.

Assessment and grading criteria

This table shows you what you must do in order to achieve a pass, merit or distinction, and where you can find activities in this book to help you.

To achieve a **pass** grade the evidence must show that the learner is able to:	To achieve a **merit** grade the evidence must show that, in addition to the pass criteria, the learner is able to:	To achieve a **distinction** grade the evidence must show that, in addition to the pass and merit criteria, the learner is able to:
P1 develop ideas and final outcomes to meet interactive media briefs **Assessment activity 12.2 Task 2 Page 197**	**M1** develop effective ideas and outcomes to purposefully meet interactive media briefs **Assessment activity 12.2 Task 2 Page 197**	**D1** independently develop imaginative ideas and outcomes to meet interactive media briefs **Assessment activity 12.2 Task 2 Page 197**
P2 select materials, techniques and processes for an interactive media brief **Assessment activity 12.2 Task 2 Page 197**	**M2** select a diverse range of materials, techniques and processes for an interactive media brief **Assessment activity 12.2 Task 2 Page 197**	**D2** independently select a diverse and well-chosen range of materials, techniques and processes for an interactive media brief **Assessment activity 12.2 Task 2 Page 197**
P3 explore the use of interactive media products **Assessment activity 12.1 Page 196**	**M3** explore and compare the use of a diverse range of interactive media products **Assessment activity 12.1 Page 196**	**D3** explore and evaluate the use of a comprehensive range of interactive media products independently **Assessment activity 12.1 Page 196**
P4 produce an interactive media product with integration of images, text and sound **Assessment activity 12.2 Task 3 Page 197**	**M4** produce an effective and informed interactive media product with integration of images, text and sound **Assessment activity 12.2 Task 3 Page 197**	**D4** independently produce an imaginative interactive media product with integration of images, text and sound **Assessment activity 12.2 Task 3 Page 197**
P5 describe interactive media work **Assessment activity 12.2 Task 1 Page 197** **Assessment activity 12.2 Task 4 Page 197**	**M5** compare and contrast interactive media work **Assessment activity 12.2 Task 1 Page 197** **Assessment activity 12.2 Task 4 Page 197**	**D5** evaluate interactive media work **Assessment activity 12.2 Task 1 Page 197** **Assessment activity 12.2 Task 4 Page 197**

How you will be assessed

You will be assessed through practical project work. You will need to produce work that shows you can develop ideas and explore multimedia techniques and technology. You will need to demonstrate your understanding of the factors in interactive media products, and show you can review your outcomes.

Case study: Adam Oliver, freelance animator

Adam Oliver works as a freelance animator, and a creative in motion graphics. This field includes television, film and corporate-based work. Motion graphics is used to generate moving or animated type, especially in areas such as television titles and credits.

You work as a freelancer – what does this actually mean?

It means self-discipline and inner motivation. Sometimes it's quite an uphill toil but the benefits of being your own boss run high.

What is your main job role in the industry?

I work as an animator and general creative in motion graphics.

Are you employed directly, or as a freelance artist/designer?

I'm freelance, often as an 'overspill' for larger studios or projects.

How do you find your work?

Through hard work and always being out there. You need to be the whole package, which includes advertising, marketing and promotion. I use my website as my business card to the world, and when I attend industry events I make sure I'm prepared: business cards, questions and show-reels. It's important to ask studios what they want from you, and how you can be of service to them – it's about building a relationship.

Can you describe a recent job?

Because I am still a young gun, I do a lot of smaller jobs and move from project to project. I try to only take on work that I have a drive for, but inevitably I sometimes have to do work that I'm not that keen on. So, for my average day I'll plan out a rough course of action the night before; I'll read up on the various news sites (industry and general), then I'll get started on my first piece.

I find most people underestimate the power of phone calls and leave it all to email. If I'm starting something new or have work to show a client, I'll give them a ring. That way you get an idea of the kind of person you're working for, which often adds a bit more soul to the job.

What materials, techniques and processes did you use in the job?

I use anything from a sketchbook and pencils to Wacom Cintiq. I like to keep my work as 'on paper' as possible, so I don't get bogged down in software shortcuts.

In general terms, what are the successful characteristics of interactive media work?

Professionalism, innovation, timing, strong sense of audience, brilliant communication.

What skills do you need for your job roles?

Creative flare is important for obvious reasons, but nowadays an ability to constantly look ahead of the current trend is a must. Because of the constant connectivity in our society and the media's increasing thirst for content, something seemingly original becomes yesterday's news within weeks. There are so many other money men out there looking for fresh angles that you need a thick skin to survive. That said, great ideas (and story) will outlast any trend.

What other skills are important in your job role, such as communication?

The ability to communicate is essential – my job is about delivering messages visually, which comes above everything else. If it's a personal piece, artistic experimentation will take a front seat.

What things do you enjoy about your work?

The constant change and challenge. The ability to bring ideas to life in the medium of time, which really does make things live.

How would you sum up your experience in the industry?

A learning curve. I'm still the new kid, so I get the odd helpful word here and there, but generally making a sustainable living is what worries me. The industry seems so volatile that I think 'exhilarating' would also be an accurate description.

What advice would you give to anyone thinking of going into the industry?

Do your homework and have a backup. If you're still at school, don't put all your eggs in one basket and end up with no life skills. You may not think it, but maths, English and even history will come into play more than you can imagine. Having a wide range of traditional skills also helps, so keep the sketchpad out!

Here are some of the key terms and issues you will need to think about when working with interactive media briefs.

Key terms	Meaning and context
mass media	• a term defining media-based communication designed to reach a large volume of people • broadcasting • newspapers • radio
HTML	• stands for HyperText Mark-up Language • shows text-based information in a website • can also provide links to another site • can show the nature/emphasis of the site
buttons	• a visually tabbed area or point on a screen that links one area to another, or actions a task/command
capture	• digital-based recording and storing of still and/or moving imagery
compression	• a way of making large digital files much smaller by encoding bits • aids rapid transfer of files and information • both sender and receiver need the decoding software systems
fitness for purpose	• if your outcome meets the needs it was intended to • if an existing interactive media product actually does what it sets out to do
user interface	• the methods and systems by which a user works with an interactive media product • how the user can affect the input of information • how the user can affect the output of information

BTEC Assessment activity 12.1: Evaluating interactive media products

Take three examples of interactive media products that you can find. These could include:

- games consoles
- mobile phones
- examples of interactive websites.

Look for characteristics by which you can assess the **user interface** and how easy/friendly this is. Success criteria might look like the following:

- How easy to use is the product?
- How interesting/entertaining is it?
- Does it always work?
- If not, why not?
- Do you use it a lot?
- Do others use it a lot?
- How are visuals, sound and text used?

Now rate the products in order of preference. Work through the stages of exploring the products **P3**, comparing them **M3** and evaluating them **D3**. Extend this by covering a wider range of products, in order to reach the merit and distinction criteria.

BTEC

Assessment activity 12.2: Creating a website for your centre

Working as part of a small team, develop and produce an interactive website for your school or college, based on the art and design department.

Task 1: Analysing and critiquing

Working in a team of four, look at the current website that your school or college uses and review the section that covers the art and design department. Think about the criteria you will use to gauge its success:

- Is it easy to use?
- Do all the links work?
- Does it contain useful and up-to-date information?
- Is it interesting?
- Does it contain things like strong visuals of learner's work, or case studies?
- Does it have any useful external links?

Bring your team's findings together and summarise them in a short presentation to your group.

Task 2: Planning

Produce a plan for an updated version of the art and design department's website. You might want to consult the marketing and IT departments for advice. You will also have to conform to the school or college's corporate branding or identity – this will mean using logos and set colours. Your plan should show:

- results of your evaluation and research
- thumbnail sketches showing potential layout of static screens
- diagram – called a flowchart – showing the links between screens and where the user can be taken to
- visuals you intend to use
- text you intend to use
- materials you intend to use.

Task 3: Designing

Working in your team, allocate each member a set of two static screens to develop, including the visuals and text you want to use. Work with your tutor to add a link to the pages. You might also explore adding **buttons**, depending on the level of skill you have and the software available.

Task 4: Communicating and presenting

In your team, make a presentation to your peers. You should show the links working, and relate these to the overall plan. You should also explain your team's choice of visual information and text.

Assignment tips

The way to achieve the higher grade profiles in this unit is to continually review and evaluate your ideas as they develop. Explain and articulate the reasons why you choose to use certain visual, text and sound information in your outcomes. Your development work also needs to be produced with fitness for purpose and user friendliness in mind.

When you produce an interactive product, think about how you can tell if it works. Why not include a peer feedback session in your evaluation of earlier development work and final outcomes? Get their feedback and use it to inform your work.

You can even use your peers as Beta testers – compile a short response sheet and ask them to complete this after testing your product. They can help you by scoring things like user friendliness, graphic content, use of images and sound, information and so on.

13 Working with visual arts briefs

The visual arts cover a wide range of activities, media and materials. In this unit, you may be working in 2D or 3D, craft, time-based media or a combination to complete your piece for a visual arts brief.

You will have the opportunity to find out about current professionals, techniques and processes and to research people from the past, before working in a studio or workshop to develop your work.

Mark Glean is a 3D visualisation and optical artist who describes his work in the case study on page 201. Much of Mark's current work is technical visuals and animations in a digital format for artists and architects. He also works on his own optical pieces in which he tries to create eye movement in the viewer.

contemporary
historical
techniques
experiment
media
materials
cultural

Learning outcomes

After completing this unit you should:

1. be able to research and record from primary and secondary sources in response to visual arts briefs

2. be able to use visual arts materials, techniques and processes

3. be able to develop ideas and outcomes to meet visual arts briefs

4. understand the successful characteristics and quality of visual arts work.

Assessment and grading criteria

This table shows you what you must do in order to achieve a pass, merit or distinction, and where you can find activities in this book to help you.

To achieve a **pass** grade the evidence must show that the learner is able to:	To achieve a **merit** grade the evidence must show that, in addition to the pass criteria, the learner is able to:	To achieve a **distinction** grade the evidence must show that, in addition to the pass and merit criteria, the learner is able to:
P1 research and record from primary and secondary sources in response to visual arts briefs **Assessment activity 13.1** **Page 204**	**M1** conduct competent research and record appropriate visual and other information from primary and secondary sources in response to visual arts briefs **Assessment activity 13.1** **Page 203**	**D1** independently research and record diverse visual and other information from primary and secondary sources in response to visual arts briefs **Assessment activity 13.1** **Page 203**
P2 use materials, techniques and processes safely **Assessment activity 13.2** **Page 205**	**M2** explore materials, equipment and techniques effectively **Assessment activity 13.2** **Page 205**	**D2** explore diverse materials, equipment and techniques imaginatively and independently **Assessment activity 13.2** **Page 205**
P3 develop appropriate ideas and outcomes to meet visual arts briefs **Assessment activity 13.2** **Page 205**	**M3** develop coherent ideas and outcomes to meet visual arts briefs **Assessment activity 13.2** **Page 205**	**D3** develop imaginative ideas and outcomes to meet visual arts briefs **Assessment activity 13.2** **Page 205**
P4 discuss successful visual arts work **Assessment activity 13.1** **Page 204**	**M4** compare and contrast experimental, development and final creative works **Assessment activity 13.1** **Page 204**	**D4** evaluate experimental, development and final creative works **Assessment activity 13.1** **Page 204**

How you will be assessed

You will be assessed by your tutor, not only on your final piece, but also on how you have worked during your assignments. This means that you will need to provide to evidence of:

- your research
- the materials, techniques and processes you have used
- how you have planned and developed ideas to meet the brief
- your reflections on your final work.

Case study: Mark Glean 3D, visualisation and optical artist

Mark Glean is a freelance artist who has worked on projects for a wide range of clients including architects, the music industry, business organisations and a major sculpture project that links science and art. In the past, he has worked in art education, both as a lecturer and a technician.

Can you tell me a bit about yourself and the work that you do?

I create technical visuals and animations for artists and architects in a digital format, while my P S Y O P T I C Z project is an outlet for my own personal visual expression.

When I get a chance I work on my own optical pieces. My premise is that art should be accessible, fun and engaging. I love playing with scale and colour and the idea of infinity. I try to make the images create a lot of eye movement.

What do you think inspired optical artists like Mark Glean?

Can you tell me about a recent piece that you have been working on?

I have been working on a series of pieces, each of which builds on the concepts or techniques of the last. They are meant to be fun, immediate and, hopefully, meditative.

How do you plan and approach your work?

I feel comfortable using different media, adapting my old ideas in new ways. Ideas still come from sketchbook work I did as a student. The three images (right) from my sketchbook were originally done by hand, in pen and ink.
I used to paint very large 'mural size' fluorescent backdrops, for which I devised a method of screen-printing repeating patterns to cover large areas of canvas quickly. I made my own paints and screen-printing inks, and used photocopy machines to help mock ideas together quickly.

Nowadays, I really appreciate computers as tools: I carefully plan ahead and tend to program special scripts for Illustrator. What used to take me days I can now achieve in hours. I also don't have to worry about finish as much as I did when I was a painter.
I archive all of my prep work and the final pieces. It's essential to make multiple backups of your work if you are working digitally.

These are images from Mark's sketchbook. How has he translated his ideas into his final pieces?

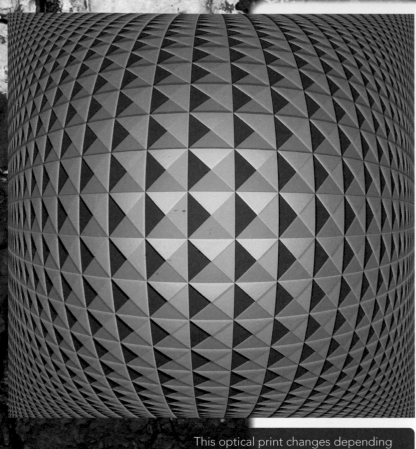

This optical print changes depending on where you view it from. How can you use form and techniques to engage people in your work?

What materials, techniques and processes do you use?

My laptop, Illustrator, Script Editor, Photoshop, digital camera, flatbed scanner, backs of envelopes and scraps of colour possibilities on paper are the main things. I also use Quartz Composer and processing which are new additions to my tool belt. I do not rely on 3D applications and use Photoshop once I have my basic grid worked out.

- I always start with a final size in mind.

- I then create the grids and basic colour in Illustrator.

- I'll pull it about, paint on it, use lighting, add textures and make decisions about which detail to bring forward and which to push back.

- I finalise the contrast and balance carefully so that all the detail is clear. The smallest clearly definable shape is always set to a square 2 mm. If you step close to the finished images, you can see every detail, but when you step back, all those little details become a haze, an animated blur. I set the contrast to obtain the fullest dynamic range, without losing any detail.

I work with lots of layers and try out many colour schemes using complementary colours – red and green, blue and orange, yellow and violet. Eventually I arrive at a hypnotic balance. The digital images are then archived to DVD along with all the prep work files, and then the final image file is turned into **giclée** prints and stretched on frames.

Where do you get your ideas and inspiration?

I love the art of M C Escher and the use of colour in the illusions of Victor Vasarely. I also find inspiration in numbers, sacred geometry, fractals, colour, music and my garden.

I am also a musician, so rhythm, dynamics and flow are important to me.

Key term

Giclée – a print created by digital and inkjet printing techniques.

What has helped you to become a successful visual artist?

- a good part-time job

- a good network of people from various backgrounds and disciplines

- having the time and patience to develop lots of ideas

- putting in extra effort can take things to a surprising higher level

- passion – it's important to enjoy what you do

- other interests

- travel to foreign places

- keeping records of everything I create and never throwing anything away.

Mark's use of ICT is central to his work. How might you use technologies to respond to your brief?

BTEC Assessment activity 13.1: Creating visual responses

P1 M1 D1 P4 M4 D4

Brief: You have been asked to produce a piece of artwork for a client who is opening a new health spa. They want the work you produce to reflect the theme of 'Natural Beauty'. In preparation for your work you are to produce a sketchbook that records the research you have done into this theme before you begin generating ideas for your work.

Task 1: Begin by collecting visual materials that reflect the theme of nature and natural beauty. This might include photographs from magazines or Internet-based resources, photocopies from books or images from leaflets or promotional materials. Annotate the images you choose to explain what elements of the image you feel would be important for inclusion in your own work.

Task 2: In your sketchbook start by creating your own visual responses to natural themes. This should include work that demonstrates that you have taken care to look at natural artefacts carefully. This could include life drawing and sketches using charcoal, pencil or conté crayon. You could also use your own photographs. Create sketches that focus on elements of your secondary research from Task 1. You also need to annotate these carefully to explain what you have noticed about natural forms and how this might inform your own ideas.

Task 3: When you have completed your research, discuss your responses to the work you have found with your tutor and peers. Compare and contrast different works and your ideas, commenting on what makes each idea successful.

Grading tips

- Make sure you include plenty of visual information collected from both primary research (such as your own photographs and life drawing) and secondary sources (based on images created by other people).

- Collect work from as wide a range of sources as you can. **D1** asks you to produce 'diverse' work which will come from thorough and thoughtful research.

- Careful annotation is essential to explain why you have chosen to include the material you have collected or created. This will help show just how much thought you have put into the collection and creation of your sketchbook work.

- When discussing your work, and other artists' work, aim to make comparisons about specific materials, techniques and processes. Draw out what you think makes each piece/idea successful (or not).

Assessment activity 13.2: Experimenting with different media

Brief: In the next stage of your brief, you need to begin experimenting with different media and methods to further explore your ideas.

Task 1: You need to utilise a wide range of methods to create 2D and 3D work. This might include mark-making techniques using pencil, pastels, crayons, ink, paint or mixed media. You should also experiment with 3D processes using textiles, papier maché, modroc and clay. Your work needs to demonstrate how you have attempted to experiment with these different methods in developing your ideas. You need to carefully annotate and record your thoughts on how useful you feel these methods might be when working on your final piece. Note the strengths and weaknesses of each method and what considerations you might have to make to use them.

You will need to detail carefully how you have worked safely when using these methods and techniques within your sketchbook.

Grading tips

- Recording carefully in your sketchbook how you have worked safely in your experimentations is an essential part of **P2** – without which you cannot go on to achieve higher marks.

- You need to show that you are working as independently as possible, so make sure you include careful annotation that records how you have employed these materials and processes.

- Make sure that the ideas you choose to develop match the requirements of the specific brief you are working to. **P3** The more thorough and imaginative your ideas are, the better your grade should be. **M3** **D3**

- **D2** requires you to show that you can use a 'diverse' range of materials, techniques and equipment. Therefore you need to demonstrate that you have explored as many different media and processes as you have access to.

Assignment tips

Be inspired: inspiration comes from many people and places. Take a leaf out of Mark's book and keep records (visual and otherwise) of things that interest you from as many sources as possible.

Learn to experiment: make sure that you have a good understanding of any equipment and software packages before you experiment. Knowing what technology can and can't do will help you to innovate.

Work to the brief: your assignment brief may have constraints that are obvious, such as deadlines and budgets. But what about less immediate restrictions, such as the final space that you will show your work in? If you are working for a client, you may have to consider their preferences and previous work. Check the brief thoroughly and ask questions before you start.

Plan your time and plan ahead: plan in enough time to come up with more ideas than you need – then pick the best ones to take further. Be patient and put the effort in at the start of your assignment – it will pay later on!

14 Working with 3D design crafts briefs

In this unit you will explore working in 3D design crafts. This is an area that covers furniture, jewellery, accessories, glass, metal, plastics and ceramics among others.

Many designers and makers in this area work as freelancers. Their work is often in demand for specialist commissions and one-off jobs. Designers need to be able to work to the clients brief and manage their time and resources – let's look at an example of a ceramics designer and maker on page 209.

jewellery
ceramics
metals
glass
accessories
felt
papier maché
craft
card
paper
design ideas
fitness for purpose
design process
research
drawing
surface pattern

Learning outcomes

After completing this unit you should:

1 be able to research and record primary and secondary sources in response to 3D design crafts briefs

2 be able to explore and develop ideas to meet 3D design crafts briefs

3 be able to use 3D design crafts materials, techniques and processes

4 understand the successful characteristics and quality of 3D design crafts work.

Assessment and grading criteria

This table shows you what you must do in order to achieve a pass, merit or distinction, and where you can find activities in this book to help you.

To achieve a **pass** grade the evidence must show that the learner is able to:	To achieve a **merit** grade the evidence must show that, in addition to the pass criteria, the learner is able to:	To achieve a **distinction** grade the evidence must show that, in addition to the pass and merit criteria, the learner is able to:
P1 research and record primary and secondary sources in response to 3D design crafts briefs **Assessment activity 14.1** **Page 211** **Assessment activity 14.2** **Task 1 Page 213**	**M1** conduct effective research and record appropriate visual and other information from primary and secondary sources in response to 3D design crafts briefs **Assessment activity 14.1** **Page 211** **Assessment activity 14.2** **Task 1 Page 213**	**D1** independently research and record diverse visual and other information from primary and secondary sources in response to 3D design crafts briefs **Assessment activity 14.1** **Page 211** **Assessment activity 14.2** **Task 1 Page 213**
P2 develop ideas and outcomes to meet 3D design crafts briefs **Assessment activity 14.2** **Task 2 Page 213**	**M2** develop coherent ideas and outcomes to meet 3D design crafts briefs **Assessment activity 14.2** **Task 2 Page 213**	**D2** develop imaginative ideas and outcomes to meet 3D design crafts briefs **Assessment activity 14.2** **Task 2 Page 213**
P3 use 3D design crafts materials, techniques and processes safely **Assessment activity 14.2** **Task 3 Page 213**	**M3** explore materials, equipment and techniques effectively **Assessment activity 14.2** **Task 3 Page 213**	**D3** explore diverse materials, equipment and techniques imaginatively and independently **Assessment activity 14.2** **Task 3 Page 213**
P4 discuss successful 3D design crafts work **Assessment activity 14.2** **Task 4 Page 213**	**M4** compare and contrast experimental, development and final creative works **Assessment activity 14.2** **Task 4 Page 213**	**D4** evaluate experimental, development and final creative works **Assessment activity 14.2** **Task 4 Page 213**

How you will be assessed

You will be assessed through practical projects, which will ask you to demonstrate the full range of skills and abilities related to the outcomes. This will include:

- research from primary and secondary sources, such as drawing, painting, collecting, collaging, photographing and generally gathering visual and some written information

- developing design ideas to meet the purpose of the brief

- using 3D materials and making techniques to communicate your ideas

- evaluating your final outcomes and developmental work against the brief, so as to identify strengths and development areas.

Case study: Ruth Parsfield, ceramics designer and maker

Ruth Parsfield designs and makes ceramics. She is a full-time art and design tutor in further and higher education, and also works as a freelance designer and a sole-trader designer/maker.

What does running your own art and design practice involve?

It involves designing and prototyping for the ceramic giftware industry, and also designing and making one-off ceramic pots and sculptural pieces for individual clients or exhibitions.

How do you find work?

My freelance work usually comes through an agent, who provides me with a brief from the client company. I develop the design and the agent presents it to the company. If the design is selected, it goes into production and eventually appears in the shops.

Can you describe a recent job?

One of my most interesting commissions this year was to design an ornate 'cheese wedge' (a covered dish for cheese) for Fortnum and Mason. I was given a guideline retail price for the finished product, and was encouraged to submit a few variations on the design rather than just one idea.

What research did you do in response to this 3D design craft brief?

I used both the Internet and library books to investigate the ethos of Fortnum and Mason, and historical examples of old English pottery cheese wedges and surface patterns to embellish the dish and cover. I also visited a museum to see antique examples of covered cheese plates, and visited the Fortnum and Mason store to see the quality of comparable products.

Did you know?

To be a practitioner in the field of crafts you would probably be self-employed. This way of working can be extremely rewarding – you are your 'own boss', but it also requires an organised, disciplined approach to work and sound planning.

Do you know anyone who is self-employed in this area, or maybe another area like construction? If so, ask about being self-employed – the good bits and the not so good bits.

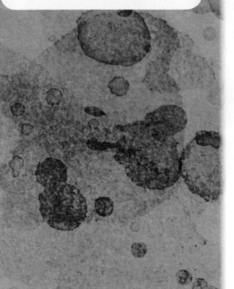

Did you know?

In the Crafts Council Survey 'A socio-economic survey of crafts activity in England and Wales, 2002–03':

- the main areas of activity in the crafts were ceramics, textiles, wood, metal and jewellery

- the estimated value of the sector had risen from £400m in 1994 to £826m

- more young people in their twenties, particularly female, are entering the crafts as a career.

How did you find ideas and inspiration?

For the shape and form of the cheese dish and cover, I referred to both secondary and primary sources. I paid particular attention to the proportions, as well as to variations in shape and form. I also took measurements and made sketches, which led to sketches for my own design. In the final artwork I used photocopies of the logo and surface design, along with loose sketching to show how these would look on the finished object.

What 3D materials, techniques and processes did you use in the job?

For this type of work the design process is all 2D, though it is informed by my knowledge of ceramic materials and processes. For example, I need to know that the piece must be suitable for slip casting and how many pieces the moulds will consist of, which is important for the economic viability of the design. I specify the type of clay to be used, the glaze, materials and method of application for the surface pattern.

Was this job a success? If so, why?

Yes, very successful – the client approved the design and it is in production as we speak.

In general terms, what are the successful characteristics of 3D design crafts work

Originality and quality are the key characteristics that make a design, especially a hand-crafted item, successful over a mass-produced one.

What skills do you need for your work?

I need a thorough knowledge of ceramic materials and processes. I also need the ability to produce the items, whether prototypes or working models for the ceramics industry or one-off hand-crafted items to exhibit or sell. I need to be able to complete a design process, which I do using traditional drawing techniques – sketches, working drawings and technical drawings. I am now attempting to update my skills with digital 3D modelling (CAD).

What other skills are important in the different roles you take on?

Communication is probably the most important, as well as time-management. Being flexible and adaptable is also helpful, especially when working as a sole trader, where one has to do everything for the business – designing, making, promotions, sales, book-keeping, customer service, packing, transporting, cleaning… the list is endless.

What do you enjoy about your work?

I have been making things from clay for 35 years, and I still love the feel of the material and the magic of its transformation during the firing process. I also enjoy the satisfaction of seeing a finished piece, whether it's a one-off or an array of identical pieces on a supermarket shelf.

How would you sum up your experience in the industry?

Varied. I seem to have diversified and adapted over the years. The commissions I work on are always enjoyable and never boring.

 Assessment activity 14.1: Designs for jewellery

You are asked to submit design ideas for low-budget unisex jewellery targeted towards a young market:

- Research into examples of jewellery – look at small independent makers and craftspeople. Try to define what they use as primary and secondary source materials to inspire their work.

- Use the theme of 'natural shapes' as the basis for your jewellery range. Source and gather together a range of natural forms that you feel have interesting shapes. Draw them using different media – pencils, pastels, paint, inks and mixed media. Evaluate your work and see if you can identify which drawings or ideas would act as starting points for jewellery designs.

Here are some of the key terms and issues you will need to think about when working with 3D design crafts briefs.

Key terms	Meanings and context
non-resistant 3D materials	• plaster • clay • card • paper • string • wire • felt • fabrics
resistant 3D materials	• metal • wood • plastics • glass
3D techniques and processes	• making techniques • cutting • drilling • joining • carving • constructing • fusing • bonding
design crafts briefs	• jewellery • furniture • accessories • ceramics • metalwork • plastics
target audience	• who or which group your craftwork is aimed at
design process	• the process of taking a theme and developing it to a final outcome • includes sourcing primary and secondary materials • designing • making
self-employed	• someone who directs and manages their own working pattern • involves finding work, pricing jobs or estimating • doing the work • keeping all relevant financial information for scrutiny

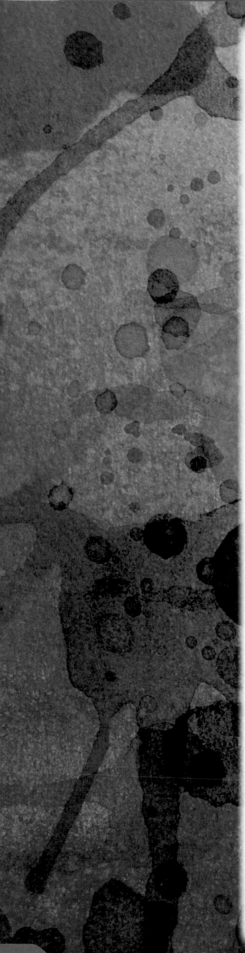

Assessment activity 14.2: Recycled crafts

You are concerned about the volume of materials and resources used in the production of art, craft and design work. You want to produce a range of 3D crafts pieces from recycled materials that can be both inspiring and environmentally sustainable.

Task 1: Develop design ideas for a wall hanging, light and storage box system made from recycled materials. Draw examples of forms and shapes from buildings and the natural world influenced by both primary and secondary sources. Look through your local directories and see if you can source scrap materials, such as the ends of rolls of paper in the printing industry, conservation board off-cuts used by framers, off-cuts of metals used in fabrication and so on. **P1 M1 D1**

Task 2: Develop your initial research into design ideas. Keep the designs simple and explain how you intend to make the pieces. You will need to show the techniques you will use to make the surfaces and shapes. Evaluate your collected materials and select some of them to make the different items, thinking about their suitability and fitness for purpose. **P2 M2 D2**

Task 3: Use the materials to explore 3D different techniques, such as cutting, joining, gluing, binding and so on. Record your findings and select the most suitable materials for production. Photograph all your work in progress and document it in your sketchbook/work journal. **P3 M3 D3**

Task 4: Produce your final pieces. When this is done, mount your work and display it. Present this to your tutor and peers, explaining what you have done – the inspirations, design ideas and processes, explorations and production methods you used. Describe your working processes and what you feel is successful. Compare and contrast your work and evaluate it – did it achieve what you set out to do? Did your tutor and peers agree?
P4 M4 D4

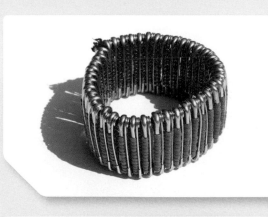

edexcel :::

Assignment tips

Assessment activity 14.2 Task 1 – You can influence your grade by making your research and recording effective and by working as independently as possible. Make sure you know what is required and manage your time well.

Assessment activity 14.2 Task 2 – To meet the Merit criteria, make sure your ideas answer the brief fully and in a practical way. If you can apply imaginative ideas and solutions to the brief, you will be assessed at **D2** .

Assessment activity 14.2 Task 3 – This is about using and exploring materials – think about words like *effectively*, *imaginatively* and *independently*.

Assessment activity 14.2 Task 4 – This is about reviewing the process and outcomes – keep notes and maintain an ongoing evaluation throughout the development process.

Websites

For additional help go to Hotlinks to view the following websites:

- Crafts Council

- Creative & Cultural Skills Council

15 Working with digital art and design briefs

When you are working with digital art and design briefs you will be exploring the potential of using digital techniques to create art and design work. This may involve using a mixture of traditional and digital techniques.

Artists and designers working in digital media need to be flexible and able to work in different ways. The ever-increasing potential of the digital environment means they have to continually adapt and refine their work and be aware of new directions made available by technology. On page 217 is an example of a digital artist and designer who works in different ways.

digital illustration
photographic-based work
digital-based fine art
online publications
websites
blogs
vlogs
animatics
animation

Learning outcomes

After completing this unit you should:

1   be able to create visual material using digital technology

2   be able to plan and develop ideas for a digital art and design brief

3   understand the successful characteristics and quality of digital art and design work.

Assessment and grading criteria

This table shows you what you must do in order to achieve a pass, merit or distinction, and where you can find activities in this book to help you.

To achieve a **pass** grade the evidence must show that the learner is able to:	To achieve a **merit** grade the evidence must show that, in addition to the pass criteria, the learner is able to:	To achieve a **distinction** grade the evidence must show that, in addition to the pass and merit criteria, the learner is able to:
P1 create visual material using digital technology safely **Assessment activity 15.1 Page 216**	**M1** create effective and coherent visual material using digital technologies **Assessment activity 15.1 Page 216**	**D1** independently and imaginatively, create visual material using an assortment of digital technologies **Assessment activity 15.1 Page 216**
P2 plan and develop ideas and outcomes for a digital art and design project **Assessment activity 15.2 Page 216**	**M2** purposefully present coherent ideas for a digital art and design project **Assessment activity 15.2 Page 216**	**D2** independently present imaginative ideas for a digital art and design project **Assessment activity 15.2 Page 216**
P3 select materials, techniques and processes for a digital art and design brief **Assessment activity 15.3 Page 217**	**M3** select materials, techniques and processes, using them effectively for a digital art and design brief **Assessment activity 15.3 Page 217**	**D3** integrate diverse materials, techniques and processes, using them creatively and independently for a digital art and design brief **Assessment activity 15.3 Page 217**
P4 discuss successful digital art and design work **Assessment activity 15.1 Page 216 Assessment activity 15.2 Page 216 Assessment activity 15.3 Page 217**	**M4** compare and contrast experimental, development and final creative works **Assessment activity 15.3 Page 217**	**D4** evaluate experimental, development and final creative works **Assessment activity 15.3 Page 217**

How you will be assessed

You will be assessed through practical project work. You will be asked to plan and develop ideas for a brief and explore digital technologies. You will then need to evaluate the characteristics of the work you have produced, with reference to examples of others' digital art and design work.

Case study: Deanne Cheuk, freelance art director, designer and artist

Deanne Cheuk works as a freelance illustrator, designer and art director. She also continues to work as an artist. Her commissions have included illustrations for Dell Design Studio laptop series.

What is your main job role in the industry?

I work as an illustrator, designer and art director, and am also an artist.

Are you employed directly, or as a freelance artist/designer?

Freelance – I work from a home office.

How do you find your work?

Clients and agencies come to me through connections with friends, or through seeing my work published in design publications, or seeing my website.

Can you describe a recent job?

I was approached by the Mother Agency in New York to be an illustrator for the Dell Design Studio laptop series.

Normally, a client or agency could just email me from my website, but my site wasn't working that week. Luckily, the agency found a link that I had posted years ago on altpick.com and contacted me. Through email we agreed on the fee for four illustrations and usage. There was also a contract and 'Letter of Intent', as there were many details to agree on, including usage fees, public appearances associated with promoting the project and a video project. As with most of my projects, I rarely meet my clients face to face. There were two rounds of sketches that were worked on before approval, then final art was sent to the agency and the job was completed.

What research did you do in response to this digital art and design brief?

Dell Design Studio had already produced one season of customised laptop art designs, so I looked at those online before starting. I also got direction from the client as to which images they liked from my archive of work.

Deanne in her studio

How did you create visual materials using digital technologies for the brief?

I made four different illustrations, one created in Adobe Illustrator using shapes and repetition, and the other three were drawn by hand, scanned in and coloured in Photoshop.

How do you develop ideas in response to the brief?

I make sketches and notes based on what ideas come to me when I am talking to the client, or when I hear the brief, and my ideas develop from there.

Was this job a success, and why?

Yes, the client is happy and the designs have sold well online.

In general terms what are the successful characteristics of digital art and design work in the fields that you work in?

Work that is captivating and original. I always tell younger designers to strive to make something truly original and it will get noticed.

What skills do you need for your job roles?

I start a lot of my illustrations by hand, but then finish everything on the computer, so retouching and Photoshop skills are invaluable.

What other skills are important in your job, such as communication?

Multi-tasking is a good skill to have, as I am often working on multiple projects and tasks. It also helps to be able to work fast and to keep the ideas coming.

What things do you enjoy about your work?

I really enjoy how varied my projects are. I work in print and with textiles, as well as on products and environments. It keeps me excited and interested when everything is so different.

How would you sum up your experience in the industry?

It is a great industry to be a part of. A good way to feel more connected is to join the professional association for design, AIGA or the customer elations management, ATC or the marketing and management consultants for small businesses, TDC and go to their events.

What advice would you give to anyone thinking of going into the industry?

Create, don't imitate!

Here are some of the key terms and issues you will need to think about when working with digital art and design briefs.

Key terms	Meaning and context
JPEG	• stands for Joint Photographic Experts Group • a way of compressing digital photographic imagery
TIFF	• stands for Tagged Image File Format • used for storing digital images and line art
capture	• digital-based recording and storing of still and/or moving imagery
compression	• a way of making large digital files much smaller by encoding bits • aids rapid transfer of files and information • both sender and receiver need the decoding software systems
blog	• short for weblog – normally a website set-up and hosted by an individual, with regular contributions/updates
vlog	• video log – another version of a weblog with the addition of video-based materials uploaded by the hosting individual or organisation

Assessment activity 15.1: Developing visual media

This activity uses a collage technique and digital technology. Make a series of four art and design pieces, using a variety of techniques. All should be A4 size:

- paint
- collaged photography
- relief printing
- fabric collage.

Scan the four images into image manipulation software and explore ways of combining them, using scale and layering, or by incorporating text. Evaluate the pieces you have produced – if they are successful, say why.

Assessment activity 15.2: Magazine cover – cultural identity

You have been asked to produce an illustration for the front page of a magazine, celebrating your town's cultural heritage. You are going to combine different images to make a visual composition without text.

Produce a plan that shows:

- which images you plan to use
- why these are important
- how you are going to capture them in a digital format
- how you plan to combine them.

Be as imaginative as possible. Look for different ways of summing up the cultures in your area. Make a short presentation to your group, showing your ideas in the form of:

- research
- thumbnail sketches showing potential layout
- examples of hand-produced collages
- examples of preliminary work using image manipulation software
- your evaluations showing your reasons and justification for choosing the images.

Assessment activity 15.3: Magazine cover – final outcome

Based on you work in Assessment activity 15.2, develop a set of final images to submit for the magazine cover. Source any images you want to use and check out copyright permissions. If you can't use an image, make your own pencil and paint version of it and include it as a student piece.

Produce at least two different versions and present these to your group and tutor. Record feedback in your work journal, and explain the inspirations you had for the pieces. Present the development work as well as the finals – you can get higher grades by contrasting and comparing your development work with final outcomes and by evaluating them.

Grading tips

It's important to aim for a balance between technical issues and creativity. To achieve a distinction grade you also need to work independently. Look at the definitions for these terms in the grading criteria and discuss them with your tutor.

To help you understand the differences between ordinary and distinctive work, look at some examples of digital art and design, such as imagery from websites, digital illustration, commercial digital work and so on.

Assignment tips

Here are some tips that might help you to achieve a higher grade in Assessment activities 15.2 on page 216 and 15.3 on page 217.

Assessment activity 15.2: The first part of this activity involves planning, and getting source materials. It's really about looking at examples that currently exist, and making judgements about how well they work. Once you have done this then you can develop the second part – your plan. The research into cultures within your area should be thorough. If you look at the assessment criteria for P2, M2 and D2, you will see that the emphasis changes – you'll be doing the same kind of task, but you can reach higher grades by presenting ideas that are coherent **M2** and imaginative **D2** – to reach **D2** you will also need to present your ideas independently. Talk to your tutor about the differences between the grades.

Assessment activity 15.3: This asks you to develop the final ideas. You might be working with photographs that you need to get permission to use. You can also do your own drawings based on them if you can't get permission – but avoid doing straight copies. Again, the differences between P3, M3 and D3 are important – if you can understand these now, you can target your work to meet them – read through them on the assessment grid on page 212. What are the differences? Can you clarify how you can meet the higher grades?

You also need to present your work – a highly important skill in the world of art and design. Again, look at P4, M4 and D4 – the differences are described in the terms: **P4** asks you to describe your work; **M4** asks you to compare and contrast different parts of experimental, development and final work – so to do this you have to go beyond a single idea; **D4** asks you to evaluate – use analysis and reflection on what you have done (you can refer to the Evaluation section in the book, on page 135 for more information).

Websites

For more information go to Hotlinks and view the following websites:

- The Association of Illustrators
- Creative & Cultural Skills.

16 Working with accessory briefs

In this unit you will learn how to make an accessory. You will research different accessories through looking at historical and contemporary designs. Taking ideas from this research and your own ideas you will be taught how to design and make an accessory. This could be a bag, millinery, footwear, glove or even a body adornment or a piece of jewellery. You will use materials and techniques that are appropriate to the accessory.

Sarah Cant, milliner and textile artist, is the case study on page 225. Millinery is Sarah's second career as she studied French literature before retraining. Sarah makes unique one-off hats for individuals, as well as producing twice-yearly collections.

Learning outcomes

After completing this unit you should:

1. be able to develop ideas to meet accessory briefs
2. be able to produce outcomes to meet accessory briefs
3. understand the successful characteristics and quality of accessory briefs work.

Assessment and grading criteria

This table shows you what you must do in order to achieve a pass, merit or distinction, and where you can find activities in this book to help you.

To achieve a **pass** grade the evidence must show that the learner is able to:	To achieve a **merit** grade the evidence must show that, in addition to the pass criteria, the learner is able to:	To achieve a **distinction** grade the evidence must show that, in addition to the pass and merit criteria, the learner is able to:
P1 research and develop designs for accessories **Assessment activity 16.1** **Page 227** **Assessment activity 16.2** **Page 227**	**M1** create an accessory which realises design intentions and shows competence in application of technical skills **Assessment activity 16.1** **Page 227** **Assessment activity 16.2** **Page 227**	**D1** create an accessory that demonstrates a high standard of practical competence, and independent working **Assessment activity 16.1** **Page 227** **Assessment activity 16.2** **Page 227**
P2 make maquettes to meet design requirements **Assessment activity 16.3** **Page 229**	**M2** compare how own and others' work meets the demands of a brief **Assessment activity 16.1** **Page 217**	**D2** evaluate perceptively how own and others' work meets the demands of a brief **Assessment activity 16.1** **Page 217**
P3 use appropriate processes to assemble, produce and present an accessory **Assessment activity 16.3** **Page 229**		
P4 safely operate appropriate equipment and machinery **Assessment activity 16.3** **Page 229**		
P5 discuss successful accessory briefs work **Assessment activity 16.1** **Page 227**		

How you will be assessed

You will be assessed by your tutor on presentation of a portfolio of work. You might present the following for assessment:

- research about accessories – this might be presented in a folder, sketchbook, or on worksheets
- design ideas for making an accessory – this will include ideas sheets, maquettes and samples
- sample accessory – show you have mastered techniques and processes and understood how to work safely
- evaluation of your work and the work of other accessory makers.

Case study: Sarah Cant, milliner

Sarah Cant is a milliner and textile artist who took an HNC at Kensington and Chelsea College before becoming a junior milliner at Stephen Jones Millinery. Since then she has been steadily building a reputation with her striking and unusual style. Sarah specialises in making one-of-a-kind individual designs, which offer the wearer a truly unique look.

Have you made anything unusual recently?

I recently made three cups for an exhibition for the Devon Guild of Craftsmen. The brief was to make three cups in any medium. I made one in straw, one in organza and one in straw and paper.

What did you have to consider in order to meet the demands of this brief?

My proposal had to explain how I intended to answer the brief. I had to think how my millinery skills could respond to the non-millinery brief of 'three cups', and how to combine the techniques and materials I use in millinery to make three cups and saucers of a normal teacup size. I decided to enter because I liked the idea of a challenge: to take hat skills into a different context, I would be using all my skills to make things to go on a head, without going on the head.

Lots of artists put in proposals, and from this the Devon Guild of Craftsmen selected a group of makers.

Sarah in her studio

Designs made by Sarah

How did you develop your ideas?

The theme of my cups and saucers was 'Nostalgia'. I linked this to treasures from the past, such as your grandma's worn teacup that you've kept. I was thinking about bits of text that reflect nostalgia and used words by T. S. Eliot to inspire me. Together, I used these ideas to inspire and develop my ideas.

Which processes did you use?

To plan the techniques, I looked at the work I was currently doing. For a year or so I have been making mixed-media textile objects such as brooches, necklaces, camisoles and wall hangings. These pieces had allowed me to play with ideas which you can't usually do with a hat. I experimented with a collage technique and started marrying techniques together, such as stitch and collage. I already had a vocabulary of hat-making techniques, but the cups were much harder to make although they were very three dimensional.

To make my millinery and the teacups I use steam from a kettle, specialist fabrics and hand-sewing equipment. I shape the hats over a block (usually made from wood) or by hand.

Tell me about your millinery work

All my hats are one-off pieces for special occasions such as weddings, Ascot, or parties such as a royal garden party. My signature style hats are hand sculpted, they would be hard to reproduce and the buyer knows she is getting a unique piece.

People order my hats either because they have seen one on someone's head or they have seen a collection of my hats at a craft fair. For craft fairs I make twice-yearly collections that reflect a colour palette and theme. I work out a visual language of trimmings, and it is from these pieces that I generate commissions. Hats that are sold or customers who return help me evaluate my designs and ideas.

Key terms

Bag – e.g. handbag, clutch bag, shoulder bag, shopping bag, rucksack.

Millinery – the art of making hats.

Footwear – e.g. shoes, boots, slippers, sandals.

Gloves – items made to cover hands and sometimes the arm as far as the elbow.

Body adornments – decorative wear that is often large and flamboyant which might focus on the neckline or arm.

Jewellery – decorative pieces made from precious or non-precious metals and stones as well as from junk, e.g. earrings, necklaces, bracelets, brooches or hairclips.

 BTEC ## Assessment activity 16.1: Comparing hats

Look at the work of Sarah Cant, Philip Treacy and Stephen Jones and choose one hat from each milliner.

Compare and contrast the hats. Consider the materials, design, aesthetic qualities, technical qualities, their purpose and whether or not you think they are successful.

To view examples of their work go to Hotlinks and click on:

* **Sarah Cant**
* **Philip Treacy**
* **Stephen Jones Millinery**

BTEC ## Assessment activity 16.2: Client needs

A client carries a designer's creations into the world. Each client will require something different. In your group, divide types of accessories between you, such as millinery, bags or footwear. Working in pairs, think about the different clients you may have and list why their needs would be similar or different from each other. Use the headings – Occupational, Designer and Private Clients.

Illustrate your findings and make a brief presentation to your peers.

Did you know?

Straw hats are recorded as far back as the 13th century. Straw hats are made by plaiting the straw. By the 1800s, hundreds of people were earning their livings by plaiting straw for hat making. In order to do this, large areas of the countryside in Hertfordshire and Bedfordshire grew straw for hat making. London was a large manufacturing area for straw hats.

Activity: As mad as a hatter – why was the hatter mad?

Workshops are bound by the Health and Safety at Work Act 1974. Employers are responsible for ensuring their workers' safety, but years ago accessories were often made in unsatisfactory working conditions by workers who weren't paid very much. Workers didn't complain because they would have lost their jobs.

Explore the history of the accessory you are studying. Can you list at least five things that practitioners needed to be careful about in the past and five things that need to be considered today?

Think of the time and effort that goes into making straw hats like this one!

Assessment activity 16.3: Make do and make better

During the Second World War the clothing and fashion industries had to make uniforms including shoes and bags for the armed forces. This meant that clothing was rationed for everyone else. People began to alter their old clothes to make new items. Ladies' fashion hats were even made out of cardboard and trimmed with feathers and other found objects.

- Collect one pair of denim jeans.
- Working directly with maquettes made from paper and card, work through design ideas for either a clutch-style bag or a pull-on hat with a brim.
- Decide which design works well and make sketches of it to record your idea.
- Pull the maquettes carefully apart to make a pattern for the hat or bag.
- Carefully cut the jeans open from the inside of the legs and iron out flat. Work out the best way to lay out the pattern so that you maximise the best bits of fabric and the design features of the jeans.
- Add any interfacing that is needed now, and using machinery correctly and safely, make up your final design item.

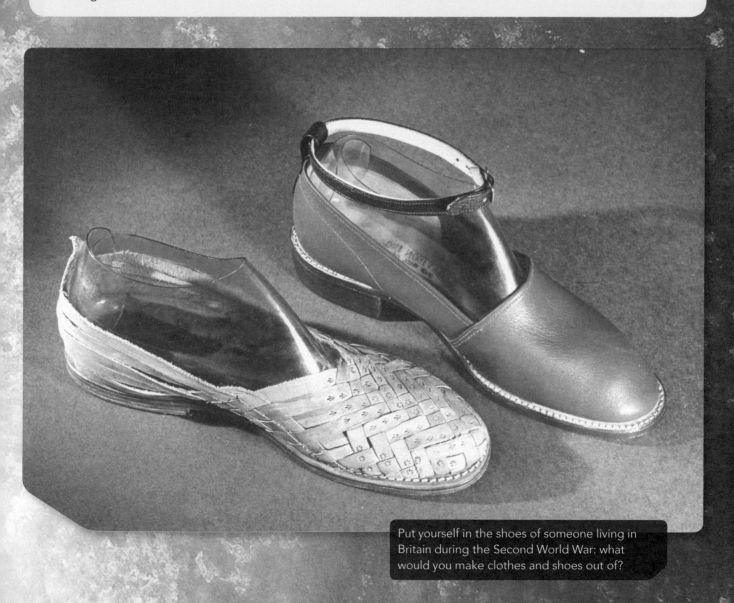

Put yourself in the shoes of someone living in Britain during the Second World War: what would you make clothes and shoes out of?

Assignment tips

Here are some tips that might help you to achieve a higher grade in Assessment activities 16.1 on page 227, 16.2 on page 227 and 16.3 on page 229.

Researching and developing design ideas   D1

Read the brief carefully and use a variety of sources to get ideas. Look at the work of historical and contemporary designers and find out what they have made. See if you can find out what has inspired other designers. Can you get inspiration from similar sources? Look at Unit 1 to find tips on researching and the Skills section for Planning.

Maquettes

Maquettes are either scaled down or full-size mock-ups, usually made of cheap materials such as paper or card. Don't just stop at one – challenge yourself by adapting and refining your ideas.

Plan your work (see Planning chapter in the Skills section) so that you have time to make a mock-up of your accessory from card, paper or fabric. This will give you the opportunity to see the size and shape. Review your work and revise your ideas. Have you been too ambitious? Is your design too simple? Will your chosen materials work? Are you able to work with the materials? Maybe you should make up a small sample of the product so you can see how the materials and techniques work together.

Improve your technical skills.

Making the accessory

Make sure you have enough knowledge to make your accessory and take every opportunity to perfect your practical work to a high standard. Do you need to brush up your skills? Work towards creating an accessory that demonstrates a high standard of practical competence and independent working. Care taken with accurate cutting and joining always improves the overall look of a piece.

Have your ideas worked?

Does your finished piece look like your design ideas? Remind yourself how to evaluate by looking at the Evaluation chapter. Do you remember how to compare and contrast, as you need to look at the work of others too?

Websites

There are many useful websites for accessory designers. To view some of these websites go to Hotlinks.

* Worn Again – for recycled materials to make new accessories
* Lulu Guinness
* Victoria and Albert Museum, London
* Bata Shoe Museum

17 Working with moving image briefs

When working to moving image briefs it is important to plan what you are going to do. In this field you need to use techniques and technologies safely and to their full potential. This means understanding cameras, lighting, general equipment, pre-production, production and post-production.

Practitioners in the moving image industry sometimes need to be skilled in working at different jobs. This can range from being able to manage a production through to operating cameras and lighting, under the watchful eye of the director. Read the case study on page 233 of an example of a freelancer in the film industry.

using technologies
post-production
shooting list
using equipment
designing lighting
image capture
editing list
close-ups
talking heads
working to the brief
timescale
budget
features
documentaries
short films

Learning outcomes

After completing this unit you should:

1 be able to use materials, techniques and technology for moving image briefs

2 be able to plan and develop ideas for a moving image brief

3 understand the successful characteristics and quality of moving image work.

Assessment and grading criteria

This table shows you what you must do in order to achieve a pass, merit or distinction, and where you can find activities in this book to help you.

To achieve a **pass** grade the evidence must show that the learner is able to:	To achieve a **merit** grade the evidence must show that, in addition to the pass criteria, the learner is able to:	To achieve a **distinction** grade the evidence must show that, in addition to the pass and merit criteria, the learner is able to:
P1 use materials, techniques and technology safely **Assessment activity 17.1 Page 236** **Assessment activity 17.2 Page 236**	**M1** explore materials, techniques and technology effectively **Assessment activity 17.1 Page 236** **Assessment activity 17.2 Page 236**	**D1** integrate materials, techniques and technology creatively and independently **Assessment activity 17.1 Page 236** **Assessment activity 17.2 Page 236**
P2 plan and develop ideas and outcomes for a moving image brief **Assessment activity 17.1 Page 236** **Assessment activity 17.2 Page 236**	**M2** purposefully present coherent ideas for a moving image project **Assessment activity 17.1 Page 236** **Assessment activity 17.2 Page 236**	**D2** independently present imaginative ideas for a moving image project **Assessment activity 17.1 Page 236** **Assessment activity 17.2 Page 236**
P3 select materials, techniques and processes for a moving image brief **Assessment activity 17.1 Page 236** **Assessment activity 17.2 Page 236**	**M3** select materials, techniques and processes, using them effectively for a moving image brief **Assessment activity 17.1 Page 236** **Assessment activity 17.2 Page 236**	**D3** integrate diverse materials, techniques and processes, using creatively and independently for a moving image brief **Assessment activity 17.1 Page 236** **Assessment activity 17.2 Page 236**
P4 discuss successful moving image work **Assessment activity 17.1 Page 236** **Assessment activity 17.2 Page 236**	**M4** compare and contrast experimental, development and final creative works **Assessment activity 17.1 Page 236** **Assessment activity 17.2 Page 236**	**D4** evaluate experimental, development and final creative works **Assessment activity 17.1 Page 236** **Assessment activity 17.2 Page 236**

How you will be assessed

You will be assessed through a submission of practical work for a project or projects. The project work will have themes. You may be able to negotiate your own theme. Your submission will include work on the key stages of pre-production, production and post-production. You'll need to keep examples of planning stages, evidence of meetings, as well as the storyboarding and actual film-based production.

Case study: Gennie Atlas, freelancer in the film industry

Gennie Atlas works as a freelance camera operator and lighting technician in the film industry. She also works as an editor using digital video editing techniques. She teaches film, video and PhotoShop on a part-time basis.
Brief: To work on the production team for a music video for The Madame Project.

Can you describe the job in more detail?

I was employed as a camera assistant and lighting technician on the first day, which entails ensuring that all equipment is working and operating efficiently. I start with an inventory of the camera and lighting equipment and check to see if there are any technical problems.

The job took two days to shoot and another day to edit. We filmed in a hotel, where we had access to all areas and staff. The filming schedule for the second evening was more complicated and time-consuming, with a lot of preparation and rehearsals. We experienced a few problems with camera lenses, so were allocated more time to fix these.

How long was each working day?

We started at 7.30 a.m. and finished about 8.00 p.m. I often work long hours and there can be a lot of waiting around.

How did you get this job?

I work as freelancer on a regular basis for three companies. For this job I was contacted by the company and I then negotiated my fee.

What sort of materials and techniques do you use on moving-image briefs like the music video?

It depends on the job. I work with the director/producer and director of photography to confirm what kinds of sets are being used, or what kind of lighting equipment and camera set-ups are needed. For the video I had to set up two HD cameras on tripods and attach TV monitors for the director and lighting cameraman. The equipment used was two Sony EX1 HD cameras with a variety of prime lenses and camera filters.

What do you need to think about when providing lighting for a film?

For the lighting of the reception area we used a selection of Kino Flo lights, Arri 300 and 650 lights, Dedos, blondes, red heads and ground row lights. For the smaller areas such as hotel rooms only a few lights were needed, such as small Arri 300 lights or Dedos. The video was edited by the director and the lighting cameraman using appropriate software. All of this has to be in the pre-production plan.

So it's fair to say that the plan is vital?

Definitely – the better the plan the more chance of the job going well. I have to integrate all the materials, techniques and processes to make sure the result works. In this case the plan showed the location and all the camera and lighting floor plans for each camera set-up. There were at least 75 camera set-ups in total over the two-day shoot because we had to film in so many locations, but because of the floor plans the camera set-ups were easy to accomplish. Pre-production planning can save a low-budget shoot a great deal of time and effort.

Did the actual production follow the plan?

Yes, though there are always small changes. It was shot on HD because this is the format used in the industry. This footage was then captured to the editing software, where eight hours of footage were condensed into the three-minute video.

Did you have to evaluate the footage as you shot the sequences?

Yes – we had to check the playback footage matched the intentions of the brief, that the lighting was correct and that the shots were what the director wanted.

What job roles can you mind map for the film industry?

How independently do you have to work?

I am always part of the team, so I am aware of my responsibilities to others. I also have a good knowledge of what other people should be doing, which helps me plan. Sometimes I have ideas for suggestions, such as changing camera settings or lighting. Depending on the director, I can be left to get on with it, which means I have to be extremely independent. Working in moving image means thinking on your feet, especially if there are technical problems. It's surprising how much of a problem the smallest details can be.

What was the outcome of the music video?

The final piece was a strong promotional video, and the shots and lighting helped to create visuals that matched the feel of the music. It will be a good advertisement for the band.

Experimental video stills: what atmosphere does the lighting give the video?

Assessment activity 17.1: Interviews

Plan and carry out a series of interviews of people in your art, design and media department. Decide on a theme or subject, such as 'A Typical Day in a Media Department'. Write your pre-production plan. **P1 M2 D2**

Carry out the shoot, making sure you have organised and piloted a set of interesting questions. How important are things like lighting, backdrop, location and so on?

Assessment activity 17.2: Music video

Come up with a pre-production plan for a music video. You can base this on a re-make of an existing video that you like or an invented one. First, write a synopsis – an explanation of the theme and intention – this forms the basis of the brief.

Now compare and contrast existing examples of the music video genre, describing the videos you feel are successful and why **P4** . Develop your skills in comparing and contrasting different types of music video, including experimental examples, by looking at a broad range of different types **M4** .

Write a pre-production plan that shows how you will develop your ideas and the outcome for the brief **P2** . If you can work this plan up purposefully, with coherent ideas that clearly develop the theme, you will be moving to the merit level **M2** . Try to develop the ideas further, to show an imaginative approach – think of alternative camera shots, colour treatments, close ups and so on. If you can achieve this then you will be working at distinction level **D2** . Include information about:

- the type of music
- the image or look that you want to portray
- target audience
- what materials, techniques and technology you will be using (extras, sets, techniques, such as green screen or chromakey, etc.)
- what processes you will use
- timescale
- budget – research this to find out the likely cost of camera operators and so on.

Write up your notes into a pre-production folder and shoot the video.

Grading tips

You need to demonstrate that you can produce a plan for a moving image brief, which identifies the subject matter and uses storyboarding to develop the theme. You will also need to write a script and list the kinds of shots you intend to use. If you can select and explore your materials, techniques and technology effectively you will be working at merit level. **M1 M3** If you can independently integrate the different things you are working with – actors, use of sets or locations, camera work, lighting, sound and post-production, and present a creative final outcome, you will be working at distinction level. **D1 D3 D4**

Here are some of the key terms and issues you will need to think about when working with moving image briefs.

Key terms	Meaning and context
technology	• still cameras • movie cameras • computers • lighting • microphones • TV studio
in-camera editing	• involves shooting scenes in correct order, without post-production editing
image capture	• downloading digital imagery onto software platform
pre-production	• plan for a moving image project, using storyboarding, shot list, script, budget, location list, permissions
production	• the shooting or filming of the piece
post-production	• process of editing, adding titles, special effects and outputting
resources	• location • actors • costumes • hired equipment • sets • props

camera operator
lighting technician
producer
director
grip
runner
sound engineer

make-up artist and hairdresser
assistant director
art directors and props
continuity and script editors

Assignment tips

Always look closely at the grading grid or grading criteria. The differences between grade bands (pass, merit and distinction) are often defined by the range of things you do or ideas you develop, and how effectively and purposefully you apply them. If you can develop ideas, work, outcomes and evaluations independently and creatively, you are working at Distinction level.

There are different aspects to moving image briefs – pre-production, production and post-production. Treat all of the stages as equally important – don't rush out filming, make sure you have a plan.

Websites

For more information go to Hotlinks to view the following websites:

- Creative & Cultural Skills – information about careers in the design sector, including job descriptions.

- Skillset – the skills council for the audio visual industries has a page dedicated to careers.

- Channel 4 – '*Three Minute Wonders*' has examples of directors' statements and films.

18 Working with site-specific briefs

Site-specific art is artwork created to exist in and for a certain place.

For this unit you will identify (or be given) a site indoors or outdoors that would be suitable for a piece of artwork, such as a **mural**, **fabric hanging** or **sculpture**. You then design the artwork for this space. This will involve relating the design to the suggested surroundings. You will also make a scale model of your idea and present drawings of the site to suggest how the final piece will look.

Jon Buck is a site-specific artist and his work is described in the case study on page 241. Jon specialises in making large sculptures designed especially for specific outdoor spaces. Most of his sculptures are permanent and will be seen by generations to come.

Learning outcomes

After completing this unit you should:

1 be able to use materials, techniques and technology for site-specific briefs

2 be able to plan and develop ideas for a site-specific brief

3 understand the successful characteristics and quality of work for site-specific briefs.

Assessment and grading criteria

This table shows you what you must do in order to achieve a pass, merit or distinction, and where you can find activities in this book to help you.

To achieve a **pass** grade the evidence must show that the learner is able to:	To achieve a **merit** grade the evidence must show that, in addition to the pass criteria, the learner is able to:	To achieve a **distinction** grade the evidence must show that, in addition to the pass and merit criteria, the learner is able to:
P1 use site-specific materials, techniques and processes safely **Assessment activity 18.2 Page 243**	**M1** explore materials, techniques and processes effectively **Assessment activity 18.2 Page 243**	**D1** integrate diverse materials, techniques and processes creatively and independently **Assessment activity 18.2 Page 243**
P2 develop effective ideas and outcomes for site-specific briefs **Assessment activity 18.1 Page 243**	**M2** purposefully present coherent ideas for site-specific briefs **Assessment activity 18.1 Page 243**	**D2** independently present imaginative ideas and outcomes for site-specific briefs **Assessment activity 18.1 Page 243**
P3 select materials, techniques and processes for site-specific briefs **Assessment activity 18.2 Page 243**	**M3** compare and contrast experimental, development and final creative works **Assessment activity 18.2 Page 243**	**D3** evaluate experimental, development and final creative works **Assessment activity 18.2 Page 243**
P4 discuss successful work for site-specific briefs **Assessment activity 18.2 Page 243**		

How you will be assessed

You will be assessed by your tutor on presentation of a portfolio of work. You might present the following for assessment:

- photographs or drawings of a potential site
- research about the area you are proposing to place art in to show that you can link the area to your design ideas
- design ideas including maquettes and scale models – these will show that you can use a variety of materials
- final project proposal including ideas about costings and a scale drawing of the artwork
- evidence that you understand how site-specific art needs planning permission and funding
- evaluation of your ideas and the work of other site-specific artists.

Case study:
Jon Buck, sculptor and site-specific artist

Jon Buck has completed numerous public commissions and has exhibited widely. He is currently an associate lecturer at Southampton Solent University and has a studio in Bath.

Can you tell me about a recent job that you've done?

In 2007 I completed *Ship to Shore* (on right), which is a 300-cm bronze sculpture with patination, paint and pigment. This was commissioned for Portishead Quays, North Somerset, by Persimmon Special Projects Western.

The brief was to produce a quality sculpture that reflected the high specification of the proposed architecture being built around Portishead Quays. This was an exciting project for me to undertake. I grew up in this area and my father and his family have been Bristol Channel pilots for many generations. The work looks out over the traditional moorings where the pilot cutters waited for incoming ships.

Ship to Shore, Jon Buck, Bronze, 2007

What did you consider first in order to meet the demands of the brief?

There are two distinct elements to take into consideration for a sculpture in a given site: first, its physicality – for example, its size, shape, form and colour.
And second, its content – the conceptual message. If the sculpture was to have sufficient stature to operate as a landmark on the headland and to act as a beacon on the coastal pathway, it had to have a scale that allowed it to compete with the surrounding architecture and paraphernalia of the public realm (lighting, signage, general street furniture and so on).

What was your inspiration?

The new buildings were built around what was Portishead Dock. I wanted to make a sculpture that in some way resembled some of the old harbour-side equipment; I was particularly interested in the old iron mooring bollards.

Did you know?

Installation art can be site-specific and made for a particular space.
Land art by its definition is site-specific – it was made in the land for the land. Neon light can also be installed as site-specific art. Visit the website of Tamar Frank, to see examples of lighting installations, by going to Hotlinks.

Key terms

Mural – a piece of 2D art work for a wall usually painted or made in mosaic or clay tiles.

Fabric hanging – usually a large piece of 2D fabric art displayed on a wall, but could also be in the form of a banner or flag.

Sculpture – 3D art can be made from any material – site-specific art placed outside is usually made from metal, plastics, carved stone, glass or fibreglass.

How did you develop your first ideas?

The idea of the large heads takes its precedent from ancient cultures, such as that of Easter Island, which often produced sculptures of sentinel-like heads of their ancestors looking out to sea. In my case I have taken this quite literally, and based the design of the sculpture on my own parents' appearance. The male's face looks out to sea, which is of course entirely fitting, while the female head takes the top position and looks towards the land, which is much as it was in my own family.

How did you get the work?

A proposal was presented to the commission panel, represented by a 3-metre high maquette, along with a plan to show where the sculpture would be situated. The proposal also gave information about lighting and installing the sculpture and how to maintain it, and there were design sheets showing how the sculpture would look against the proposed environment.

Describe the finished work

The finished sculpture is in bronze. Inside the sculpture is a stainless steel armature, which is welded and bolted to a raft of the same material which in turn is bolted to a concrete foundation. The surface of the work is stained red, with blue pigmentation in the incised lines that define the features. The bold colouration not only allows the work to compete with the environment but also helps continue the theme of shipping, beacons and buoys.

Which equipment did you use to resolve the idea?

The finished full-scale sculpture was cast into bronze by the Pangolin Editions foundry. Once completed, it was transported from the foundry and craned into position on site.

Ship to Shore, Jon Buck, Bronze, 2007

Assessment activity 18.1: Site-specific art

To get ideas for this unit, make a collection of pictures of different and varied site-specific art. Find out about the artists who made the art, the materials used and the methods. Note down the sizes where appropriate.

Site-specific art can be indoors or outdoors. Don't muddle site-specific art with a piece of art that has been bought and then put in a certain place.

- How much work can you find made for specific indoor sites?

- Look up the work of Alice Kettle and Polly Binns who both work in textiles and design and make commissioned work for specific places.

- From your examples identify which artworks you prefer and why?

To view the work of Polly Binns and Alice Kettle go to Hotlinks.

Town and county councils frequently commission and invest in site-specific art. This is usually called public art. There is a growing awareness of the importance of good-quality public art in relation to successful neighbourhoods and city centres.

Look on your local council or county website and search for public art or site-specific art. If you can't find anything, look on the website of the nearest large town to you.

For examples of the public art in Southampton, go to Hotlinks and click on the link for Southampton Council. For more about public art see Unit 1.

 Assessment activity 18.2: Design in situ

For this activity you need to propose a design for a site. You should plan your work in drawings and sketches. Take photographs of the proposed site and draw ideas on tracing paper over the photographs. This will show you how your ideas might look in situ. Then you need to focus your time on making maquettes or a scale model of your idea.

The case study is a great way of looking at someone else's work and commenting on whether or not you think it works.

- Were the original design intentions resolved?

- Now look at your own work – does it work well in the proposed site?

- Are the proposed materials, techniques and processes going to make the project work?

- What do other people think of your ideas?

Assignment tips

Working out ideas

To be successful, site-specific artists need to develop proposals that are easy to understand for a client.

Make the site work

Jon Buck explained in the case study that it is essential for a site-specific artist to understand the proposed site. In Jon's case this included the history of the site.

Temporary works

An outcome could be anything suitable for the site you have identified and could be a temporary structure. Look, for example, at the work of Andy Goldsworthy, who has made work from stone, slates, leaves, twigs and snow.

The fourth plinth in Trafalgar Square in London has recently had different sculptures placed on it. These have been designed specifically for the plinth. If working to a commission, you must determine whether or not the work will be permanent or temporary.

Indoor/outdoor

Site-specific works can be indoors as well as outdoors and could also be a painting, or made of any materials you can imagine. It could also be a performance. Read more about site-specific performance art in the Planning chapter.

For further information on bronze casting foundries and some of the work they have made, go to Hotlinks:

- Pangolin Editions – which cast *Ship to Shore*
- Bronze Age Sculpture Casting Foundry
- Morris Singer Art Founders

Glossary

3D graphics applications – software and animation techniques used to create 3D characters and environments for websites, games and interactive platforms.

Aesthetics – how something looks and feels. The aesthetics of a piece involve aspects such as beauty, balance and use of materials. If something is clumsily made, or difficult to use, or looks awkward, it might be described as having poor aesthetics.

Application of brief – what the products are used for, for example, packaging, signposting, advertising, promotion, typography, corporate identity, layout, logos, titles and idents.

Bag – examples include handbag, clutch bag, shoulder bag, shopping bag, rucksack.

Blog – short for weblog – normally a website set-up and hosted by an individual, with regular contributions/updates.

Body adornment – decorative wear that is often large and flamboyant which might focus on the neckline or arm.

Buttons – a visually tabbed area or point on a screen that links one area to another, or actions a task/command.

CAD/CAM – stands for Computer Aided Design (CAD) and Computer Aided Manufacture (CAM). Used by designers to test, develop and create designs in computer technologies.

Capture – digital-based recording and storing of still and/or moving imagery.

Collage – from the French coller, to glue.

Communicate ideas – by responding to themes, identifying the constraints of a design brief, investigating materials, techniques and processes, presenting ideas (such as through maquettes), creating working models through sketchbooks/work journals and by completing a finished piece.

Compression – method of making digital files smaller and easier to access from web-based or DVD/disk presentations.

Conceptual art – a term used in the 1960s to describe art where the idea behind the work is more important than the end result.

Constraints – factors that need to be considered when working such as budget, target audience, message, timescale, materials, health and safety and ethics.

Contemporary – usually means 'of now' but often means trendy/cutting edge.

Contextual – the context in which something was made. For example, Picasso painted Guernica in 1937 as his response to a town being bombed in the Spanish Civil War.

COSHH – stands for Control of Substances Hazardous to Health. COSHH relates to hazards that have to be controlled by safety measures and equipment.

Design process – the process of taking a theme and developing it to a final outcome, including sourcing materials, designing and making.

Drape modelling – designing a garment on a stand then translating this into a flat pattern.

Dyeing – immersing cloth into a dye bath to infuse colour into fibres.

Embellish – to decorate something.

Fabric hanging – usually a large piece of 2D fabric art displayed on a wall, but could also be in the form of a banner or flag.

Facings – a finish, such as for an arm hole or neckline.

Felting – traditionally, taking wool fibres and layering them on a flat surface before applying hot water and friction to help the fibres mat together to make a cloth.

Fitness for purpose – a way of gauging if your project is going to do what it was meant to do, often a key consideration in design work.

Foam board – Stiff, lightweight sandwich board used for model making and mounting work.

Footwear – examples include shoes, boots, slippers, sandals.

Giclée – a print created by digital and inkjet printing techniques.

Gloves – items made to cover hands and sometimes the arm as far as the elbow.

Hand and machine embroidery – applying threads in a pattern to cloth.

HTML – stands for Hyper Text Mark-up Language and shows text-based information in a website. It can also provide links to another site and can show the nature/emphasis of the site.

Ideas generation – process of developing ideas for a brief. An essential part of the design process.

Image capture – downloading digital imagery onto software platform.

In-camera editing – involves shooting scenes in correct order, without post-production editing.

Jewellery – decorative pieces made from precious or non-precious metals and stones as well as from junk. Examples include earrings, necklaces, bracelets, brooches or hairclips.

JPEG – stands for Joint Photographic Experts Group and is a way of compressing digital photographic imagery.

Key light – the main light used in photographic work.

Knitting – making a fabric with yarn and needles, fingers or French knitting with a knitting dolly.

Letterforms – study of individual letters.

Maquette – a model or rough version of a sculpture or 3D form or product.

Mass media – a term defining media-based communication designed to reach a large volume of people. Examples include broadcasting, newspapers and radio.

Mount cutter – Specialist device used to cut window mounts. Used in exhibition mounting.

Mural – a piece of 2D artwork for a wall usually painted or made in mosaic or clay tiles.

Narrative – the story.

Painting – applying a design by hand with a paintbrush.

Pattern block – a basic body shape which is used as the starting point for garment design.

Plastic fantastic – a model heavily made-up to look like a doll.

Polygonal lasso tool – creates polygonal selections in Photoshop and allows you to cut away shapes.

Post-production – process of editing, adding titles, special effects and outputting.

PPE – stands for Personal Protective Equipment. PPE includes respirators, safety goggles, gloves, gauntlets and so on.

Preliminary work – work that can show the developmental stages of your work and highlight how you think.

Pre-production – plan for a moving image project, using storyboarding, shot list, script, budget, location list, permissions.

Primary sources – those that you experience for yourself first-hand.

Printing – applying colour to cloth through a screen or directly with a stamp.

Production – the shooting or filming of the piece.

Purpose – the aim of something.

Raku – Raku ceramics are of Japanese origin and were associated with the Tea Ceremony. Work is rapidly fired in kilns where it can be extracted quickly and placed red-hot in the reduction chamber, where the oxygen is burnt away and then quenched. Alternatively it can be left to cool gradually. This produces the range of crackle glazes and metallic or iridescent effects associated with this way of firing ceramics.

Rationale – statement that explains your reasons for doing something. Used as a statement in project proposals.

Recording from primary sources – using any combination of drawing, lens-based and written techniques to record directly from sources first-hand.

Recording from secondary sources – using images and examples from postcards, magazines, video, film, printed materials and so on, as starting points for a design.

Roughs – visuals produced normally to the intended size. Communicates more information than thumbnails.

Running order – denotes the order that you put your work in. It can determine the 'hook people in' factor if strong work is shown at the beginning.

Sample seams – practising machine stitching such as open seams, French seams or machine and fell seams which you find on jeans.

Sculpture – 3D art that can be made from any material. Site-specific art placed outside is usually made from metal, plastics, carved stone, glass or fibreglass.

Secondary illustrations – drawings to help form initial ideas.

Secondary sources – are those that another person has reviewed or experienced for you to refer to.

Self-employed – someone who directs and manages their own working pattern. It involves finding work, pricing jobs, doing the work and keeping all relevant financial information.

Surface decoration – applying a pattern to a fabric through using print, paint, stitch or tiny objects like beads.

Surreal – sur-real means unreal, something which is bizarre or relates to surrealism.

Synopsis – a short (brief) outline version of, for example, a story, an article, a film or a television programme.

Target audience – who or which group your project is aimed at.

Thumbnail sketches – small, quick drawings, made without correction, normally in line/pencil/pen. Used to explore ideas visually in an abbreviated manner.

TIFF – stands for Tagged Image File Format and is used for storing digital images and line art.

Tonal range – the different shades of grey between solid black and absolute white.

Tone – the variation of light and dark areas which can be used to describe 3D forms in 2D.

Typography – study of groups of letterforms or typefaces/type families.

User interface – the methods and systems by which a user works with an interactive media product and how the user can affect the input and output of information.

Vlog – **video log** – another version of a weblog with the addition of video-based materials uploaded by the hosting individual or organisation.

Weaving – making fabric using looms strung with the warp and threading a weft yarn across in a pattern.

Window mounting – cutting of an aperture or window, behind which the work is taped. Creates a neat viewing window.

Zip insertions – practising putting in a zip.

Index

2D visual communication
  assessment and grading criteria   26
  assignment tips   48
  communication of design ideas 36–41
  evaluation   147
  example work   27
  formal elements of   41–46
  functional skills   35
  health and safety   33
  mark-making   28–30
  materials   29–30, 32
  personal, learning and thinking
  skills (PLTS)   34
  planning   115
  preparing and making skills   132
  recording ideas   33–34
  techniques   31–32
  use of   28
3D design briefs
  assessment and grading criteria   184
  assignment tips   190
  case study   185–86
  evaluation   148
  model making   187
  planning   116
  preparing and making skills   132
  recycling bins   189
3D design crafts briefs
  assessment and grading criteria   208
  assignment tips   214
  case study   209–211
  ceramics design   209–211
  evaluation   148
  jewellery design   211
  key terms   212
  materials   212
  planning   116
  preparing and making skills   132
  recycling   213
  techniques and processes   212
3D graphics applications   188
3D visual communication
  assessment and grading criteria   50
  assignment tips   68
  communicating ideas   57
  design briefs   59
  digital techniques   63
  evaluation   147
  example of work   51, 67
  formal elements in   62–66
  functional skills   58, 60
  health and safety   56–57
  materials   53
  personal, learning and thinking
  skills (PLTS)   57, 60, 62
  planning   115
  preparing and making skills   132
  presentation of work   98–99
  techniques   52–54

A

Abstract Expressionism   8
accessory briefs
  assessment and grading criteria   224
  assignment tips   230
  case study   225–26
  client needs   227
  comparison of hats   227
  evaluation   148
  health and safety in the past   228
  key terms   227
  millinery   225–26
  planning   116
  preparing and making skills   132
  recycling jeans   229
  straw hats   228
acrylic paint   10, 32
aesthetics   52
Allington, Clare   173–74
analysis   135, 138–41, 175
Angel of the North (Gormley)   57
animators   37, 46
annotation of work   81
application of briefs   161
art and design industry
  assessment and grading criteria   152
  evaluation   148
  planning   115
  preparing and making skills   132
  researching   153–56
artist's houses, visiting   16–17
assessment criteria
  2D visual communication   26
  3D design briefs   184
  3D design crafts briefs   208
  3D visual communication   50
  accessory briefs   224
  art and design industry   152
  contextual references in art and
  design   2
  digital art and design briefs   216
  fashion design briefs   172
  graphic design briefs   158
  ideas   70
  interactive media briefs   192
  moving image briefs   232
  photography briefs   166
  planning   115–16
  portfolios   88
  site-specific briefs   240
  textile briefs   178
  using ideas   70
  visual arts briefs   200

B

bags   227
Banksy   14

blogs   14, 219
body adornments   227
Braque, Georges   6
briefs, design
  3D visual communication   59
  project proposal briefs   73
  responses to   58
Brody, Neville   159, 160
buttons   195

C

CAD/CAM   188
Cant, Sarah   225–26
capture   195, 219
card   53
Carrington, Dora   74
cartridge paper   30
ceramicists   46
ceramics   63
ceramics design   209–211
clay   53
collage   3, 220
colour, use of in different
disciplines   45–46
communication
  of design ideas   36–41, 57–61
  of evaluation conclusions   144
  uses of techniques   36–37
  of work and outcomes   80–81
composition   41, 45
compression   100, 195, 219
Conceptual Art   14
constraints   161
contemporary developments   14–15
contextual references in art and design
  assessment and grading criteria   2
  assignment tips   24
  contemporary developments   14–15
  evaluation   147
  example work   3
  historical developments   12–13
  influences from a wider context   10–12
  movement in art and design   5–9
  planning   115
  preparing and making skills   132
  presenting information   20–22
  research   16–20
contextual understanding   16
Copperwheat, Ben   101
COSHH (Control of Substances
Hazardous to Health)   52, 57
critiquing   135, 142–143
cropping   141
Cubism   6
CVs   99

D

Dadaism   7
Dali, Salvador   8

Daphnis and Chloë (Boucher) 4
de Kooning, Willem 8
Delauney, Robert 10
design briefs
  3D visual communication 59
  responses to 58
design ideas
  communication of 36–41, 52, 57–61
  recording 33–34, 52, 54–55
developmental work
  communicating 80–81
  experimentation 77
  functional skills 82, 83
  materials, equipment and
  techniques 78
  personal, learning and thinking
  skills (PLTS) 84
  recording ideas 111–12
  reviewing and evaluating ideas 78
  strengths and weaknesses of 82–83
  techniques for 75–77
diaries, visual 110
digital art
  2D techniques 32
  mark-making 30
digital art and design briefs
  assessment and grading criteria 216
  assignment tips 222
  case study 217–18
  collage technique 220
  evaluation 148
  key terms 219
  magazine cover 220–21
  planning 116
  preparing and making skills 132
digital media 44
digital technology 63
drawing 44
  materials 29–30
  techniques 31–32
Duchamp, Marcel 7
dyeing 181

E

embellishment 179, 181
embroidery 181
Emin, Tracey 14
equipment 131
evaluation
  analysis 135, 138–41
  communication of
  conclusions 135, 144
  critiquing 135, 142–43
  cropping 141
  example of 146
  example work 136
  factors influencing 149
  fit for purpose 137–38
  importance of 149
  interactive media products 196
  key terms 147
  presentation of 135, 145
  recycling bins 189

stages to 150
textile briefs 182
exhibitions 12–13
experimentation 77, 127–28, 134, 175,
  182, 205
explanations of work 99–100
Exposition International des Arts
Decoratifs et Industriels Modernes
Paris, 1925 13

F

Facey, Ruth 23
fashion, punk rock 4
fashion design briefs
  analysis 175
  assessment and grading criteria 172
  assignment tips 176
  case study 173–74
  evaluation 148
  experimentation 175
  planning 116
  preparing and making skills 132
  sources of inspiration 173
fashion designers 38, 46
felting 179, 181
Festival of Britain, London 1951 13
fitness for purpose 137–38, 188, 195
foam board 100
footwear 227
formal elements
  of 2D visual communication 41–46
  in 3D visual communication 62–66
Friend, Mark 67, 149
full colour drawing, analysis of
example 140
functional skills
  2D visual communication 35
  3D visual communication 58, 60
  development work 82, 83
  examples of artist's work 44
  making notes 139
  photography briefs 169
  portfolios 93, 94, 100
  primary and secondary sources 55
  recording design ideas 39
Futurism 6–7

G

galleries
  interaction 15
  visiting 16
Gauguin, Paul 11
Gaynor, Mark 114
gloves 227
Gormley, Antony 57
grading criteria
  2D visual communication 26
  3D design briefs 184
  3D design crafts briefs 208
  3D visual communication 50
  analysis 141
  accessory briefs 224

art and design industry 152
contextual references in art
and design 2
digital art and design briefs 216
experimentation 128
fashion design briefs 172
graphic design briefs 158
ideas 70
interactive media briefs 192
moving image briefs 232
photography briefs 166
planning 115–16, 118
site-specific briefs 240
portfolios 88
textile briefs 178
use of sketchbooks 126
visual arts briefs 200
graph paper 30
graphic design briefs
  assessment and grading criteria 158
  assignment tips 164
  case study 159–160
  evaluation 148
  key terms 161
  planning 115
  preparing and making skills 132
graphic designers 46, 47
Great Exhibition, London 1851 12–13
group work and planning 114

H

Hamilton, Richard 13
hats 225 – 28
health and safety 33, 56–7, 130,181
height, impact of gaining 10
historical developments 12–13
HTML (Hyper Text Mark-up
Language) 195
Hyperrealist 62

I

ideas
  for advertising 163
  assessment and grading criteria 70
  assignment tips 86
  communication of 36–41, 57–61
  developing 120–28
  development of 75–77
  evaluation 147
  example work 71
  and experimentation 77
  finding 129–30
  gathering 105–110, 133
  generating 164, 188

  materials, equipment and
  techniques for 78
  museum collections as starting
  points 85
  personal, learning and thinking
  skills (PLTS) 123, 130
  planning 115

planning research 105
preparing and making skills 132
presentation of work and outcomes 80–81
recording 33–34, 52, 54–55, 111–12
reviewing and evaluating 78–79
sources of inspiration 173
textile briefs 182
image capture 237
Impressionism 5
in-camera editing 237
industry, art and design
   assessment and grading criteria 152
   evaluation 148
   planning 115
   preparing and making skills 132
   researching 153–56
influences from a wider context 10–12, 23
information graphics 162
inks 29, 32
inspiration
   from historical and contemporary art 23
   Morisot, Berthe 5
   sources of 173
   see also ideas
installation art 241
interaction in museums and galleries 15
interactive media briefs
   assessment and grading criteria 192
   assignment tips 198
   case study 193–94
   evaluating products 196
   evaluation 148
   key terms 195
   planning 116
   preparing and making skills 132
   website creation 197
interior designers 36, 45
Internet
   blogs 14
   websites 15

J

jewellery 227
jewellery design 211
jewellery designers 36
John, Gwen 74
JPEG 219

K

key light 100
knitting 179, 181
Khalo, Frida 3

L

land art 241
landscape photography 167
layout paper 30
letterforms 161
line drawing, analysis of example 139

line studies 41
lines 46
logos 161–62

M

MacLellan, Donald 167–69
maquettes 52, 225, 226
Marinetti, Filippo 6
mark-making 28–30
mass media 195
materials
   3D visual communication 53
   drawing 29–30
   non-resistant 188
   own collection of 44
   resistant 188
Matisse, Henri 72
metal 53
millinery 225–26, 227
mind maps 105–106, 122–123
Minimalism 9
model making 187
mood boards 107
Monet, Claude 5
Moret, Sally 133
mount cutters 95, 100
mounting work 95–96
movements in art and design 5–9
moving image briefs
   assessment and grading criteria 232
   assignment tips 238
   case study 233–35
   evaluation 148
   interviews 236
   key terms 237
   music video 236
   planning 116
   preparing and making skills 132
Mueck, Ron 62
museums
   examples 134
   interaction 15
   visiting 16

N

non-resistant materials 188, 212
Nude Descending a Staircase (Duchamp) 7

O

observation skills 34
Oliver, Adam 193–94
organisations, art and design 115
outcomes, factors affecting 36

P

painting 32, 44
paper 30, 53
Parsfield, Ruth 209–211
pastels 29
pencils 29

personal, learning and thinking skills (PLTS)
   2D visual communication 34
   3D visual communication 57, 60, 62
   analysis 141
   critiquing 143
   development work 84
   experimentation 127, 128
   finding ideas 130
   formal elements of 2D visual communication 42
   generation of ideas 123
   group and individual workings 131
   photography briefs 167
   planning 110
   portfolios 92–100
   presentation of design ideas 40
photographers 36, 45
photographic paper 30
photographs for evidence 134
photography 44
   impact of 11
   mark-making 30
   techniques 32
photography briefs
   assessment and grading criteria 166
   assignment tips 170
   case study 167–69
   evaluation 148
   functional skills 169
   landscape 169
   personal, learning and thinking skills (PLTS) 167
   planning 116
   portraits 170
   preparing and making skills 132
Picasso, Pablo 80
Pissaro, Camille 5
planning
   example work 104
   gathering ideas 105–110
   and group work 114
   importance of 103
   improving grades with 118
   personal, learning and thinking skills (PLTS) 110
   researching ideas 105
   story illustration 117
   time 73, 105, 112, 134
plaster 53
plastics 53
Pollock, Jackson 8
polygonal lasso tool 71
polymer technology 10
portfolios
   assessment and grading criteria 88
   assignment tips 102
   checklist and tips 102
   evaluation 147
   example work 89, 101
   explaining work 99–100
   functional skills 93, 94, 100
   key terms 100

personal, learning and thinking skills (PLTS) 92, 94, 98, 100
planning 115
preliminary work 100
preparing and making skills 132
presentation of 92–102
purpose of 90–91
types of 90
portrait photography 170
Post Impressionism 6
post-production 237
PPE (Personal Protective Equipment) 52
preliminary work in portfolios 100
preparing and making skills
  developing ideas 120–28
  experimentation 127–28
  relevant units 131–32
  target market 127
  technical skills and techniques 130–31
pre-production 237
presentation
  of evaluation 135
  of final ideas 39–40
  of research 20–22
  techniques 145
  types of 145
primary sources
  project proposal briefs 73
  for recording ideas 33, 52, 54–55
  for research 16–17
printing 181
  designing for 45
  mark-making 30
printmakers 46
printmaking 31, 32, 44
production 237
project proposal briefs 73, 83–84
proportion 41
public art 17, 241–44
punk rock
  fashion 4
  Sex Pistols record cover 12

R

rationale 100
records of ideas 33–34, 52, 54–55, 73
recycling 213, 229
recycling bins 189
Reid, Jamie 12
research
  files 130
  own response to 19
  presentation of 20–22
  primary sources 16–17
  recording sources 18
  secondary sources 17
Renoir, Pierre Auguste 5
resin 53
resistant materials 188, 212
resources 237
Riley, Bridget 10
Robinson, Dave 47
roughs 161

Rousseau, Henri 11
running order 100
Ryles, Jessica 77, 179

S

safety 33, 56–57, 130, 181
sand paper 30
scale 62
sculptors 46
sculpture 63
secondary sources
  project proposal briefs 73
  for recording ideas 33, 52, 54–55
  for research 17
self-employment 212
Sex Pistols record cover 12
Sisley, Alfred 5
site-specific briefs
  assessment and grading criteria 240
  assignment tips 244
  case study 241–42
  evaluation 148
  generating ideas 243
  planning 116
  preparing and making skills 132
sketchbooks 21, 122–26
software 188
sources for research
  primary 16–17
  recording 17
  secondary 17
spider diagrams 105–106, 122–23
Stijelja, Danny 159–60
storyboard artists 45
straw hats 224
studios, artist's, visiting 17
sugar paper 30
surface decoration 181
Surrealism 8

T

target audience/market 127, 161, 188, 212
technical logs 56
techniques
  2D 31–32
  3D visual communication 52–54, 63
technology 237
temporary art 240
textile briefs
  assessment and grading criteria 178
  assignment tips 182
  case study 180
  embellishment 181
  evaluation 148, 182
  example work 179
  experimentation 182
  health and safety 181
  idea development 182
  key terms 181
  planning 116
  preparing and making skills 132

surface decoration 181
textile designers 45
texture 41
This is Tomorrow, 1956 13
thumbnail sketches 161
TIFF 219
time 105, 112, 134
tissue paper 30
tonal drawing, analysis of example 140
tonal range 28
tonal work 41
tone 28
trade, overseas, impact of 11
travel, impact of 11
typography 161

U

user interface 195
user-interface software designers 36

V

van Gogh, Vincent 74
visual arts briefs
  assessment and grading criteria 200
  assignment tips 206
  case study 201–203
  creating visual responses 204
  evaluation 148
  experimentation 205
  planning 116
  preparing and making skills 132
visual diaries 110
vlogs 219

W

watercolour paper 30
weaving 181
website creation 197
websites
  museums and galleries 15, 24, 68
Westwood, Vivienne 4
Williams, Nicki 76, 81
Williams, Tim 117
Willoughby, Alison 180
window mounting 95, 100
wire 53
Wise, Ann 85
wood 53